The College of Law
of England and Wales
2 BUNHILL ROW
LONDON
EC1Y 8HQ

ELGAR EUROPEAN LAW

Founding editor: John Usher, *formerly Professor of European Law and Head, School of Law, University of Exeter, UK*

European integration is the driving force behind constant evolution and change in the laws of the member states and the institutions of the European Union. This important series will offer short, state-of-the-art overviews of many specific areas of EU law, from competition law to consumer law and from environmental law to labour law. Whilst most books will take a thematic, vertical approach, others will offer a more horizontal approach and consider the overarching themes of EU law.

Distilled from rigorous substantive analysis, and written by some of the best names in the field, as well as the new generation of scholars, these books are designed both to guide the reader through the changing legislation itself, and to provide a firm theoretical foundation for advanced study. They will be an invaluable source of reference for scholars and postgraduate students in the fields of EU law and European integration, as well as lawyers from the respective individual fields and policymakers within the EU.

Titles in the series include:

EU Public Procurement Law
Christopher H. Bovis

EU Criminal Law and Justice
Maria Fletcher and Robin Lööf with Bill Gilmore

Judicial Review in EU Law
Alexander H. Türk

EU Intellectual Property Law and Policy
Catherine Seville

EU Private International Law
Second Edition
Peter Stone

EU Labour Law
A.C.L. Davies

EU Public Procurement Law, Second Edition
Christopher H. Bovis

EU Internet Law
Andrej Savin

EU Internet Law

Andrej Savin

Associate Professor, Copenhagen Business School, Denmark

ELGAR EUROPEAN LAW

Edward Elgar

Cheltenham, UK • Northampton, MA, USA

Published by
Edward Elgar Publishing Limited
The Lypiatts
15 Lansdown Road
Cheltenham
Glos GL50 2JA
UK

Edward Elgar Publishing, Inc.
William Pratt House
9 Dewey Court
Northampton
Massachusetts 01060
USA

A catalogue record for this book
is available from the British Library

Library of Congress Control Number: 2012943536

This book is available electronically in the ElgarOnline.com Law Subject Collection, E-ISBN 978 1 78100 601 6

ISBN 978 1 84542 937 9

Typeset by Columns Design XML Ltd, Reading
Printed and bound by MPG Books Group, UK

To Henriette

Contents

Preface

This book analyses Internet regulation in the European Union (EU). Frank Easterbrook, pointing out the danger of collecting different strands of study into a unified one, famously called Internet law 'the Law of the Horse'.[1] His warning is still valid today. Assuming that Internet law is a unified field, we run the danger of forgetting that its regulation arises out of more general, older legal disciplines. Nevertheless, the Internet has been part of our reality for two decades. Today it penetrates our lives to an unprecedented extent and we can no longer be happy attempting to view it through the prism of other disciplines. Although it may have earlier been true to say that intellectual property or contract law was sufficient to explain the Internet, this is no longer true. There are two reasons for this. First, as a result of the digital revolution, rather than applying the inherited concepts to the digital world, the traditional phenomena such as property, privacy and identity need to be reconceptualized in a broader non-digital frame. Second, the ubiquitous new phenomena, such as user-generated content or social networks, bring new rules, a new language and a new social context which do not easily lend themselves to traditional legal classification.

In this book we understand the Internet to mean a world-wide web of interconnected computers which use the same language (protocol) to communicate. As such, we do not distinguish between the Internet provided through the regular broadband pipe and through other means (LAN networks, new generation 3G or 4G mobile networks, etc.) This approach inevitably means that a range of phenomena typically relevant in information technology (but which do not involve publicly accessible connected networks) are out of the scope of this book. In other words, this book is not about information technology systems in general but only those which operate on the publicly accessible World Wide Web.

Three other remarks about this book's scope are in order.

First, a number of works have already been written on the subject of electronic commerce, both in the EU and abroad. Although it is tempting

---

[1]   Easterbrook, F.H., 'Cyberspace and the Law of the Horse' (1996) *University of Chicago Legal Forum* 207.

to view the Internet purely as an electronic commerce phenomenon, this would be both wrong and misleading. Although most activities on the World Wide Web have commercial aspects, only some of them take place in the purchase–sale form. A regular visit to a free news website, for instance, is commercial only in that the site generates revenue from advertising, but does not take place in the form of a purchase of a subscription and is outside the scope of a simple electronic sales contract. In other words, Internet regulation is wider than the regulation of sales transactions that take place on the Internet.

Second, excellent works exist on EU intellectual property, EU copyright, EU telecommunications, EU privacy or EU consumer protection. The work which we offer is meant neither to replace nor to compete with them. Instead, we attempt to provide an overview of how these disciplines fit together in situations concerning Internet regulation. As such, the work is not meant as a simple catalogue of disparate legal disciplines but as an attempt to understand their interaction. The chapters that follow represent a collection of what are typically encountered as legal problems in Member States' courts.

Third, the Internet has two components. The first is the infrastructure on which the content is transmitted. The second is the content itself. The former is subject to a separate and relatively complex legal discipline called telecommunications law. The second is the subject of various legal disciplines that are covered in this book. The decision not to talk about telecommunications regulation is a result of two factors. The first are space constraints. The second is the existence of a conceptual difference between the regulatory environment which applies to the wires as opposed to that which applies to the content. Although other media (such as television or radio) share many features with the Internet, they are, as a rule, non-interactive and distributed from the centre to the periphery and therefore subject to different principles.

This book is not an attempt to analyse the Internet as a Single Market phenomenon. Although the European Commission often uses Article 114 of the Treaty on the Functioning of the European Union (TFEU) as a legal basis when regulating the Internet, the main reason for harmonization is arguably not the fear that disparity between Member States' laws would slow the economic development but rather that a lack of a coherent vision would have a negative impact on such development in the EU. The EU lawmaker, in other words, acts not so much as a harmonizer as it acts as a policy-maker.

The EU's efforts in Internet regulation may at first appear confusing. Instruments are numerous, policies difficult to distinguish, court decisions conflicting, official statements contradictory, proposals incoherent.

But these problems can only partially be attributed to systemic or bureaucratic failures. Arguably, there are two reasons for this apparent failure. The first concerns the radical rethinking of the user/consumer's role. Few media have contributed to turning the world into McLuhan's 'global village'[2] as much as the Internet has. The reason why it surpassed newspapers, radio, television and other communication media is simple: it allows participation. It turns passive consumers into active players and contributors. The implications of such a new global village for the economy and society at large are as yet unknown. But some elements of the picture are already beginning to emerge. We know that participation increases the number of players (and therefore interests) on the board exponentially. This is the second reason for the apparent failure. We are aware that holders of vested rights are fighting innovation which they perceive is endangering their interests. We know that governments, corporations and other individuals all have their own interests in violating privacy. We are aware of the crucial role of consumers. These disparate interests are not easy to balance.

The Internet gives us the opportunity to rethink the world we live in. It is a thought experiment in developing legal rules for new social contexts. But the Internet also creates these new social contexts. The motivation for this book on EU Internet law comes from the desire to systematize many instruments that either apply to Internet regulation or have been specifically drafted for that purpose. Today, the United States stands at the forefront of Internet development. Most of what other jurisdictions do can be interpreted as a response or reaction to a trend that comes from the US. The European Union has answered most of these challenges. Sometimes, these answers are distinct, even original or unique. That is the case with at least the introduction of the country of origin principle in the Electronic Commerce Directive. On the other hand, occasionally, the solutions are questioned by businesses and the wider public alike. In any case, European regulation of the Internet is a reality.

* * *

This book is a result of a long-lasting interest in Internet regulation. Thanks are due to many individuals and institutions with which the author was fortunate to interact over many years. The author wishes to specially thank the staff and colleagues at the Law Faculty, University of Cambridge, Emmanuel College and Kings College, Cambridge, where he

---

[2] McLuhan, M., *The Gutenberg Galaxy: The Making of Typographic Man* (University of Toronto Press, Toronto 1962), p. 21

lectured and was a fellow from 2001–07. I am grateful to my colleagues at the Law Department, Copenhagen Business School, where I have worked since 2007. Finally, I am greatly in debt to my family and in particular to my wife, Henriette, whose patience and support has been material to this work's completion.

* * *

The law is up to date as of 1 June 2012.

Cases of the European Court

Secondary legislation

1. Internet regulation in the European Union

1. CHALLENGES OF CYBERSPACE

The modern world has been subject to information and communication technology (ICT) penetration at an unprecedented level. The main aspect of this phenomenon has been the ability to distribute information and knowledge widely and at great speed. This is a phenomenon that predates our decade and even the last century. But the Internet, as its latest manifestation, is fundamentally different from a television transmission or a newspaper, neither in its purpose nor in its ability to reach audiences instantaneously but in its capacity to involve them as active participants. This active participation and its networking potential are unique to the Internet and a direct result of its architecture, which promises low costs, decentralization and anonymity. To maintain this liberating potential, prudent regulation is needed. At the beginning of the Internet's history, however, it was believed that cyberspace cannot be regulated at all and ought to be left to its own means. We now know this not to be true, but we still do not know how to regulate it.

The Internet attracts and empowers people but at the same time makes itself a target of control and a battleground of interests. On one hand, with its vast potential for information distribution, the Internet is often viewed by the general public only or primarily in light of its liberating potential. Regulation is here perceived as something restrictive that endangers and limits the acquired liberties. On the other, a different trend is emerging: the Internet is gaining a reputation as dangerous, morally dubious and difficult to control. Consumers are attracted to the potential that the Internet opens up for them but are afraid of the lack of protection. Businesses are eager to benefit from electronic commerce (e-commerce) but weary of having to become accustomed to different legal systems or of becoming liable in different jurisdictions. Content producers see new business opportunities but are loath to abandon habits formed in the old world. In this duality of its character lie the power, the danger and the difficulty of governing the Internet.

Both the United States and the European Union have decisively shaped the Internet as we know it today.[1] As a result of its economic strength and of its strong starting position, the United States has been the dominant force behind the Internet's expansion, although the European Union followed in its steps. The Internet's emergence as a global medium of communication made a quick impression on the European Union. In little more than a decade, it adopted laws on issues as wide in range as intellectual property, electronic commerce, data protection and privacy, consumer protection and criminal law. Initiatives were tabled as quickly as various technological developments allowed and policies were drafted with an atypical enthusiasm.[2] To an outside observer, this flurry of activity and abundance of documents in the EU makes clear the perceived importance of the Internet but at the same time disguises the fact that Internet regulation remains difficult and ambiguous.

Towards the end of the last century, the number of Internet users started to increase dramatically.[3] Two ideas moved the EU's intervention in this area. First, the European Union acknowledged that the Internet promises further economic development, which cannot be tapped into without intervention in the areas where it directly bears on the Internal Market. On the other hand, the EU also realized that the development and spreading of the Internet had a direct influence on the protection of individuals as consumers and as private persons. The EU began to view electronic commerce as a vital tool in keeping the Single Market competitive. But, the global impact of the Internet was felt in everyday activities too, including the actions of private individuals. The intervention, therefore, could not concentrate on furthering only the Single Market aims but had to include individual freedoms. As a result of this tension, two focal points of EU intervention in the field of Internet law began to crystallize: one centered around the Single Market and the other

---

[1]   On why *nation states* are still primary actors in Internet regulation, see Drezner, D., 'The Global Governance of the Internet: Bringing the State Back In' (2004) 119 *Political Science Quarterly* 477.

[2]   Dickie has aptly called this state of affairs a mixture of 'soft- and hard-law, and of established, pending and proposed law', Dickie, J., *Internet and Electronic Commerce Law in the EU* (Hart, Oxford and Portland, OR 1999), p. 103.

[3]   For statistics on Internet usage in the EU, see European Commission, *Science, Technology and Innovation in Europe* (Publications Office of the European Union, Luxembourg 2011).

around consumers.[4] The first reflected the ideal of a unified European market for goods, services, people and capital and the belief that this aim cannot be achieved without a single market for electronic commerce. The second reflected the EU's determination to protect the individual. Both aims were asserted strongly, beginning from treaty provisions, through directives and judgments. The presence of both aims in EU instruments gave, as will be argued elsewhere in this book, conflicting results.

As a result of fast-paced legislative activity in many loosely connected areas, the Community body of laws relating to the Internet, at present, is not joined in a common overarching structure, guided by Single Market-informed policies. Instead, it is an aggregate of loosely connected secondary laws reliant on the European Commission's (the Commission) interpretation as the first cases slowly trickle through the Court of Justice (the Court). The instruments normally referred to as 'framework directives' act as frameworks only for the specific areas they cover (such as electronic commerce or telecommunications). The policy instruments (such as Action Plans or Green and White Papers) have indirect influence on the multitude of directives in fields other than their own. Many projects were begun in the 1990s, at a time when the Internet was in its infancy and its potential impact poorly understood. Other projects were drafted in fulfilment of the European Union's international obligations, partially under the influence of commercial forces and lobbies. Others yet were a result of the work of the Council of Europe, the EU lacking the required competence.

At the same time, policies and legislation on the other side of the Atlantic appeared more transparent, individual interests were easier to trace and public debate seemed louder. The drafting of such laws as the hotly disputed 1998 Digital Millennium Copyright Act (DMCA)[5] in the US was followed by a public and academic debate, the formation of interest groups and clashes in the Congress. In the US the battles also raged over speech regulation on the Internet in light of the First Amendment, as well as over privacy and the role of intermediaries. In Europe, some of these issues remained altogether unnoticed while many others were observed dispassionately. Where even stricter regimes than those found in the United States came into place beginning in the 2000s, none of the public excitement seen in the US was evident and general

---

[4] Cf. Dickie, J., *Consumers and Producers in EU E-Commerce Law* (Hart, Oxford and Portland, OR 2005), especially Chapters 1 and 7.

[5] H.R. 2281.

interests seemed to be lost in complicated law-making procedures that demonstrated the less democratic traits of EU law-making only too well.

In the meantime, the Internet as it was in the 1990s and early 2000s had gradually transformed. What influenced the Internet of the twenty-first century more than any other development was the presence and expansion of collaborative efforts.[6] The exclusive and limited network of the early 1990s has turned into a global decentralized phenomenon. From a linear model characterized by exclusive content being placed by individual corporations, the web has moved towards a collaborative, interoperable, user-centred platform sometimes referred to as Web 2.0 and, further, to a platform enabling large degrees of personalization.

But it is not only the content distribution model that has changed. The web itself has evolved from a passive medium into a platform, from a released and finished package into a constantly changing, dynamic 'permanent beta'.[7] The concepts of open access and open source are some examples of not only how the Internet can transform the social milieu from which it arose but also of how traditional patterns of regulation can be transformed. At the same time, much of daily life had migrated to the Internet to the extent that the Internet became representative of our culture. We, the users, at the same time, have transformed our identities. The Internet, whose regulation in the hands of the European Union, we observe, is built on an architecture different from any other medium before it.

2. INTERNET ARCHITECTURE

The uniqueness of Internet architecture rests on three groups of features: its layered structure, its end-to-end nature and its neutrality. This architecture led some authors to declare that it also determines its governance method.[8] Technology here determines regulatory policy, which then influences that very technology.

---

   6   Ghosh, R. (ed.), *Code: Collaborative Ownership and the Digital Economy* (MIT Press, Cambridge, MA 2005); Benkler, Y., *The Wealth of Networks: How Social Production Transforms Markets and Freedom* (Yale University Press, New Haven, CT and London 2006).
   7   On Web 2.0, see O'Reilly, T., 'What is Web 2.0? Design Patterns and Business Models for the Next Generation of Software', accessed 1.8.2012 at http://www.oreillynet.com/pub/a/oreilly/tim/news/2005/09/30/what-is-web-20.html.
   8   The clearest exposition of this term is Lessig's 'code is law' thesis. See Lessig, L., *Code 2.0* (Basic Books, New York 2006).

The idea of the *layered structure* describes the Internet's heterogeneous nature and the complexities of its hardware, software and substance: the Internet is not homogenous but rather composed of different layers.[9] In order to regulate the Internet properly one has to embrace and understand its layered structure. Or, in other words, 'regulation should be directed at or match the layer where the problematic conduct arises'.[10]

The *end-to-end architecture* refers to the Internet's decentralized nature and its lack of dependency on a central distribution system. This architecture depends on packet switching, decentralized standard-setting, cryptography and anonymity.[11]

Packet switching is a technology that is inherently difficult to control by traditional mechanisms applied to telecommunications. The computers are independently managed but connected in a network and adhere to a common standard enabling them to communicate (the TCP/IP protocol). The most important feature of the protocol is that it enables the data to be broken into packets, which are then transmitted through the network of intermediaries and reassembled in the target computer. The data can use any route available on the way but the route chosen does not have an impact on the quality of the ultimate information received. This feature of the Internet is a result of the original client's (the US Defense Department) desire to make the network resistant to failures of individual communication lines.

Directly in connection with this is the decentralized standard-setting. Although the original network arose under the auspices of the US government, the actual standard-setting is performed by non-governmental bodies. The first among these is the Internet Engineering Task Force (IETF). Another significant body is the World Wide Web Consortium (W3C). The very influential organization in charge of the domain names is the Internet Corporation for Assigned Names and Numbers (ICANN).[12]

---

[9] Solum, L.B. and Chung, M., 'The Layers Principle: Internet Architecture and the Law' U San Diego Public Law Research Paper No. 55, accessed 1.8.2012 at http://ssrn.com/abstract=416263.

[10] Solum, L.B. and Chung, M., op. cit., p. 104.

[11] Froomkin, M., 'The Internet as a Source of Regulatory Arbitrage', in Kahin, B. and Nesson, C. (eds), *Borders in Cyberspace* (MIT Press, Cambridge, MA 1996), pp. 129–63.

[12] On the role that the US plays here, see Wu, T., Dyson, E., Froomkin, M. and Gross, D., 'On the Future of Internet Governance', American Society of International Law, Proceedings of the Annual Meeting, Vol. 101, accessed 1.8.2012 at http://ssrn.com/abstract=992805.

Connected with these features are anonymity and cryptography. A varying degree of anonymity is available and even guaranteed to users on the Internet.

Following from this last feature is what Froomkin[13] calls regulatory arbitrage – the ability of Internet users to evade unfavourable regulatory regimes by choosing to subject their transaction to more liberal ones. The first consequence of this is that proper censorship is difficult. A website can be registered under any one of a multitude of domain names (every country has one plus there are a number of universal ones such as .biz, .org, .eu, or others). The content itself can be offered for hosting to any one of the thousands of hosting services across the globe. Cryptography can be used on any content crossing the borders. The second consequence is that it is often easier to speak freely on the Internet than it is on traditional media. The countries that do control the Internet with varying degrees of success[14] face rising costs and difficulties as the customer base and the number of services grow.

Alongside its architecture, which opens up its liberal potential, the Internet is also influenced by the regulatory regime to which it is subject. That regime has been described by Oxman[15] as having succeeded due to three factors. First, no legacy solutions were imposed on new technologies. The Federal Communications Commission (FCC) has treated information technology (IT) services as unregulated from the moment they appeared. They were transmitted through telephone infrastructure, and yet they were not regulated as telephone services. Second, as Internet services began replacing legacy services, the former were not forced into regulatory models of the latter but, rather, remained unregulated. As services such as Voice over Internet Protocol (VoIP) and wireless access spread, this should have the effect of removing the regulatory burdens from legacy services. Finally, competition was strictly monitored and preserved, and the responses to violations were targeted and minimal – they addressed specific problems rather than the whole industry.

---

[13]   Froomkin, M., see note 11, p. 142.
[14]   Such as China, Saudi Arabia or Iran. On this see Goldsmith, J. and Wu, T., *Who Controls the Internet: Illusions of a Borderless World* (OUP, Oxford 2006).
[15]   Oxman, J., 'The FCC and the Unregulation of the Internet', OPP Working Paper No. 31, in Fitzgerald, B., *Cyberlaw I & II* (Ashgate, Dartmouth 2006), vol. 1, p. 77, at pp. 78 and 99–101.

The final of the three defining features of the Internet is its *neutrality*.[16] In simplest terms it is a concept that describes how the Internet relates to the content posted on it or, in other words, the relationship of the Internet towards applications or services that run on it. More precisely, it refers to the belief that governments should step in to actively prevent the Internet service providers (ISPs) from discriminating between types of data on the network. Presently, the Internet provides the same standards of service (upstream and downstream download speeds, bandwidth, quality of signal) irrespective of the application or content used and distributed. The problem of network neutrality relates to the desire of content providers to gain faster and more capacious access to the infrastructure and thereby charge higher fees for provision of premium content. The question has distinctly political undertones. Yet, this issue, more than any other has the capacity to determine the way the Internet will operate in the present century.

Importantly, network neutrality is a result of Internet architecture. This architecture, as was indicated above, rests on the end-to-end principle: the core of the network is simply a protocol that describes *how* the neutral machines placed at the end of the network communicate. *What* exactly is placed on the network is not a result of a decision made at the core but, on the contrary, on the periphery, where ultimate users reside[17] and changing this balance may damage the Internet.

As a consequence of the described architecture, the Internet is open – not susceptible to authorizations either at the production or at the user end. At the same time, these features make it a subject and target of numerous interests: international, national, corporate and individual.[18] In summary, understanding the Internet's architecture is a prerequisite for good governance of the Internet. Although this point does not have a particularly European flavour it is perhaps worth recalling the complexities of the EU law-making process and emphasizing that good flexible solutions, although much needed, are also the most difficult to achieve.

---

[16] See Nunizato, D., *Virtual Freedom: Net Neutrality and Free Speech in the Internet Age* (Stanford University Press, Stanford, CA 2009). See also Hazlett, T.W., *The Fallacy of Net Neutrality* (Encounter Books, New York 2011).

[17] For more on the consequences of this design and the potential dangers, see Zittrain, J., 'The Generative Internet' (2005–2006) 119 *Harvard Law Review* 1975.

[18] Specifically, on the unobserved security concerns of such an Internet, see Zittrain, J., *The Future of the Internet and How to Stop It* (Allen Lane, London 2008).

3. MAKING LAWS FOR THE INTERNET – INTERNET GOVERNANCE[19]

Many ideas about governing the Internet have crystallized since its emergence. Some are idealistic.[20] Others repeat the metaphor of cyberspace as separate place.[21] A preliminary question, popular at the onset of the debate about Internet regulation, asked whether the Internet can be governed at all. The wave of popular enthusiasm that followed the discovery of the medium's potential dictated a certain kind of optimism that was empowering but ill-suited to the Internet of today. The best representative of that mood is the famous 'A Declaration of the Independence of Cyberspace' written by John Parry Barlow.[22] In memorable words, Barlow said:

> We have no elected government, nor are we likely to have one, so I address you with no greater authority than that with which liberty itself always speaks. I declare the global social space we are building to be naturally independent of the tyrannies you seek to impose on us. You have no moral right to rule us nor do you possess any methods of enforcement we have true reason to fear.

We now know that the 'global social space we are building' is not naturally independent of tyrannies[23] and that governments do have methods of enforcement that both corporations and individuals have reasons to fear.

---

[19] For a detailed overview of issues concerning governance and policies in the IT sector in the EU, see Christou, G. and Simpson, S., *The New Electronic Marketplace: European Governance Strategies in a Globalising Economy* (Edward Elgar, Cheltenham, UK and Northampton, MA 2007). See also Bygrave, L. and Bing, J., *Internet Governance: Infrastructure and Institutions* (OUP, Oxford 2009). In this book we understand 'governance' to mean the problem of ruling the Internet in general and not just the issue of domain name regulation.

[20] Barlow, J.P., 'A Declaration of Independence of Cyberspace', in Fitzgerald, B. (ed.), *Cyberlaw I & II* (Ashgate, Dartmouth 2006), Vol. I, p. 129.

[21] On the problems associated with this and the dangers arising from it for the judiciary, see Hunter, D., 'Cyberspace as Place' (2003) 91 *California Law Review* 439 and Lemely, M., 'Place and Cyberspace' (2003) 91 *California Law Review* 521.

[22] Barlow, J.P., op. cit.

[23] For an empirical study of the Chinese government's measures to control the Internet, see Zitrain, J., 'Internet Filtering in China', Harvard Law School Public Law Research Paper No. 62, IEEE Computing, March/April 2003, p. 70.

Other ideas, however, have crystallized into policy and decidedly shaped the Internet. Among these, few are as indicative of the formative phase of the Internet or as important for the course that it took as ex-President William Clinton's 'A Framework for Global Electronic Commerce'.[24] The principles which it contains, informed by the liberal 1990s, have pushed the Internet from a purely regulatory environment into governance, from hard to soft law and from public to private regulation.

The Clinton framework notes that the expansion of the Internet has been driven primarily by investment from private corporations. In order to maintain the acquired freedom, the regulatory 'nudge' is supplied in the form of a simple idea that the Internet must not be regulated but ought to be market-driven, and that markets and not governments are the most efficient regulators. To ensure future development, businesses and consumers should maintain their central role with as little government intervention as possible. On the contrary, governments should encourage self-regulation and create such environments that would enable free and unhindered development of the Internet. Following from that, governments should avoid undue restrictions and, where their involvement is needed, 'its aim should be to support and enforce a predictable, minimalist, consistent and simple legal environment for commerce'. Governments should also recognize the unique qualities of the Internet and not attempt to fit the Internet to the legacy regime developed for telecommunication services. Finally, e-commerce should be facilitated on a global basis. The ideas developed here were followed and copied in the European Union's Initiative in Electronic Commerce from 1997.[25]

Internet governance does not have a precise definition. The Working Group of Internet Governance defines Internet governance in the following manner:[26]

> Internet governance is the development and application by governments, the private sector and civil society, in their respective roles, of shared principles, norms, rules, decision-making procedures, and programmes that shape the evolution and use of the Internet.

---

[24]   Clinton, W., 'A Framework for Global Electronic Commerce', in Fitzgerald, B. (ed.), *Cyberlaw I & II* (Ashgate, Dartmouth 2006), Vol. I, p. 133.

[25]   European Commission, *A European Initiative in Electronic Commerce, Communication to the European Parliament, the Council, the Economic and Social Committee and the Committee of the Regions,,* COM(97) 157, 15.4.1997.

[26]   Working Group on Internet Governance, Report July 2005, accessed on 1.8.2012 at http://www.wgig.org/docs/WGIGREPORT.pdf.

As is apparent, one important feature distinguishes 'governance' from pure 'regulation': governance applies to international organizations, citizens and businesses in addition to governments understood in a traditional sense. Governance, in other words, is an attempt to address a global phenomenon by global action. The importance of the above definition lies in the recognition of the fact that the Internet is not ruled or shaped purely by *laws* or *regulation* but also by the fact that the idea of governance itself is not limited to domain name regulation but spreads to all 'principles, norms, rules, decision-making procedures, and programmes' that shape the Internet. The Internet, in other words, requires something more than pure traditional 'regulation'.

In recent years, the concept of 'new governance' has been extensively discussed in the European Union.[27] Although the term does not have a firm definition many of its features are known. It suggests alternative legal paradigms for regulating issues ranging from environment to education and others. It was said[28] that the mere usage of the term governance suggests that the approach in the EU is already changing from 'command-and-control' towards a 'regulatory' one. Some of the features that can be used to describe it include diversity, revisability and provisional character. Others are participation of the affected, transparency, openness, evaluation and review. A central authority would have the task of coordinating the new governance and facilitating 'the emergence of new infrastructure'.

We suggest, and will demonstrate in different parts of this book, that the dominant EU paradigm is, therefore, that the Internet ought to be *governed* rather than purely *regulated*. But how is the right balance chosen between intervention of national governments, involvement of independent bodies and of corporations and the power of the medium, which has, it seems, a significant potential to regulate itself?[29] Which governance model preserves the autonomy of the Internet, its liberalizing potential and its networking power while enabling the state to regulate?

---

[27]   For an overview of the issues involved, see De Búrca, G. and Scott, J. (eds), *Law and New Governance in the EU and the US* (Hart Publishing, Oxford and Portland, OR 2006).

[28]   De Búrca, G. and Scott, J., op. cit., p. 2.

[29]   On the issue of regulating cyberspace through technology, see Reidenberg, J., 'Lex Informatica: The Formulation of Information Policy Rules Through Technology' (1998) 76 *Texas Law Review* 553. See also Lessig, L., 'The Law of the Horse: What Cyberlaw Might Teach' (1999) 113 *Harvard Law Review* 501.

Looking purely in terms of traditional regulation, there are four (exclusive or concurrent) potentially applicable governance models.[30] They can briefly be described as follows.

The first model presupposes the extension of territorial sovereignty. This model assumes that the present legal paradigm based on state territorial sovereignty is adequate for Internet regulation, and its proponents say that the state can simply adapt its current laws to apply to the Internet. The latter is not a separate entity that exists outside national borders, but, on the contrary, is largely subject to national jurisdictions which states can and should take advantage of. A large proportion of activity on the web does rely on this model, ranging from protection and enforcement of intellectual property rights to data protection, taxation or consumer protection. In fact, it would be difficult to claim that this model is anything but dominant today. This, of course, does not mean that the Internet is illiberal and subject to government restrictions, or liable to adapt to the standard of the most restrictive state. The application of this model simply means that the Internet can be contained. In as much as this localization is present, that is, to the extent that the users and the networks are found in individual geographic locations, the rules that apply to them will also be local. This prevents neither the globalizing nor the liberalizing effect of the Internet which both derive from its architecture. In fact, one can go as far as to say that Internet architecture encourages regulatory competition and forces governments to be liberal rather than restrictive regulators. This competition has been especially evident in the case of electronic commerce, where businesses tend to place themselves in jurisdictions legally and financially more favourable to them.

At the same time, it would be wrong to say that complete reliance on national regulation is a desirable model. First, the relationship between regulation and innovation is still largely unknown. An overly restrictive regulatory climate *may* create a less competitive, less innovative digital economy. Second, a significant number of areas (such as regulation of spam, child pornography, domain names or data transfer between states) require either cooperation between states or corporate involvement, or both.

The second model relies on international agreements and international regulatory efforts. The Internet, its proponents argue, should be left to international agreements, concluded between sovereign Member States. The record of such achievements is, at least at the present time, poor

---

[30] See Johnson, D.R. and Post, D.G., 'Law and Borders: The Rise of Law in Cyberspace' (1996) 48 *Stanford Law Review* 1367.

although existent.[31] An interesting example of this approach is found in
the EU–US Agreement on transfers of passenger data.[32] The EU regime
forbids private data transfer outside the European Union unless specific,
very strict conditions have been met. This transfer agreement introduces a
special regime for data transfer across the Atlantic as a way of over-
coming these limitations. The US security regulations require that all
passenger airline data is transferred, and the two parties managed to
negotiate a deal setting the conditions on which such data can be
provided to the US.

The third model of regulation relies on new international organizations.
This model presupposes the creation of new international organizations
formed specifically to deal with the Internet and entrusted with its
regulation. Examples of organizations which have operated with success
include the Internet Corporation for Assigned Names and Numbers
(ICANN), the World Wide Web Consortium (W3C) or the Internet
Society (ISOC).

The nature of these organizations varies. The first, ICANN, is a
non-profit organization created in 1998 to supervise the performance of a
number of Internet-related tasks of which the most notable is the
assignment of Internet names and addresses. The second, the World Wide
Web Consortium, is a standards organization for the World Wide Web. It
is a consortium of member organizations, of which there are presently
over 400, which it coordinates in their job of setting Internet standards.
The third, the Internet Society, is an international organization for the
promotion of Internet use.

Some of the organizations are unique and historical. Such is the position
of ICANN, whose importance cannot be replicated any more than its
control can be wrested away from the United States. Others, such as W3C,
are, although successful, entrusted with standard-setting rather than regulation. Others, yet, play a limited role. Arguably, this model has not had a
significant success rate in any of the Internet governance areas today.

The final model emphasizes Internet architecture and its regulatory
potential.[33] This idea has in the past been influential and important but

---

[31]   For the Cybercrime Treaty, see Chapter 10.

[32]   Council Decision, Brussels, 24 June 2010, 11222/1/10 REV 1. A previous
Council Decision, 2004/496/EC, 17 May 2004, on the conclusion of an Agree-
ment was annulled by the European Court of Justice. See C-317/04 and C-318/04
*European Parliament v Council of the European Union and Commission of the
European Communities* [2006] ECR I-4721, 30 May 2006.

[33]   Although Lessig is usually credited with the metaphor, it originated with
Mitchell, see Mitchell, W., *City of Bits: Space, Place, and the Infobahn* (MIT

also poorly understood.[34] In simple terms, the architecture or 'code' of the Internet produces regulatory effects. The Internet is governed not only by traditional regulatory methods in the form of legal norms but also and primarily by the architecture it is based on. Any impact on the regulatory regime also brings changes to the architecture itself, making it more or less restrictive. The present Internet is liberal only because it is built on architecture not easily subject to centralized control. But, although this may evoke the vision of the invisible hand leading the Internet, one of Lessig's most important ideas is that cyberspace should *not* be left to the invisible hand:

> [W]e have every reason to believe that cyberspace, left to itself, will not fulfil the promise of freedom. Left to itself, cyberspace will become a perfect tool of control. ... The invisible hand, through commerce, is constructing an architecture that perfects control[35]

Or, in another place:

> We can build, or architect, or code cyberspace to protect values that we believe are fundamental. Or we can build, or architect, or code cyberspace to allow those values to disappear.[36]

However, the issues are of considerable complexity.[37] The idea that code can have a regulatory effect seems foreign to an ordinary legal mind and its implications are hotly debated.[38]

Press, Cambridge, MA 1995), p. 111. For another early version of the metaphor, see Reidenberg, J., 'Lex Informatica: The Formulation of Information Policy Rules Through Technology' (1998) 76 *Texas Law Review* 553.

[34] See Wu, T., 'When Code Isn't Law' (2003) 89 *Virginia Law Review* 103, who looks at the problem from the perspective of the interest group behaviour.

[35] Lessig, L., *Code and Other Laws of Cyberspace* (Basic Books, New York 1999), pp. 5–6.

[36] Lessig, L., *Code V 2.0* (Basic Books, New York 2006), p. 6.

[37] For a general debate about code as code and some issues that highlight the difficulties of the relationship between Information Technology and regulation, see Dommerin, E. and Asscher, L., *Coding Regulation: Essays on the Normative Role of Information Technology* (T.M.C. Asser Press, The Hague 2006). See also Wu, T., 'When Code Isn't Law', op. cit., on code as a function of interest group behaviour and on instances where code acts against regulation. On the problem with the idea that code must be subject to political action, see Post, G., 'What Larry Doesn't Get: Code, Law and Liberty in Cyberspace' (2000) 52 *Stanford Law Review* 1439.

[38] See Dommerin, E., 'Regulating Technology: Code is Not Law', in Dommerin, E. and Asscher, L., op. cit.

Closely related to the link between code and law is the idea that the Internet is not suited to direct legal control and needs a more flexible approach in the form of self-regulation.[39] In this context, self-regulation is the delegation of regulatory powers from state to non-state entities comprising of industry representatives. As such, self-regulation is not synonymous with deregulation, which is the reduction of excessive governmental control, or with non-regulation, which is complete absence of regulation. Likewise, self-regulation is not synonymous with governance, which is a general term for a move from regulation to less government-oriented approaches.

In Europe, self-regulation started to gain prominence in the Internet area in the late 1990s. Today, self-regulatory authorities and codes of conduct are widespread. In a study of Internet self-regulation in the EU, the Oxford Internet Institute found that self-regulation had worked best where there was a firm legal basis, where codes of practice were well known and where clarity and transparency were not at issue.[40] The EU itself supports self-regulation, which is mentioned in various EU policy documents,[41] but also endorses co-regulation, which is a combination of state and non-state regulation. In the 2005 EU-commissioned study on co-regulation,[42] this model was seen as a viable option as long as transparency and openness were maintained.

The European Union, as will be seen further in this book, relies on all four models of regulation. But the coexistence of the models does not ensure a 'free' Internet nor does it make the EU a liberal regulator. The perceived and desired freedom of the Internet is a function of many factors. In the European Union, first among them is the Single Market. As the *raison d'être* of the Community, this aim features prominently in all Community legislative measures. However, tensions are present between the Single Market on the one hand and other treaty values, such as the protection of private life, fundamental rights or consumer protection, on the other.

---

[39] See Price, M. and Verhulst, S., *Self-Regulation and the Internet* (Kluwer, The Hague 2005), p. 19.
[40] Oxford Internet Institute, Internet Self-Regulation: An Overview, EU No. 27180-IAPCODE.
[41] See references in section 5 of this chapter.
[42] Hans-Bredow-Institut, 'Final Report Study on Co-Regulation Measures in the Media Sector, Study for European Commission', accessed 1.8.2012 at http://ec.europa.eu/avpolicy/docs/library/studies/coregul/final_rep_en.pdf.

Furthermore, the Internet originated in the United States[43] and much of the development, control as well as legal problems, are inextricably tied to it. Solutions to problems in cyberspace are inevitably presented in the form of juxtaposition between the American ones and all the others. A large number of questions, if not all of them, have a trans-Atlantic dimension. In this book, we will also look at these problems from the United States' perspective. In fact, one of the biggest challenges placed before EU regulators today is facing the United States' regulatory power and providing an alternative to it.[44]

The Internet developed in the United States and its current 'look and feel' is a result of that development.[45] Its main features were a result of both the architecture and the deregulatory approach mandated by the Federal Communications Commission.[46] The architecture, set up in the early sixties and seventies, and careful regulation in the eighties led to the booming of the medium in the nineties and its ubiquity in the twenty-first century. The European Union can never match this historically given fact. Neither does it have to. Its regulatory choices are determined by its own history and environment.

3.1 Domain Name Regulation as an Aspect of Governance

The control of domain name assignment was from the very beginning conducted on behalf of the US government by other organizations, notably the Internet Assigned Numbers Authority (IANA). This organization was established under a contract with the US Department of Defense and put in charge of overseeing global Internet Protocol (IP) address allocation, Domain Name System (DNS) root zone management, and other Internet Protocol assignments. In reality, it was a small group of people, directly supervised by Jon Postel of the Information Society Institute of the University of South California. On 24 December 1998,

---

[43] On the Internet's origins, see Leiner, B., Cerf, V., et al., 'A Brief History of the Internet', in Fitzgerald, B. (ed.), op. cit., p. 3.

[44] For more detail on this issue, see May, B., Chen, J.C. and Wen, K.W., 'The Differences of Regulatory Models and Internet Regulation in the European Union and the United States' (2004) 13 *Information and Communication Technology Law* 259.

[45] For a concise history, see Leiner, B., Cerf, V., Clark, D., et al., 'A Brief History of the Internet', in Fitzgerald, B. (ed.), *Cyberlaw I & II* (Ashgate, Dartmouth 2006), Vol. I, p. 3.

[46] See Oxman, J., 'The FCC and the Unregulation of the Internet', OPP Working Paper No. 31, in Fitzgerald, B. (ed.), *Cyberlaw I & II* (Ashgate, Dartmouth 2006), Vol. I, p. 77.

IANA entered into a transition agreement with the Internet Corporation for Assigned Names and Numbers (ICANN) and transferred its functions to it, effective on 1 January 1999. The United States have, directly or indirectly, been in charge of assignment of names and addresses since the inception of the Internet and are very reluctant to hand over that control to an international body.[47]

At a World Summit on the Information Society held in Tunisia in 2005, a broader international participation was requested. The EU along with some other members proposed a new way of regulating the Internet which relied on cooperation between governments and the private sector.[48] These proposals were defeated at the conference. On 30 June 2005, the United States issued Principles on the Internet's Domain Name and Addressing System.[49] The principles provided:

(a)   The US will continue with its special role to guarantee the security and stability of the Internet.
(b)   The US recognizes the legitimate interests of governments over the national domain name space.
(c)   For the US, ICANN is the main body for the technical management of the Internet core resources.
(d)   The US supports a continuing dialogue on Internet governance.

The most important of these is item (c) – ICANN is the appropriate technical manager of the Internet DNS. This shows primarily that the United States is unwilling to relinquish the control of the DNS management to an international body.

The EU proposal, radically different from the American, relied on the public–private cooperation model:

(a) [the model] should not replace existing mechanisms or institutions, but should build on the existing structures of Internet Governance, with a special emphasis on the complementarity between all the actors involved

---

    47   Kleinwachter, W., 'WSIS and Internet Governance: The Struggle over the Core Resources of the Internet' (2006) 11 *Communications Law* 3–12.
    48   'Proposal for addition to Chair's paper Sub-Com A internet Governance on Paragraph 5, "Follow-up and Possible Arrangements"', WSIS-II/PC-3/DT/21-E of the WSIS Summit, 30 September 2005. For comments, see Kleinwachter, W., op. cit.
    49   National Telecommuncations & Information Administration, *Principles on the Internet's Domain Name and Addressing System*, 30 June 2005, accessed 1.8.2012 at http://www.ntia.doc.gov/legacy/reportoarchives.html.

in this process, including governments, the private sector, civil society and international organisations each of them in its field of competence;

(b) this new public-private co-operation model should contribute to the sustainable stability and robustness of the Internet by addressing appropriately public policy issues related to key elements of Internet Governance;

(c) the role of governments in the new cooperation model should be mainly focused on principle issues of public policy, excluding any involvement in the day-to-day operations;

(d) the importance of respecting the architectural principles of the Internet, including the interoperability, openness and the end-to-end principle.

The notable feature of this model is the public–private cooperation. The private sector would lead the daily operations but governments would be in charge of overseeing them. Importantly, however, this was seen as a movement away from ICANN control and towards an intergovernmental, possibly UN-led, effort. The United States government, backed by the media,[50] vigorously opposed the idea, seeing it as vague and ineffective in practice. The final agreement was a compromise that included wider participation of governments of world nations. This equality of governments, however, is limited to control of their own top-level domains.

Today it does not seem that the ability to control Internet domains really represents the feared power. In our time, the threat to the Internet comes mostly from other sides.[51] Nevertheless, it is a fact that the European Union plays but a marginal role in this sphere of Internet governance.

4. EU COMPETENCE TO REGULATE

When transferring parts of their sovereignty to the Union, Member States placed safeguards in the Treaty on European Union (TEU) ensuring that EU legislation has a proper legal basis, is proportionate to the objective to be achieved and does not violate the principle of subsidiarity.[52] The

---

[50] The papers engaged in a vigorous campaign. The US government, however, exercised pressure on the EU to withdraw the proposal. See letter from Condoleeza Rice and Carlos Guiterrez to Jack Straw, 7 November 2005, accessed 1.8.2012 at www.theregister.co.uk/2005/12/02/rice_eu_letter/. For more on EU–US policy differences, see also Drissel, D., 'Internet Governance in a Multipolar World: Challenging American Hegemony' (2006) 19 *Cambridge Review of International Affairs* 105

[51] See Zittrain, note 17 above.

[52] Article 5 TEU.

authority to legislate in the sphere of information technology, intellectual property, telecommunications or, specifically, the Internet derives from several legal bases and is subject to different procedures. Among these are free movement of services provisions, Articles 49 and 56 TFEU. The Single Market legal basis, contained in Article 114 TFEU, is the most widely used legal basis in the EU, both in general and for various laws affecting the Internet.

The use of the Single Market legal basis has been subject to judicial scrutiny since its introduction in the Single European Act in 1986. In order to speed up the completion of the Single Market, it enabled laws to be adopted more easily with only a qualified majority instead of the more common uniformity. It quickly became popular and was used even when the original purpose was not fulfilled. The culmination came in 1998 with the *Tobacco Advertising*[53] judgment in which the (then) European Court of Justice ruled that Article 114 TFEU could not be used as a general legal basis in the absence of other bases. On the contrary, that basis is available only when there is a genuine Single Market aim. After the *Tobacco Advertising* judgment, in other words, it is much more difficult to rely on the Single Market basis.

In spite of relative clarity of the basis for EU powers, doubts remain as to whether the breadth and the scope of its intervention in the field of Internet law can be squared with the principles of subsidiarity and proportionality. It is doubtful whether subsidiarity, which is the idea that law-making powers should be located at the lowest level of government, close to the citizens, is duly taken into consideration in some of the directives. Subsidiarity rests upon a dual test: not only are Member States not in a position to achieve the objective but the Community itself, by reasons of scale or effect, is better suited to the task.

The claim that serious disruptions in the Internal Market result from lack of harmonization in these areas is tenuous. A typical formulation is found in Recital 6 of the Data Retention Directive:[54]

> The legal and technical differences between national provisions concerning the retention of data for the purpose of prevention, investigation, detection and prosecution of criminal offences present obstacles to the internal market for electronic communications, since service providers are faced with different requirements regarding the types of traffic and location data to be retained and the conditions and periods of retention.

---

[53]   C-376/98 *Federal Republic of Germany v European Parliament and Council of the European Union* [2000] ECR. I-08419.

[54]   More on the Directive can be found in section 4 of Chapter 8.

No 'obstacles to the internal market for electronic communications' have been presented by industry representatives in the months leading to the adoption of the Directive. On the contrary, it is possible to argue that the new requirements present an additional burden for corporations. The principal objective, moreover, is not to contribute to the Internal Market but to help combat serious crime. Examples of these kinds of problems can be found in almost every EU directive affecting Internet law.

On the surface, the EU seems to respect the principle of proportionality as it opts for directives more often than regulations and for framework instruments when possible.[55] On the other hand, on a more substantial level, it can be argued that some community directives, at least, lack proportionality.

The TFEU provisions serve not only as a legal basis for most of the EU's Internet laws but also as a general backdrop for Internet activity in the Community. In that sense, it is to be expected that the Community Single Market law will be applicable in this area. That law, as developed in the Court's cases, states that both discriminatory and non-discriminatory obstacles to trade in goods and services are illegal unless specifically justified in the Treaty or by reference to the Court's own exceptions.

Very few cases concerning the Single Market coming from the European Court of Justice specifically focus on the Internet and those that do, do not necessarily establish far-reaching principles. Nevertheless, the cases serve to support the point that measures restricting the sale of goods or provision of services on the Internet are illegal, unless otherwise justified in the Treaty or by reference to the Court's case law. In *DocMorris*[56] the issue was whether a Dutch company which legally provided pharmaceutical services via a dispensary in Holland, by mail order and on the Internet, can also provide them on the Internet in Germany, where such sales are restricted to authorized pharmacies. The Court, after careful consideration of all the conditions of sale and the classification of drugs, decided that a national measure restricting such sales is a measure having equivalent effect, normally justifiable under Article 36 TFEU but not so if the prohibition is absolute. In *Gambelli*,[57] it was held that the Italian prohibition on online gambling was in

---

[55] See, Protocol on the Application of the Principles of Subsidiarity and Proportionality, OJ C 310/207, 16.12.2004.

[56] C-322/01 *Deutscher Apothekerverband eV v 0800 DocMorris NV* [2003] ECR 000.

[57] C-243/01 *Criminal Proceedings against Piergiorgio Gambelli and Others* [2003] ECR 0000.

violation of the provisions on free movement of services. Both cases illustrate nothing more than the Court's willingness to apply its developed Single Market doctrines to the Internet.

5. EUROPEAN POLICY ON INFORMATION TECHNOLOGY

The history of the EU's interest in Internet law is relatively brief. Although relevant intellectual property (IP) and data protection laws predate the earliest Internet laws, specific e-commerce initiatives can be dated to the mid nineties.[58] On the other hand, someone attempting to find a single EU-endorsed policy document on Internet law or even just electronic commerce would be looking in vain. Doubts remain even over the question whether the European Union actually has a coherent Internet policy rather than a set of mini policies. This is true in spite of an abundance of White and Green Papers and various official agendas. Nevertheless, several documents provide an indication of the drive behind the EU directives to be analysed further in the book.

Historically, the first document of interest to Internet law and the one to colour the EU's subsequent approach to the Internet is the European Initiative in Electronic Commerce from 1997.[59] The purpose of the document was to encourage the growth of e-commerce but its specific interest lies in the Commission's desire to create a 'coherent regulatory framework'. This was to be built on existing 'Single Market legislation which already creates the right conditions for online businesses'.[60] Four guiding principles were developed for the framework. The first related to technology: the EU must 'promote technology and infrastructure' necessary to ensure competitiveness. The second related to regulation: the EU must enable a coherent regulatory framework based on the Single Market. The third related to promotion: the EU was to make consumers

---

[58]   Poullet, Y., 'Towards Confidence: Views from Brussels: A European Internet Law? Some Thoughts on the Specific Nature of the European Regulatory Approach to Cyberspace', in Chatillon, G., *Internet International Law* (Bruylant, Brussels 2005), p. 123. For a more detailed overview, see Chapter 5 in Christou, G. and Simpson, S., op. cit.

[59]   European Commission, A European Initiative in Electronic Commerce, Communication to the European Parliament, the Council, the Economic and Social Committee and the Committee of the Regions, Brussels, COM(97) 157, 15.4.1997.

[60]   A European Initiative in Electronic Commerce, at 111(58)

and industries aware of the opportunities that electronic commerce enables. The last was related to the international dimension: the EU was to ensure effective international participation.

At the same time, four principles were to provide an 'adaptable and appropriate' framework for legislation:

- no regulation for regulation's sake
- all regulation based on Single Market Freedoms
- all regulation to take account of business realities
- all interests to be reached effectively and objectively

Several observations must be made about the Initiative. The first is that the Community is signalling its preference for a flexible approach, which includes self-regulation. This largely follows in the steps of the Clinton administration's 'A Framework for Global Electronic Commerce',[61] which is itself a model of liberal, non-state initiated regulation. The second is that the balance between producers' and consumers' interests is taken into account.[62]

A new policy on Information Technology was initiated under the Council of Europe at the Strasbourg Summit in 1997 and developed in 1999.[63] Highlighting the significant potential of digital technologies, particularly for such issues as freedom of expression, transparency, pluralism, and so on, the document is also interesting for highlighting the darker side of information technology such as cybercrime and threats to privacy. The Declaration highlights access as particularly important for any potential success of information technology. Further to this, important conventions have been drafted under the auspices of the Council of Europe, such as the Data Processing Convention.[64]

The third historically significant step was taken with the Lisbon Declaration and the e-Europe initiative.[65] The initiative was to make Europe the most dynamic 'knowledge-based economy in the world' by

---

[61] See note 23.

[62] Although, in reality, there are reasons to believe that it is tilted in favour of producers. See, for example, Dickie, J., *Consumers and Producers in EU E-Commerce Law,* op. cit. and Christou, G. and Simpson, S., op. cit., p. 99.

[63] 'Declaration on a European Policy for New Information Technologies', adopted by the Committee of Ministers, 7 May 1999.

[64] The Convention for the Protection of Individuals with regard to Automatic Processing of Personal Data, Strasbourg, 28 January 1981.

[65] Communication from the European Commission, E-Europe – An Information Society for All, COM(1999) 687 of 8 December 1999, repeated in the conclusion of the Stockholm European Council on 23 March 2001. See also

2010. Among the declared goals that were to help achieve this were those that related to Internet access (then judged to be slow, uncertain and expensive) and the development of electronic commerce. Internet penetration, it was thought, had to be wider and electronic commerce needed to meet with better acceptance. Both problems were directly related to the need to liberalize the telecommunications sector in the Member States, a difficult step taken only reluctantly, but also due to the lack of a proper legislative framework. In light of this, work was initiated on a number of directives, including the E-Commerce Directive. In addition to this, self-regulation was promoted as was the creation of a separate .eu domain name. The duration of the program, initiated in 2000, was extended in 2002 with the same goals.

Another project, the 'i2010 – A European Information Society for growth and employment',[66] is an information society initiative launched in June 2005 with three aims: to create a 'Single European Information Space'; to strengthen investment in innovation and information technology; and to improve public services and quality of life through better use of ICT. In essence, this is just a continuation of previous policy initiatives.

A Digital Agenda for Europe[67] is an action plan which aims to help deliver a digital Single Market.[68] The key aims are, among others, to improve ICT standard-setting and interoperability, improve trust and security, increase access to fast Internet and improve ICT research and innovation. The Agenda is a list of 101 actions which need to be undertaken to achieve these goals. Among these are legislative actions such as amending the Electronic Signatures and the Electronic Commerce Directives (Actions 8 and 9).

Within the general regulatory framework, inspired and informed by EU policies on information technology, individual policies (or areas) have been developed. Apart from directives discussed elsewhere in this book (such as those covering privacy or consumers), the best examples of these include what is commonly referred to as E-Health, E-Education or

European Council of Ministers, Council Resolution on the Implementation of the eEurope 2005 Action Plan, 5197/03 of 28 January 2003.

[66] Commission Staff Working Paper, Communication from the Commission, 1.6.2005, SEC(2005) 717/2.

[67] Communication from the Commission to the European Parliament, the Council, the European Economic and Social Committee and the Committee of the Regions, A Digital Agenda for Europe, Brussels, COM(2010) 245, 19.5.2010.

[68] See also study: Van Eecke, P. and Truyens, M., 'Legal Analysis of a Single Market for the Information Society' (SMART 2007/0037), 30 May 2011.

E-Government. E-Health, for instance, has been developed as a prioritized area within the e-Europe 2005 Action Plan.[69] Its aim is to implement information and communication technologies across sectors that affect health, education and government. These areas highlight some of the innovative sides of the EU approach to Internet governance.

Finally, even outside of the European Union framework, a number of initiatives have concentrated on the regulation of the Internet. The most notable of these come from the Council of Europe, which has contributed vigorously to information and communication technology regulation by drafting a number of policies, issuing policy statements and working on important conventions.[70] Importantly, the aims of the Council are markedly different from that of the European Union. Unlike the latter, whose primary concern is trade between Member States, the former deals with human rights, democracy and the rule of law.

The picture that emerges from this multitude of policies and instruments is complex and occasionally confusing. Not only is it often not clear which authority stands behind different policies but it is also evident that they may occasionally be confusing and contradictory. Nevertheless, what can be extracted from these instruments is a desire to keep Europe competitive and the idea that a link between technology and development is a key for achieving that aim.

5.1 Net Neutrality

The regulatory framework on telecommunications in the European Union is complex, consisting of over 20 different regulations, directives and decisions.[71] The Second Amending Directive[72] amends the present Framework Directive, which establishes a harmonized network for the

---

[69] E-Health – Making Healthcare better for European Citizens; An Action Plan for a European E-Health Area, Communication from the Commission to the Council, the European Parliament, the European Economic and Social Committee and the Committee of the Regions, Brussels, COM(2004) 356 final, 30.4.2004.

[70] For an overview of their efforts, see Oakley, K., *Highway to Democracy: The Council of Europe and the Information Society* (Council of Europe Publishing, Strasbourg 2003).

[71] See European Commission, *Regulatory Framework for Electronic Communications in the European Union, Situation in December 2009* (The Publications Office of the European Union 2010)

[72] Directive 2009/140/EC of the European Parliament and of the Council of 25 November 2009, OJ L 337/37, 18.12.2009.

regulation of electronic telecommunication. It applies to telecommunications and therefore has only an indirect impact on the Internet. Nevertheless, with the new telecommunications framework, the EU has taken basic measures to ensure net neutrality and some of its provisions are of great significance.

Article 3(a) of the Second Amending Directive provides that measures taken by Member States regarding end-users' access to electronic communications networks shall respect the fundamental rights and freedoms of natural persons, as guaranteed by the 1950 European Convention for the Protection of Human Rights and Fundamental Freedoms (ECHR) and general principles of Community law. Any restrictions may only be imposed if they are 'appropriate, proportionate and necessary within a democratic society' and shall in any case be subject to proper judicial safeguards.

First, under the new telecommunications framework,[73] 'national regulatory authorities' are required to promote 'the ability of end-users to access and distribute information or run applications and services of their choice'.

Article 22(3) of the Universal Service Directive[74] further allows the creation of safeguarding powers for national regulatory authorities to prevent the degradation of services and the hindering or slowing down of traffic over public networks. This provision simply means that national regulatory authorities, after consulting the Commission, can set a minimum quality of service requirements if a problem arises.

Finally, Articles 20(1)(b) and 21(3)(c) and (d) of the Universal Services Directive further strengthen transparency requirements related to the treatment of consumers. These provisions are designed to enable the consumers to better understand the Internet.

Further, the Commission has developed five principles that define net neutrality in the EU:[75]

- freedom of expression is fundamental
- transparency is non-negotiable
- the EU should invest in open networks
- fair competition
- support for innovation

---

[73]   Article 8(4)(g) Framework Directive.
[74]   Universal Service Directive, OJ L 108, 24.4.2002, pp. 51–77.
[75]   Kroes, N., 'Net neutrality in Europe', address at the ARCEP Conference (L'Autorité de Régulation des Communications Electroniques et des Postes), Paris, 13th April 2010, SPEECH/10/153, 23/04/2010.

6. EU TELECOMMUNICATIONS LAW AND THE INTERNET

While the subject of this book is mainly the top and the middle layer of the Internet, that is, the providers' network and the actual content, the EU also regulates the bottom layer – the physical layer used to provide the services. The term telecommunications regulation today refers to legislation pertaining to broadcasting (such as radio and television), regular telecommunications (fixed and mobile telephony) and information technology (provision of Internet access through broadband, wireless and other means).

The telecommunications regulatory framework does not regulate content. This is emphasized in the Framework Directive which separates the 'regulation of transmission' from the 'regulation of content'.[76] In other words, the regulatory framework says nothing about electronic contracts, about the IP status of the material provided, about the privacy of users or the providers, the appropriateness of the content or the possible criminal sanctions. These issues are covered in various other EU and national instruments on electronic commerce, copyright and others and, in the case of audiovisual services, in a separate EU directive.[77]

The EU regulates the telecommunications sector extensively.[78] Telecommunications services have for years been subject to national monopolies and were limited to radio, television and voice telephony. With the technological advances in the 1980s and 1990s, it became necessary to liberalize them and maximize the advantages of the Single Market while increasing competition. This resulted in a number of liberalizing directives in the areas of telecommunications terminals, services and infrastructure.[79]

The basis for telecommunications regulation is provided in Article 106 TFEU. The first paragraph of that article prohibits Member States from discriminating on the basis of nationality as well as violating EU competition rules. The second paragraph covers services of general economic interest and subjects them to the Treaty's rules including those

---

[76] See Recital 10, which specifically excludes most information society services because they do not consist of 'the conveyance of signals on electronic communications networks'. Web-based content is specifically excluded from the framework.

[77] Audiovisual Media Services Directive, OJ L 95/1, 15.4.2010.

[78] In detail see Nihoul, P. and Rodford, P., *EU Electronic Communications Law* (OUP, Oxford 2011).

[79] Nihoul, P. and Rodford, P., op. cit., p. 4.

on competition provided that these do not 'obstruct the performance ...
of the particular tasks assigned to them'. The last paragraph of Article
106 gives the Commission the appropriate law-making powers necessary
to ensure the application of the Article.

In order to prevent distortion of competition in services of general
interest (referred to in Article 106(2)), the Universal Services Directive
ensures the availability of a minimum standard of high-quality services
while establishing the end-users' rights and providing companies' obligations.[80]

As a result of developments in the broadcasting, telecommunications
and information technologies, the EU adopted a new regulatory framework in 2002.[81] The new framework was meant to cover both the Single
Market and competition issues and to improve the development of new
infrastructures and technologies. Additionally, the framework addresses
specifically the convergence between fixed and mobile telecommunications as well as convergence between broadcasting, telecommunications
and information technology. The new framework simply puts all telecommunications services under a single regulatory framework.

The three key instruments of the new regime are the Framework,
Authorisation and Access Directives.

The general framework of the new regime is provided in the Framework Directive.[82] Apart from specific issues, the Framework Directive
introduces national regulatory authorities (NRAs). The market entry is
regulated in the Authorisation Directive[83] while access is covered in the
Access Directive.[84]

With the new framework as updated in 2009, the general operation of
the bottom Internet layer and access to it has been submitted to a uniform
albeit complex regime at European level. The legislation has an impact
not only on neutrality of services but also on the effectiveness of EU
telecommunications services in the Single Market and their competitiveness.

---

[80]   See footnote 70 above.
[81]   The framework was revised in 2009. The amending directives are the First
Amending Directive, OJ L 337/11, 18.12.2009, and the Second Amending
Directive, OJ L 337/37, 18.12.2009.
[82]   OJ L 108/33, 24.4.2002, amended in 2009.
[83]   OJ L 108/21, 24.4.2002, amended in 2009.
[84]   OJ L 108/7, 24.4.2002.

7. CONCLUSION

The debate about Internet law is often subject to simplification as issues are politically coloured or portrayed in black and white. In fact, Internet regulation remains an elusive concept. While the early battles over Internet regulation have largely subsided, the debate about who regulates and when and the share of work between the actors has not. The latest interest in governance, self-regulation and home country control has demonstrated the Internet's adaptability in the face of increasingly complex demands put on it but it has also demonstrated its vulnerability. The Internet is remarkably susceptible to traditional methods of regulation, to traditional models of political pressure and traditional policy-making, none of which should be underestimated. Poor choices lead to an economy that is less dynamic and less competitive but also to a society that is less free.

The European Union has played a crucial part in Internet regulation in Member States. Large parts of electronic commerce, privacy, copyright protection and other areas are extensively covered by EU instruments. Globally, the European Union has a potential to hold a unique position. Its quasi-federal status, so often a source of problems, is also a starting place of regulatory competition and a drive for introducing decentralized solutions. Its desire to introduce new governance models is an asset in a battle to find the right solution, as is possibly its bias for a public over the private model of regulation. Its economic strength makes it a plausible alternative to the omnipresent power of the United States. The choice of governance model is therefore crucial for the development of a new electronic economy in the EU as it is for the preservation of the individual freedoms of its citizens.

One of the theses of this book is that the fluid status of the Internet, its little-explored consequences and its unknown impact warrant as liberal a regulatory approach as possible and a balance between governmental intervention and self-regulation, careful participation in governance efforts and recognition of the exceptional features of the Internet's architecture. As will be demonstrated in the chapters to follow, this is a task that is not always easy to fulfil.

2.   Electronic commerce

1. REGULATING ELECTRONIC COMMERCE IN EUROPE

Electronic commerce has a deceptively simple definition: it is the act of buying or selling goods or services by means of electronic resources. The straightforwardness of this explanation hides the complexity facing the regulator and the great economic importance of the phenomenon. Since the public rise of the Internet in the mid 1990s and through its wide penetration at the turn of the century, the lawmakers across the globe have repeatedly tried to address a host of questions relating to the conclusion of electronic contracts and its consequences. When can contracts be formed on the Internet? Is a simple exchange of emails sufficient? When does clicking on the words 'I Agree' on the seller's web page bind the parties? This anxiety is a result of the Internet's often real but sometimes only perceived borderlessness. In a transaction concluded on the Internet the parties are 'not present'. But this does not differ from contracts concluded over other modes of communication. Sending an offer and receiving acceptance happens in much the same way over email or by clicking the 'I Agree' button on the web page of the supplier as it does by phone, regular mail or fax transmission. From this perspective, it may be surprising that electronic commerce ever got the attention that it did.

On the other hand, the Internet brings real problems, some of which do not appear with other media. If a dispute arises, what courts will have jurisdiction? Will consumers be able to avail themselves of their local protective regime? How can an online payment be processed? The European Union as a developed industrial economy has been exposed to these dilemmas for over fifteen years. Here, like elsewhere, the key problem has been the adequacy and adaptive power of traditional rules and extent of the potential intervention. Part of the European answer to this dilemma has come in the shape of the Electronic Commerce Directive[1] which became a backbone for European regulation in this area.

The Internet's potential lies in the employment opportunities it provides and the growth it brings through investment in innovation and increased competition.[2] The Community legal order, with its liberal regime for the movement of factors of production, represents a particularly positive climate for the development of electronic commerce. Although the current volume of electronic commerce amounts to about 20 per cent of manufacturing shipments only,[3] with a growth rate of 15 per cent per annum, its future potential is considerable. After a boom in the late 1990s and a bust in 2000, the trade has recovered in the early years of the century. Medium- as well as long-term predictions seem to be optimistic. The services sector, which in the developed countries forms the larger part of gross national product, is already heavily dependent on the information society and will be more so in the future. In the first years of the present decade, the Internet penetration in Europe for households stood at about 50 per cent[4] and for businesses at well over 90 per cent. Most companies have a website and an increasing number use the Internet as a business tool. At the moment, e-commerce presents less than a quarter of retail sales in Europe but this number increased from €10 billion in 2000 to €70 billion in 2003 to several hundred billion euros in 2006 and after. Advertising can be singled out as another growing sector in recent years with businesses spending more on online advertisement placements than those in traditional media.

Few laws in the European digital context are as ambitious in their scope or as far-reaching in practice as the Electronic Commerce Directive.[5] Not only is the Directive designed to address central issues in

---

[1] Directive 2000/31/EC on certain legal aspects of information society services, in particular electronic commerce, in the Internal Market, OJ L 178, 17.7.2000. The proposal was adopted in 1998, amended by the European Parliament in 1999 and finally adopted in 2000. The Parliament's most important amendment was to allow ISP liability for breaches of intellectual property rights under certain circumstances.

[2] These are also emphasized in Recital 3 of the Directive.

[3] As of 2004, U.S. Census Bureau E-Stats, 25 May 2006.

[4] Up from 18 per cent in 2000 and 43 per cent in 2002. Source: European Commission, ICT and e-Business for an Innovative and Sustainable Economy, 7th Synthesis Report of the Sectoral e-Business Watch (2010), Office for Official Publications of the European Communities (Luxembourg 2010).

[5] On the historical development of the Directive, see Pearce, G. and Platten, N., 'Promoting the Information Society: The EU Directive on Electronic Commerce' (2000) 6 *European Law Journal* 363.

electronic commerce, a difficult achievement in any context, but also its
ambition is to provide the ground for competing with the United States in
encouraging the use of the Internet in commerce. Although the recitals of
the Directive contain the familiar EU Single Market invocation, it is also
clear that a stable regulatory environment has been set as a primary goal.

It can be said with some confidence that the Electronic Commerce
Directive is one of the more successful initiatives in electronic commerce
in modern times. The Commission reported positively on the Directive in
2003 and confirmed that there was no need for a revision.[6] The two
studies on the Directive commissioned since, the Study on the Economic
Impact of the Electronic Commerce Directive[7] and the Study on the
Liability of Internet Intermediaries[8] have also had positive results.

For Europe, the Directive was the beginning of a crucial phase of
wider regulation of the Internet, but for the outside world, in the form of
the 'country of origin rule', it proved an intriguing approach to the
difficult issue of legislative jurisdiction.

The study of the Directive is complex, involving the analysis of
preparatory work, national legislation and the implementation in Member
States. In this chapter, we will talk about the pursued aims, look at its
main provisions and analyse its modus operandi. We will also look at the
purpose of the Electronic Commerce Directive and at its provisions
concerning the conclusion of electronic contracts and the country of
origin rule. Jurisdiction issues arising out of some of the provisions of the
Directive will be addressed in Chapter 3, liability issues in Chapter 5 and
consumer issues in Chapter 7.

---

[6]   Report from the Commission to the European Parliament, the Council and
the European Economic and Social Committee, First Report on the application of
Directive 2000/31/EC of the European Parliament and of the Council of 8 June
2000 on certain legal aspects of information society services, in particular
electronic commerce, in the Internal Market (Directive on electronic commerce)
COM(2003) 0702 final, 21.11.2003.
[7]   European Commission, DG Internal Market and Services Unit E, Final
Report, 7 September 2007.
[8]   Ulys, T.V., et al. *Study on the Liability of Internet Intermediaries,*
Markt/2006/09/E, 12 November 2007.

2. E-COMMERCE FRAMEWORK

The early Community project on electronic commerce was the action plan, Europe's Way Forward to the Information Society.[9] More tangibly, in 1997 the Commission published the *European Initiative in Electronic Commerce*.[10] Its four guiding principles were to: (a) promote the technology and infrastructure; (b) capitalize on the Single Market by ensuring a coherent regulatory framework for e-commerce; (c) foster a favourable business environment; and (d) reach a common European position. It was to prove the right document for boosting both the interest in electronic commerce among Member States and the awareness of businesses and consumers alike.

In 1997, the Clinton administration published 'A Framework for Global Electronic Commerce[11] which emphasized the belief that the Internet should be market-driven and not regulated. Five principles were to inform Internet governance: (1) the private sector should lead; (2) governments should avoid undue restrictions on electronic commerce; (3) where governments do need to intervene, they should be to support a simple and minimalist legal environment; (4) governments should recognize the unique qualities of the Internet; and (5) electronic commerce should be facilitated globally. The Framework remains one of the strongest statements of a 'hands-free' approach.

In 1997, independently but approximately at the same time as the Clinton/Magaziner framework, the '*European Initiative in Electronic Commerce* identified important areas for action. Among these were the 'access to infrastructure' and the 'creation of a legal framework'. Both frameworks identified the 'new economy' as an area of utmost importance. The Europe Union observed that the initiatives had to be implemented by 2000 if Europe was to benefit from the development of the Internet.[12] The plan, the true beginning of e-commerce regulation in

---

[9] Communication to the Council, the European Parliament, the Economic and Social Committee and Committee of the Regions, COM(94) 347 final, 19.7.1994. This was preceded by the 1993 Commission White Paper on Growth, Competitiveness and Employment – The Challenges and Ways Forward into the 21st Century, which discussed new technologies and their importance for Europe's economy, COM(93) 700 final, 5.12.1993.

[10] Communication to the Council, the European Parliament, the Economic and Social Committee and Committee of the Regions, COM(97) 157, 15.4.1997.

[11] Clinton, W., 'A Framework for Global Electronic Commerce', in Fitzgerald, B. (ed.), *Cyberlaw I & II* (Ashgate, Dartmouth 2006), Vol. I, p. 133.

[12] In reality the implementation dragged well into the 2000s.

Europe, was a starting point for a number of legal initiatives discussed in this and other chapters of the book. It drew inspiration both from the American efforts and from the UNCITRAL Model Law on Electronic Commerce,[13] recasting some of the fundamental principles in a Single Market context.

Some policy values, which can also be looked at as guiding principles, were introduced in the Initiative, to control the new regulatory framework.[14] According to the general EU principle of subsidiarity, Community harmonization should only happen where other integration mechanisms prove insufficient. Accordingly, 'no regulation for regulation's sake' is the first guiding principle. Mutual recognition and home country control should take priority over full regulation. Secondly, the new rules should be compatible with the Internal Market and not conflict with it. Thirdly, the new regulation should follow the realities of the business cycle. Finally, public interests should be taken into consideration, including consumer protection.

The preparatory work on the Directive, in the form of first proposals and comments received on them, both from competent Community institutions and from the general public, reveals that the Community had a number of goals in mind. Primarily, and in accordance with Article 18 TFEU, the aim was to prevent discrimination between Member States of 'information society service providers'.[15] Further to that, the aim was to remove other 'non-discriminatory obstacles'. These were addressed throughout the Directive. To achieve this, the Community expected the Directive to be not only part of a wider scheme of instruments on e-commerce but also to rely on the *acquis communautaire.*

Possibly the most important feature of the E-Commerce Directive is its ambition to be the 'framework directive'. Directive 2000/31 is meant to be part of a larger number of initiatives covering trading that takes place on the Internet. More narrowly defined, this area encompasses measures on the protection of consumers (see Chapter 7), on electronic signatures (see Chapter 9), on e-commerce (this Chapter) and on copyright and related rights (see Chapter 6). More widely defined, it includes a number

---

[13]   UNCITRAL Model Law on Electronic Commerce with Guide to Enactment 1996, United Nations Publications, No. E.99.V.4.

[14]   Pearce, G. and Platten, N., 'Promoting the Information Society: The EU Directive on Electronic Commerce' (2000) 6 *European Law Journal* 363, at 366–7.

[15]   To distinguish them from conceptually narrower Internet service providers, information society service providers are here referred to as ISSs.

of other initiatives concerning money, financial services, taxation and others, also discussed within the mentioned chapters.

The Directive with its counterparts reflects the 'life cycle of electronic commerce activities'.[16] It starts with the establishment of information society service providers, moving on to commercial communication and contracts concluded by electronic means, to end with the liability of intermediary service providers. In spite of this, it is evident that this is not an all-encompassing law on electronic commerce. Indeed, such laws rarely exist at national levels and are of modest success at international levels.[17] The Directive covers what were believed to be the most contentious areas. Furthermore, the Community, limited by principles of subsidiarity and proportionality as expressly recognized in Recital 10, sought to address only the necessary obstacles to electronic commerce between Member States.

The Internal Market was expressly set as the framework for the Directive.[18] The purpose of the Directive and other instruments from the framework is to enable the free movement of information society services. This fits within the general concept of the four freedoms, as they are set out in the TFEU and developed by the European Court of Justice. It is worth remarking that the main idea behind the four freedoms[19] is the prohibition of any restrictions on movement of goods, services, people and capital between Member States. Initially, this was taken to mean discrimination based on nationality.[20] Very importantly, however, in the practice of the Court,[21] the freedoms have been interpreted as including non-discriminatory barriers to movement, those that place an equal burden in law (thus avoiding the difference based on nationality) but a different burden in fact (making it in practice more costly and less competitive for the provider from another Member State).

---

[16]   Lodder, A., 'Directive 2000/31 on Certain Legal Aspects of Information Society Services, in particular Electronic Commerce, in the Internal Market', in Lodder, A. and Kaspersen, H. (eds), *eDirectives: Guide to European Union Law on E-Commerce* (Kluwer Law International, The Hague, London, New York 2002), p. 69.

[17]   On the UN Convention on the Use of Electronic Communications in International Contracts, see Connolly, C. and Ravindra, P., 'First UN Convention on E-Commerce Finalized' (2006) 22 *Computer Law & Security Report* 31–8.

[18]   See Recitals 4, 5, 6 or 59.

[19]   See Articles 34–62 TFEU.

[20]   Also set out as a general Treaty principle in Article 18 TFEU.

[21]   See C-120/78 *Rewe-Zentral AG v Bundesmonopolverwaltung fhr Branntwein* [1979] ECR 649 for goods; C-55/94 *Gebhard* [1995] ECR I-4165 for establishment; and C-76/90 *Saeger* [1991] ECR I-4221 for services.

Article 114 TFEU on the Internal Market is used as a legal basis for the Directive, together with Articles 52 TFEU on establishment and 62 TFEU on services, clearly placing it in a Single Market context and suggesting its main purpose.

A total replacement of national law on contract formation, on the Internet or otherwise, was never contemplated and the framework regime is intended to supplement it only. In EU terms, this can be understood as a 'minimum harmonization' measure, providing only the harmonized basis that must be respected throughout the Community and requiring Member States to recognize that regulation is at the place of origin. This is among the more original but also controversial features as demonstrated by the recent Services Directive.[22] It is worth adding that some EU measures are full harmonization measures, pre-empting further national action even where this increases the standards.[23]

The Internal Market was not the only perspective that the legislator had in mind, however. Although the Directive is not a draft convention and only operates within the EU, relations with third states were clearly in the mind of the regulators, as they thought not only that Europe should have a strong negotiating position (Recital 59) but also that Europe and major non-European areas need to consult each other (Recital 60).

3. E-COMMERCE DIRECTIVE – AIMS AND SCOPE

The Directive applies both to business-to-business (B2B) and business-to-consumer (B2C) transactions. Consumer protection, a specifically business-to-consumer area, is not the focus of the Directive but is recognized by reference in several recitals and in the idea that consumers benefit from electronic commerce by being exposed to greater choices and lower prices. This double nature of the Directive can be explained by the desire to create a universally-enabling instrument which can be supplemented by special consumer protection rules, as needed.

The objectives of the Directive are set out in Article 1, the first paragraph of which refers to the Internal Market. The purpose of the Directive is free movement of information society services between Member States. The Preamble proclaimed that hindrance to trade and

---

[22]   See original proposal: European Commission, Proposal for a Directive of the European Parliament and of the Council on services in the internal market COM(2004) 0002 final, 25.2.2004.

[23]   Most notably the Unfair Commercial Practices Directive (UCP), OJ L 119/22, 11.6.2005.

lack of harmony in Member States in the mentioned areas were primary motivating factors for harmonization. Paragraph 2 of Article 1 states that the tool, which will be used, is the approximation of laws and summarizes the main activity areas in the Directive. These are:

- the establishment of service providers
- commercial communications
- electronic contracts
- intermediary liability
- out-of-court dispute settlement

There were several reasons for focusing the activity on the aforementioned areas of harmonization. Primarily, the problem of the form of an electronic contract was being addressed differently in Member States. Secondly, the problem of the point of creation was increasingly gaining in importance.[24] Thirdly, the issue of whether Internet service providers were liable for the content they transmitted was unresolved and was threatening to slow the Internet's development down. The Directive was therefore meant as a set of solutions to a cluster of connected problems.

Despite ambitious declarations, the authors were aware of the difficulties. Their dilemmas are apparent in the revision history and in the limitations introduced in Article 1.[25] Article 1(3) provides that the Directive does not prejudice any protection of public health or consumers 'in so far as this does not restrict the freedom to provide information society services'. Furthermore, the Directive does not establish additional rules on private international law and does not deal with the jurisdiction of the courts.[26] Paragraph 5 of Article 1 excludes the application of the Directive to taxation, data protection, telecommunications, cartel law, notaries, advocates or gambling. Finally, paragraph 6 excludes measures taken in protection of linguistic or cultural diversity or pluralism.

Each of the limitations to the Directive can be understood in its own context although not all seem entirely justified and a number are not drafted ideally. Article 1(3) would suggest that freedom to provide

---

[24]   Murray, A., 'Entering into Contract Electronically: The Real WWW', in Edwards, L. and Waelde, C. (eds), *Law and the Internet: A Framework for Electronic Commerce* (Hart Publishing, Oxford 2000).

[25]   For the history of some of the provisions of the Directive, see Murray, A., 'Articles 9–11, ECD – Contracting Electronically in the Shadow of the E-Commerce Directive', in Edwards, L. (ed.), *The New Legal Framework for E-Commerce in Europe* (Hart Publishing, Oxford 2005), p. 67.

[26]   Article 1(4). For a detailed discussion of this question, see Chapter 3.

services prevails over public health or consumer protection, as the latter are only protected in so far as they do not restrict the freedom to provide services. Since the priority is clearly set in favour of both public health and consumer protection in other provisions, not least in the Single Market Treaty provisions, this must be interpreted as a mistake. Article 1(4) concerning private international law, although seemingly written in a neutral way, created a lot of controversy over its relationship with the principle of the country of origin. Article 1(5) refers to measures where proper EU harmonization has not happened (for example, the professions) or where resistance from Member States might be too difficult to overcome.

Article 2 defines crucial terms of the Directive. Somewhat curiously, it does not define information services themselves. For that, reference must be made to Recitals 17 and 18 of the Directive. This, in turn, copies a definition given in the Technical Standards Directive.[27] Recital 17 thus says that information society services are:

> provided for remuneration, at a distance, by means of electronic equipment for the processing ... and storage of data, and at the individual request of a recipient of a service.

This is not an unusual definition, although it may sound rigid from the present perspective.

The Electronic Commerce Directive is wider in scope than its title might suggest. This is not surprising. First, as mentioned, it was designed as a framework instrument, part of a broader set. More importantly, it covers the wider business of receiving information society services rather than the narrower act of an online sale, as can be seen in the definition provisions. This makes it applicable in situations not involving trade. Importantly, Recital 18 sets out to explain the nature of the information society services beyond the above definition. In doing so, it emphasizes that they are not restricted to on-line contracting but include those services where information is provided. Another important requirement is the individual demand. Where this is lacking, the services are not covered by the Directive. Therefore, television and radio broadcasting fall without, whereas email or on-demand video are within.

The basic elements of the definition are fourfold. First, the service must be provided for remuneration although the cost need not necessarily

---

[27]   Directive 98/34 of 22 June 1998 laying down a procedure for the provision of information in the field of technical standards and regulations and of rules on Information Society Services, OJ L 204, 21.7.1998.

be borne by the final recipient. A number of extremely important information services, such as web mail or search engines, rely on advertising for their income. Second, the service must be provided at a distance. This should be taken to mean that there must have existed electronic communication between the parties at the time when the contract was concluded. Third, the service must be made by electronic means. Other distance-selling methods are not covered. Finally, the service must be provided at the individual request of a recipient. The last point was introduced to distinguish information society services from television and other broadcasting services. The question remains open, at this point, as to how web television and radio (such as TiVo, Apple TV or Sky+), television provided through mobile devices (smart phones, tablets, etc.) and television provided through personal computers ought to be classified. They contain elements both of on-demand and traditional services, in that the service is provided or requested for, usually through some form of web access, but also that they fall under broadcasting and can mostly also be accessed on traditional media.

Article 2(c) defines the place of establishment of a service provider. This will be the place where the provider has a 'fixed establishment for an indefinite period'. The presence of technical equipment does not, in itself, constitute establishment. The last is an important point, as servers and other equipment are often located in places away from the provider's establishment. The purpose behind the definition, as behind the introduction of the country of origin rule, seems to be to prevent Member States from avoiding the supervision provisions.

4. OPERATION OF THE E-COMMERCE DIRECTIVE

The Electronic Commerce Directive achieves four major goals. First, it eases the establishment and operation of information service providers throughout the EU. Second, it mandates the provision of particular kinds of information in electronic contracts. Third, it takes measures to facilitate electronic contracts. Finally, it limits liability of information society service providers. The first and the third of the features are analysed in this chapter while the second and fourth are looked at in Chapters 7 and 5 respectively.

4.1 Establishment of the Information Service Provider

The Directive's first task is to enable easy establishment of information service providers. Recital 19 sheds light on the term 'establishment' in the Internal Market context. The recital provides that the 'place at which a service provider is established should be determined in conformity with the case-law of the Court of Justice' on establishment. The concept of establishment, as developed in that case law[28] is identified by virtue of the presence of a fixed establishment pursuing activity for an indefinite period. Since establishment is a more permanent presence, and therefore subject to the more stringent control of the 'host state', providers will often seek to avail themselves of more favourable terms of the freedom to provide services. This has resulted in a Communication from the Commission helping to distinguish between the two.[29]

For information society services which operate through websites, the place of establishment is not the place where the technology supporting the website is located, nor the place where the site is accessible, but rather the place where the provider pursues its economic activity. Where the provider has several places of establishment or where it is difficult or impossible to determine one, it shall be the place where the provider has a centre of activities relating to the particular service.[30] The definitions, although helpful, are not precise and it is possible to imagine an operator pursuing economic activity in several centres.

Articles 4 and 5 deal with the establishment of information society service providers. The guiding principle behind these articles seems to be the ease of access to the information required. They demand that recipients of services be able to quickly and easily understand the kind of service they receive and its source.

Article 4 introduces the principle of exclusion of prior authorization. The taking up and pursuit of ISS activities does not depend on any prior requirement. Specifically excluded from this are authorization schemes not specifically targeted at ISS providers and telecommunications services. Article 5 establishes the obligation of the ISS provider to provide information about itself. This includes its name, address, contact details, authorization details, and so on.

A special requirement in Article 5(2) relates to prices, which are often a source of confusion. The first draft provided that 'prices of Information Society services are indicated accurately and unequivocally'. In the second draft, it was added that these prices must also include all

---

[28]   See C-55/94 *Gebhard* [1995] ECR 4165.

[29]   For difficulties in distinguishing services from establishment in banking and insurance sectors, see the Commission's Interpretative Communications on the Second Banking Directive (Brussels, SEC(97) 1193 final, 20.6.1997) and the Third Insurance Directive (Brussels, OJ C 43/5, 16.2.2000).

additional costs. The final text states that prices should be indicated 'clearly and unambiguously' and that they must specify whether they are inclusive of VAT and delivery, where applicable.

4.2 Commercial Communications

Section 2 of the second chapter (Articles 6 to 8) of the Directive deals with commercial communications directed at recipients. Advertising, marketing, unsolicited emails and similar phenomena have grown in importance as electronic commerce developed. At the same time, the development of electronic advertising has exceeded even ambitious expectations. The Directive provides minimum requirements regarding the provider of services and the commercial activity it engages in. The information requirement is not specifically targeting consumers but also applies to B2B transactions.

Article 6 establishes information obligations which are additional to any other requirements imposed on the ISS provider elsewhere. The commercial communication must, according to this Article, be identifiable as such, as must be the entity on whose behalf this is provided. The regulation of promotional offers, discounts and similar incentives is left to Member States but must be identifiable as must be any conditions necessary to qualify for them, where permitted. Finally, competitions and games are also left for regulation by Member States but the same conditions apply to them as to promotional offers. In the area of financial services, the Commission issued a Communication concerning the application to them of Articles 3(4) to 6,[31] which was a result of a concern expressed by financial service providers about the areas which did not yet converge.

Article 7 deals with unsolicited commercial communication, or spam, as this is more commonly referred to today.[32] At this stage we will only say that the provision, as adopted in the Directive, was always inadequate to cope with the shear volume of such communication. The provision leaves the legality of spam to Member States but obliges them to introduce provisions which would oblige the sender of a communication to identify it as such as soon as received. Further to that, Article 7(2) obliges the Member States to take measures to make sure that service providers respect opt-out registers containing the names of those not wishing to receive such communication.

---

[31] COM(2003) 259 final, 14.5.2003.
[32] Spam will be dealt with in more detail in Chapters 8 and 10.

Article 8 covers regulated professions. Services provided by a member of a regulated profession (such as solicitors, notaries, etc.) are allowed, subject to compliance with the general rules but also any professional rules (such as those concerning conduct, secrecy and such). Professional associations are encouraged to provide codes of conduct at Community level. The E-Commerce Directive does not prejudice other Community instruments regulating professional conduct.

In light of the recent developments in this area, it is submitted that the area of commercial communication as set out in this part of the Directive is out of date. The Community left it to Member States to actually make unsolicited commercial communication illegal and limited itself to imposing information requirements (which have already been covered in the Distance Selling Directive). More importantly, perhaps, unsolicited communication is undesirable by virtue of its high cost rather than the annoyance factor to the end-user/recipient. The Directive does little to address this or the problem of unsolicited communication coming from third states.

4.3 Concluding Contracts on the Internet

The Electronic Commerce Directive is not a model law for electronic commerce.[33] It does not replace national civil law rules and does not give the answer to such questions as existence of offer or acceptance, the place of performance or consequences of breach. Such rules come from national laws and remain unchanged (although not unrecognized) by EU rules.

In the previous chapter we have examined some of the issues concerning regulatory competence in Internet law and identified some of the powers that the EU relies on to regulate in that area. The EU, we have concluded, has the legislative competence to act. But, this is not necessarily the case in civil law where the European Union has only very limited powers to regulate and is generally not in a better position than Member States to do so.[34] These powers have always been used with

---

[33] Such a document has been created in 1996 under the auspices of UNCITRAL as the 'UNCITRAL Model Law on Electronic Commerce with Guide to Enactment', General Assembly Resolution 51/162 (United Nations 1996). See also United Nations Convention on the Use of Electronic Communications in International Contracts, UNITED NATIONS PUBLICATION, A/Res/ 60/21, 5 December 2005.

[34] For a recent attempt to create an optional European sales law, see Communication from the Commission to the European Parliament, the Council,

restraint and, despite occasional doubts, are usually well accepted by Member States.[35]

Article 9 of the E-Commerce Directive imposes a requirement that Member States make it possible for contracts to be concluded by electronic means. This reflects a desire for electronic contracts to be concluded in a manner as close as possible to normal contracts. Member States are under an obligation to ensure that legal requirements applicable to the contractual process do not create obstacles for the use of electronic contracts nor result 'in such contracts being deprived of legal effectiveness and validity on account of their having been made by electronic means'.

The E-Commerce Directive does not cover the typical life cycle of a contract, which includes negotiations, formation, performance and possible remedies and dispute resolution. Section 3 of the Directive, entitled 'Contracts concluded by electronic means' contains some important elements, but does not suggest a full harmonization of the area. It is interesting to note that the original draft for the Directive was somewhat more ambitious in including more detailed provisions on the formation of the contract. These can still be found buried in the preparatory works. Even when other e-commerce-related directives are included, no comprehensive system of electronic contracts emerges: the instruments such as the E-Money Directive[36] complement the picture but do not create a system of Internet contract law.

The answer to why this is the case can be found in the 1997 Initiative,[37] which clearly shows that the extent of the Commission's intentions were limited. Looking through the lens of concern for how the existence of multiple regulatory systems might affect electronic commerce, the following is said:

> A number of Member States' rules governing the formation and the performance of contracts are not appropriate for an electronic commerce environment and are generating uncertainties relating to the validity and enforceability of electronic contracts (for example the requirements for written documents, for hand written signatures, or the rules of evidence that do not take into account electronic documents). The Commission will take concrete steps to address

---

the European Economic and Social Committee and the Committee of the Regions, a Common European Sales Law to facilitate Cross-border Transactions in the Single Market, COM(2011) 636 final, 11.10.2011.

[35] For an overview of the EU's regulatory efforts in private law, see Twigg-Flesner, C. (ed.), *European Union Private Law* (CUP, Cambridge 2010).

[36] See section 3, Chapter 9.

[37] COM(97) 157, 15.4.1997.

the problem of how to *eliminate barriers for the legal recognition of electronic contracts* within the Single Market. Furthermore, as regards *consumer protection* in the field of electronic commerce, this point shall be dealt with in the Communication on the Consumer Dimension of the Information Society. [emphasis added]

On an international plane the Directive is also not unique. An important inspiration, the UNCITRAL Model Law, was published in 1996. It sought to improve legal certainty and predictability for e-commerce transactions.[38] The UN Convention on e-commerce followed in 2005.[39] The basic principles of the Convention are functional equivalence (paper documents equal electronic ones) and technology neutrality (the law does not discriminate between forms of technology).[40] The Convention maintains party autonomy, also present in other UNCITRAL documents.[41] Most of the solutions in the Directive correspond to those in the Model Law and this relationship is expressly referred to in the Commission's 2003 Report.[42]

The Community's legal effort regarding electronic contracts, however, should not be undervalued. The intervention is extensive with wide and varying issues covered, ranging from payment and consumer protection to various aspects of jurisdiction. Even where the instruments are general in scope, such as the European Regulation on recognition and enforcement of foreign judgements (Brussels I Regulation),[43] some thought has been given to the issue of electronic commerce and the effects it might have.

The E-Commerce Directive itself covers a range of issues. In the area of pre-offer information, for instance, the Directive requires the Information Society Providers to make certain information available,[44] regulates the establishment of providers[45] and regulates certain aspects of the placing of the order.[46] Although various aspects concerning offer and acceptance are covered in the following sections, it is sufficient to point out here the fact that the national law of a Member State will apply to

---

[38]   See footnote 34.
[39]   See footnote 34.
[40]   See in particular Articles 8 and 9.
[41]   Article 3.
[42]   See footnote 6 above, point 97.
[43]   Council Regulation No. 44/2001 on jurisdiction and the recognition and enforcement of judgments in civil and commercial matters, OJ L12/1, 16.1.2001.
[44]   Article 10.
[45]   Articles 4 and 5.
[46]   Article 11.

general issues concerning electronic contract formation. These laws will not be analysed here.[47]

4.4 Contracts in Electronic Commerce

Section 3 of the Directive covers contracts concluded by electronic means. As was said above, this section does not harmonize contract law or replace national provisions in this area. This is clear from Section 3 as it is from the preamble to the Directive. The legislative history of Section 3, however, reveals some earlier, more ambitious attempts.

The UNCITRAL Model Law on Electronic Commerce was adopted in 1998. Its aim was to ensure that electronic contracts should be recognized.[48] The Model Law itself is only concerned with recognition of electronic commerce acts. But the Electronic Commerce Directive, in Articles 10 and 11 (discussed below), actually makes an attempt at harmonizing contract formation rules in electronic contracts.[49]

Article 9 mirrors Article 6 of the Model Law. Article 9(1) obliges Member States to ensure electronic contracts are allowed. It stipulates that legal requirements must be such that they do not deprive the contracts of 'effectiveness and validity' purely on account of them having been made by electronic means.

Article 9(2), however, creates a list of contracts that Member States may exclude from the scope of the general rules. First in this list are contracts that create or transfer rights in real estate. Second are the ones requiring the involvement of courts or other public authorities. Further to that are added contracts of suretyship and those governed by family law. Member States are under an obligation to notify the Commission of those contracts which they intend to exclude from paragraph 1. Most of the exclusions are understandable, although the drafting of at least one is somewhat ambiguous. Whereas real estate contracts (under paragraph a) and family law contracts (under d) were always treated as separate,

---

[47] For an example of the relationship between national law and EU law in electronic contracts, see Part III, 'Denmark', *Cyberlaw*, in *International Encyclopaedia of Laws* (Kluwer Law International, The Netherlands 2007).

[48] Both the United States and the European Union have adopted the Model Law. In the US, this has been done in the Uniform Electronic Transactions Act (UETA), approved by the National Conference of Commissioners on Uniform State Laws (NCCUSL) on 23 July 1999 which has now been adopted in most of the federal units. In the EU, the adopting document is the Electronic Commerce Directive.

[49] See footnote 26, Murray, op. cit., p. 70.

paragraph b) originally spoke of the contracts that need to be registered in order to be valid. It is not entirely clear what had been gained by changing this requirement to contracts requiring the 'involvement of courts', as there are very few contracts that require this rather than registration.

Article 10 of the Directive addresses issues of transparency. The minimum information to be provided by the ISS providers prior to the conclusion of the transaction includes: technical steps to follow the conclusion of the contract (Article 10(a)); whether the contracts will be filed and accessible by ISPs (Article 10(b)); technical means for identifying and correcting input (Article 10(c)); and languages offered for the conclusion (Article 10(d)). Further to this, any codes of conduct (paragraph 2) must be made available as well as contractual terms and conditions (paragraph 3). The previous conditions do not apply to contracts concluded exclusively by email. There is evidence that some of the requirements introduced in this Article are of limited use, either because national laws already provide sufficient incentives to provide the requested information or because such information is not needed.

Article 11 ensures that the ISPs acknowledge the receipt of the order without delay, by electronic means. The order and acknowledgement of receipt are considered to be received when the parties to whom they are addressed can access them. The drafts of Article 11 were more ambitious. The first two drafts were entitled 'Moment at which the Contract is Concluded'[50] whereas the actual title of Article 11 is 'Placing of the Order'. Why has the final version been watered down?

Contract laws in Member States are different. In some countries, the contract is concluded after the offer has been accepted. In others, the process has three stages. In the UK, the invitation to treat is followed by the offer, which in turn is followed by the acceptance. The first draft article brought confusion by introducing the fourth step of the confirmation of the acknowledgement of receipt. It provided that:

> the contract is concluded when the recipient of the service (i) has received from the service provider, electronically, an acknowledgement of receipt of recipient's acceptance, and (ii) has confirmed receipt of the acknowledgement of receipt.

---

[50]   A Proposal for a European Parliament and Council Directive on Certain Legal Aspects of Electronic Commerce in the Internal Market, COM(1998) 586, 18 11 1998

Acknowledgement of receipt is deemed to be received and confirmation is deemed to have been given when the parties to whom they are addressed are able to access them.

Two crucial elements exist in the draft which are absent from the final version. First, draft Article 11(1) seeks to regulate the moment when the contract is concluded. This, it will be observed from above, is at the moment when the confirmation of the acknowledgement of the receipt is received by the recipient of the service. This step is unnecessary and it is not clear what the draft wanted to achieve with this. The fourth step is counterproductive, making the process more cumbersome. This is reflected in the second draft, where Article 11 provides that the contract is concluded when the recipient of the service has received the acknowledgement of the receipt from the provider. This solution was better, closer to systems in many states and more practical for consumers and traders alike.

The existing solution in the E-Commerce Directive is modest. Article 11 demands that the service provider has to acknowledge the receipt of the recipient's order without undue delay and by electronic means. The order and the acknowledgement of receipt are deemed to be received when the parties to whom they are addressed are able to access them. Finally, the service provider must make available to the recipient of the service appropriate, effective and accessible technical means allowing him to identify and correct input errors, prior to the placing of the order. Business (non-consumer) parties are allowed to contract out of these provisions and regulate the relationship differently.

5. COUNTRY OF ORIGIN PRINCIPLE

The country of origin principle is a potentially wide-reaching idea that Internet services should be entitled to free movement if they are legal according to the law of the state where they originate. A simple definition is that the country of origin rule is a rule of international law allocating competence between Member States.[51] More precisely, it is a rule that gives the competence to the state where the service (in this case, information society) originates. This is a term from the arsenal of

---

[51] See Hörnle, J., 'The UK Perspective on the Country of Origin Rule in the E-Commerce Directive: A Rule of Administrative Law Applicable to Private Law Disputes?' (2004) 12 *International Journal of Law and Information Technology* 333.

legislative competence and determines which state, among several that possess the competence, shall exercise it.

To those proponents of the country of origin as a wider solution to problems of regulation on the Internet, this idea must seem attractive. The countless problems caused by borderlessness of the Internet disappear by a simple stroke, giving the competence to a single state. But, even if the idea has the potential to resolve these difficulties, is it not confined to the relative order of the European Union that benefits from clear competence rules and a well though-out system of remedies?

Article 3 of the E-Commerce Directive provides that, where the ISS provider is established on the territory of a Member State, that state shall ensure that its national laws apply to the provider. This is the basic provision of the country of origin rule, giving the legislative competence to the 'home state'. Article 3(2) then adds that Member States will not, for reasons falling within *coordinated field*,[52] restrict the freedom to provide information society services. This article applies to host states, sending them a signal that they are, in principle, not allowed to regulate information society services where these originate outside that Member State. Paragraph 3 then adds that the following two shall only operate within the coordinated field. The list of information services that fall within this category is given in the Annex to the Directive. This is largely on account of them being covered by other measures from the European Union arsenal. The mentioned areas, copyright and neighbouring rights, electronic money, choice of law, consumer contracts, real estate contracts and spam, have all been covered in other EU instruments.[53]

In further derogation from the principle of country of origin, and in consistency with other EU directives and the general approach to the Internal Market, Member States shall be able to derogate from paragraph 2. Host states will therefore be able to impose their own regulation for reasons of public policy, public health, public security or protection of consumers. The measures thus imposed must be: (a) necessary for one of the mentioned reasons; (b) taken against an ISS provider that endangers the objectives mentioned or presents a serious and grave risk to them; and (c) be proportionate. To ensure that the spirit of the country of origin rule is preserved, paragraph 4 also provides that the host state shall request that the home state takes the measures in question and waits for

---

[52] Coordinated field is defined in Article 2 as 'requirements laid down in Member States' legal systems applicable to information society service providers or information society services, regardless of whether they are of a general nature or specifically designed for them'

[53] Covered in Chapters 6, 9, 3 and 7 respectively.

their outcome. Only if the home state has not taken them or if they prove to be inadequate will the host state act. Furthermore, the host state will notify the Commission and the home state of the measures that it intends to take. These precautions will only be derogated from in cases of urgency.[54] The Commission is given the power of monitoring the derogations taken under Article 3(4) and it has the power to ask the host state to refrain from taking them or put an end to them.[55] It is not clear what sanction might be available to the Commission in case of non-compliance.

It is apparent from these provisions that the legislator has proposed a system of communication between Member States. The latter are supposed to notify each other of contentious areas and resolve possible disputes in an amiable way. The restrictive use of Article 3(4), furthermore, fits very well with the general idea of the protection of certainty, which seems to be the highlight of the E-Commerce Directive. The evidence suggests that derogations have, so far, been used very restrictively.[56] This, in turn, might indicate both that the area of regulation does not seem to be problematic and that Member States are tolerant and willing to recognize rules of the home state.

The country of origin principle is an idea often repeated in recent writings on Internet law. Some authors claim that 'country of origin regulation ... is the only regulatory model so far attempted which ... is capable of resolving the conflicts between the multifarious and overlapping claims by national jurisdictions to regulate particular Internet activities'.[57] In the view of the author, the key is in the word 'capable'. If by capable we mean that the concept, if agreed on universally and enforced properly, can resolve the legislative jurisdiction disputes and conflicts where two or more states both purport to regulate the same subject matter, then there is a fair chance that this, in theory, is possible. The concept, taken on its own, has that potential. On the other hand, it is unrealistic to expect that aim ever to be truly achieved.

It is fair to say that, in its present incarnation in the Electronic Commerce Directive, the country of origin principle achieved some

---

[54]   Article 3(5).

[55]   Article 3(6).

[56]   The Report from the Commission on Directive 2000/31/EC, (COM(2003) 702 final, Brussels, 21.11.2003) suggests (see paragraph 4.1) that there have only been five notifications under Article 3, of which only two used the emergency procedure of paragraph 5.

[57]   Reed, C., *Internet Law: Text and Materials* (Cambridge University Press, Cambridge 2004).

limited, if welcome, success. In a recent judgment,[58] the Court rejected the principle's conflict-of-laws operation and further clarified its true scope:

> Article 3 ... must be interpreted as not requiring transposition in the form of a specific conflict-of-laws rule. Nevertheless, in relation to the coordinated field, Member States must ensure that, subject to the derogations authorised in accordance with the conditions set out in Article 3(4) of Directive 2000/31, the provider of an electronic commerce service is not made subject to stricter requirements than those provided for by the substantive law applicable in the Member State in which that service provider is established.

The present situation (minimum harmonization accompanied by mutual recognition and mandatory requirements) grants the host state significant space for maintaining its potentially restrictive laws in place. Article 3 was necessary as a broadly drafted warning not to subject e-commerce services to stricter domestic laws.

In addition to the mentioned difficulties, which arise out of the context in which the country of origin rule developed, there are others. The country of origin rule can be described as a rule of legislative jurisdiction, in other words – a rule of competence, not a rule of adjudicative jurisdiction. It determines which state's laws apply to information society services but does not determine which courts have jurisdiction. Arguably, a large number of Internet issues concern adjudicative rather than legislative jurisdiction. Similarly, country of origin is not a choice of law principle and, in spite of the *eDate* case[59] purporting to limit its operation to public law cases, it is unclear how this can be achieved in practice.

6. COMMON EUROPEAN SALES LAW

A Common European Sales Law[60] was proposed as a way of partially addressing differences between contract laws of Member States. In order to avoid the uncertainties of foreign laws in unfamiliar states, the parties

---

[58]   Joined cases C-509/09 and C-161/10 *eDate Advertising GmbH v X, Olivier Martinez, Robert Martinez v MGN Limited*, 25 October 2011, not yet reported.

[59]   *eDate* case, paragraphs 53–68.

[60]   Proposal for a Regulation of the European Parliament and of the Council on a Common European Sales Law, COM(2011) 635, 11.10.2011. See Micklitz, H.W. and Reich, N., 'The Commission Proposal for a "Regulation on a Common European Sales Law (CESL)" – Too Broad or Not Broad Enough?', EUI LAW WORKING PAPER, NO. 2012/04, February 2012

would get an option to resort to one EU-wide sales law. Traders' fear of contract law barriers is quoted in the proposal as the main reason for the initiative.[61] By opting for the sales law, the traders get the opportunity to rely on a common set of contract rules.

Article 3 of the proposed Regulation emphasizes the law's optional nature. The law is activated only if the parties specifically opt in. In that case, the law governs the sale of goods, the supply of digital content and the provision of services. The law is used for cross-border contracts between traders, which are defined as contracts between parties who have habitual residences in different countries where at least one is a Member State.[62] If, on the other hand, the contract is between a trader and a consumer, it will be considered cross-border if either the address the consumer indicated, the delivery address or the billing address are located in a country other than the trader's habitual residence and if at least one of these is a Member State.

Common European Sales Law can be used for sales contracts including contracts for the supply of digital content.[63] This may but need not be on a tangible medium. In light of the fact that digital content is often supplied in combination with goods or in exchange for information (such as shopping habits), the proposed law applies irrespective of whether the content is supplied in exchange for a price. The law also applies to service contracts. The law may only be used if the supplier is a trader.[64] The trader, on the other hand, can be either a legal or a natural person acting for the purposes of that person's business (Article 2e of the Regulation). If both parties are traders, one needs to be a small or medium-sized enterprise (SME), a term which has an autonomous definition in the Regulation.

Digital content is defined in Article 2 of the Regulation as:

data which are produced and supplied in digital form, whether or not according to the buyer's specifications, including video, audio, picture or written digital content, digital games, software and digital content which makes it possible to personalise existing hardware or software;

but excluding financial services and advice, online banking, legal advice, electronic healthcare, electronic communications (i.e., telecoms), gambling and:

---

[61] Recital 3.
[62] See Article 4(2).
[63] Article 5(b) of the Proposal.
[64] Article 7 of the Proposal.

the creation of new digital content and the amendment of existing digital content by consumers or any other interaction with the creations of other users.

The last exclusion seems to be targeting private content and user-generated content (UGC). If so, the definition chosen is peculiar as is the exclusion. User-generated content may and does have a commercial dimension and can be traded.

The law contains a number of provisions of interest to electronic commerce. Section I contains a list of pre-contractual requirements to be given by a trader. Article 13 contains a special list of information for distance contracts. These conditions are largely similar to general information requirements arising from the E-Commerce Directive and special requirements arising from consumer or financial directives. Of particular interest is the obligation to give information on any technological protection (such as digital rights management) or interoperability.[65]

Section 3 covers contracts concluded by electronic means. Article 24 stipulates that such contracts are concluded by electronic means except in cases where emails only have been used, presumably because emails have been equated with ordinary mail communication. The trader is obliged to give the other party technical means for correcting errors. The trader is obliged to provide information on a number of technical and other issues. Contractual terms, in particular, need to be accessible. In contracts requiring payment, the trader is under a special obligation (Article 25) to inform the consumer of the general information from Article 13, including price information under Article 14 and the duration of the contract. In particular, the consumer must be informed of the contract's duration. The trader must, under Article 25(3), indicate any delivery restrictions and methods of payment.

The rest of the law contains much of what is expected in such documents, with rights and obligations of the parties, withdrawal, unfair terms, remedies, damages, risk passing and other provisions. Of interest to Internet users is Article 100 which contains criteria for conformity of, among other things, digital goods. These must be fit for any particular purpose and in particular the purpose which they ordinarily have. Paragraph (h) says that, when determining what qualities digital goods must possess, regard is to be had as to whether or not the content is supplied free of charge or not. This would seem to establish a presumption that goods supplied free of charge may be of lower quality than those provided for remuneration. This is the case, for instance, when

---

65   Article 13(1)(h) (i) of the law.

audio and video content is streamed at different qualities to paying and non-paying customers.

Article 101 contains a peculiar provision according to which the incorrect installation of 'goods or digital content' must be regarded as inconformity either when the seller installs it or when the consumer who is so authorized does but the incorrect installation is due to poor instructions. There is no guidance as to what constitutes poor instructions and it must be presumed that the courts would, in due course, form an opinion on this.

Under Article 103, digital content is not to be considered as non-conforming simply because an updated version had become available in the meantime. Furthermore, Article 105 obliges the trader to keep the digital content conforming even in cases where the content must be subsequently updated. For content not supplied in exchange of payment, the buyer can resort to one remedy only – damages to property resulting from non-conformity.[66]

7. CONCLUSION

Electronic commerce keeps playing an ever increasing part in the EU. The regulatory climate is stable with the relatively uncontroversial Electronic Commerce Directive and with more recent proposals such as the European Sales Law.

The success and importance of the Electronic Commerce Directive can be summarized in three points. Firstly, it creates a framework for other directives in the field and forms a basis for an evolving flexible system. Secondly, it uses the principle of the country of origin creatively, opening up a possibly new avenue of regulation. Finally, it encourages alternative dispute resolution mechanisms.

As a legislative model, the Electronic Commerce Directive, in spite of containing a number of good solutions, has its limitations. It is a law designed to operate within the European Union environment. As such, it reaps all the benefits that that the organization offers, but is also subject to its weaknesses. Ultimately, the success of the Electronic Commerce Directive depends on the success of the approach it has chosen to take. In the United States, self-regulation has been the model for regulating the

---

[66] Articles 106 and 107 of the law.

Internet since its inception.[67] The lawmaker has occasionally intervened, sometimes strongly, but the bulk of regulation was left to businesses.

Contrary to this, the European Union advocates a combined approach, following direct regulation in a number of areas but relying on the principle of subsidiarity, which involves less direct intervention, through minimum harmonization and mutual recognition. Additionally, the core of the regulatory interest in EU Internet law revolves around balancing the rights of producers with those of consumers, where the former lobby for liberalization and the latter for greater protection. The E-Commerce Directive addresses the interests of both with the emphasis on businesses.[68] The Directive is an Internal Market instrument, a fact that put limits on its scope from the outset. Furthermore, as a framework directive, it chose a flexible structure that has the potential to adapt itself to further changes.

In the light of these circumstances, it is important to see the Electronic Commerce Directive in a proper perspective – as a successful Internal Market instrument and to give it credit for what it has achieved. Ultimately, the main objective of the Directive, for Europe 'to become the most competitive and dynamic knowledge-based economy in the world capable of sustainable economic growth with more and better jobs and greater social cohesion',[69] may not depend on the choice and design of that specific regulatory instrument.

---

[67]   *A Framework for Global Electronic Commerce*, see footnote 11 above. See also Cox, N., 'The Regulation of Cyberspace and the Loss of National Sovereignty' (2002) 11 *Information and Communication Technology Law* 241, p. 249.
[68]   Consumers have largely been neglected in the Directive itself but are addressed in other directives (see Chapter 7).
[69]   Lisbon European Council, 23 and 24 March 2000, Presidency Conclusions.

3. International jurisdiction and applicable law

1. THE INTERNET AND MODERN CONFLICT OF LAWS

One of the most important and most difficult questions surrounding the Internet concerns resolving civil disputes in regular courts. The claim that the Internet should be subject to regular civil courts and regular civil procedure today seems natural although it has not always been so. In its early days, it was thought that the Internet, inherently present or accessible 'everywhere', makes the traditional premises upon which private international law rests unworkable.[1] Courts ought to exercise care, these arguments ran, when they assume jurisdiction over web pages not connected in any way with their own forum. The Internet is borderless and should not be subject to the same rules as regular transactions.[2] It would be impossible or improper to impose local jurisdiction and local laws on a global phenomenon with little or no local presence.[3] The courts should let the Internet develop as freely as possible and should approach the issue with an eye for the medium's particular qualities.

Today, few if any of these claims have support. The courts do assert jurisdiction locally over absent defendants who post globally and apply

---

[1] For an early overview of the field, see Boele-Woelki, K. and Kessedjian, C., *Internet: Which Court Decides? Which Law Applies?* (Kluwer, The Hague 1998). For a more recent American perspective: Hawkins, E., 'General Jurisdiction and Internet Contacts: What Role, if any, Should the Zippo Sliding Scale Test Play in the Analysis?' (2006) 74 *Fordham Law Review* 2371. For an overview in the EU: Makowski, P., 'Jurisdiction and Enforcement in the Information Society', in Nielssen, R., Jacobsen, S.S. and Trzaskowski, J. (eds), *EU Electronic Commerce Law* (Djøf, Copenhagen 2004), p. 125.

[2] Goldsmith, D., 'The Internet and the Abiding Significance of Territorial Sovereignty' (1998) 5 *Indiana Journal of Global Legal Studies* 475; Post, D., 'Against "Against Cyberanarchy"' (2002) 17 *Berkeley Technology Law Journal* 1365.

[3] See Johnson, D. and Post, D., 'Law and Borders – The Rise of Law in Cyberspace' (1996) 48 *Stanford Law Review* 1367.

national laws to trans-border cases. Since the majority of situations in a cyberspace setting differ little from their non-electronic counterparts there are today no separate private international law rules for cyberspace, although newer instruments (such as the Brussels I Regulation and the Rome II Regulation, discussed below) do recognize some situations specific to electronic communications.

In spite of the willingness to take Internet disputes, both the courts and the litigants keep struggling to understand how to localize disputes that arise from a medium which in its very nature seem to be delocalized. From the viewpoint of the claimant, the successful outcome of a dispute in international civil litigation depends on whether a particular set of facts can be connected to a state more favourable to their interests. Once the location has been established, the courts can proceed to resolve the dispute by applying the proper law. With the Internet the certainty which traditional conflicts rules provide disappears and is replaced by a recurrent fear that one's actions will be subject to jurisdictions of remote courts and unknown laws.

Legal uncertainties surrounding the Internet begin with determining the courts' jurisdiction. Events on cyberspace, which appear to happen simultaneously in several jurisdictions, are difficult to localize and connect to a particular court. In civil law traditions, *general jurisdiction,* which is the court's authority to hear all cases irrespective of the nature of the claim, is based on the defendant's nationality, domicile or habitual residence, depending on the context. While it may be possible to sue the defendant in, for example, the place where it is domiciled, this may not be a very suitable forum if the web pages were accessed remotely in another land. *Special jurisdiction* is exercised only if there is a connection between a claim and the jurisdiction in question. The fact that goods are ordered by a consumer from a particular country or that a personal reputation had been harmed in that country may or may not amount to a connection.

Choice-of-law questions are conceptually equally difficult. What law applies to the Internet will be decided by rules which typically refer to party autonomy or, in its absence, assign the matter to laws of the state with which the dispute is, in one manner or another, most closely connected. But in such situations, a number of difficulties arise. What law will apply to claims where the defendant accessed the material posted globally in the state where she is resident? Will consumers who bought online be able to avail themselves of a more favourable regime of their place of habitual residence in case they want to sue or are sued?

Finally, judgments obtained in one state may have to be recognized in others, in recognition and enforcement procedures which may be controversial and are subject to local public policy standards. In a typical example, a judgment delivered in state A awarding damages for a defamatory publication on a web page may not be recognizable in state B where free speech enjoys constitutional protection.

This chapter will look at dispute resolution in the European Union, beginning with an overview of the rules concerning jurisdiction in civil and commercial disputes and enforcement of judgements. Applicable law will be looked at next, including the implications of the country of origin rule. The chapter will conclude with some observations on the approach taken in the United States. Consumer protection rules in private international law are analysed in section 5 of Chapter 7.

2. JURISDICTION IN DISPUTES CONCERNING THE INTERNET

2.1 General and Special Jurisdiction

The European Union conflicts system consists of rules on jurisdiction in civil and commercial matters,[4] rules on law applicable to contract[5] and tort[6] and various secondary instruments.[7] In addition to this, the primary Community law (treaties) and secondary Community law (directives, regulations, court judgments) also have an impact on private international law. This section explores the EU rules on civil jurisdiction and their impact on the Internet.

Jurisdiction rules for civil and commercial cases in the European Union are located in the European Regulation on Recognition and

---

[4] Council Regulation (EC) 44/2001 of 22 December 2000 on jurisdiction and the recognition and enforcement of judgments in civil and commercial matters, OJ L 012, 16.1.2001. For a detailed overview of the field, see Stone, P., *EU Private International Law* (2nd ed., Edward Elgar, Cheltenham and Northampton, MA 2011).

[5] Rome I Regulation on the law applicable to contractual obligations (formerly Rome Convention), OJ L 177/6, 4.7.2008.

[6] Rome II Regulation on the law applicable to non-contractual obligations, OJ L 199/40, 31.7.2007.

[7] A detailed overview of these can be found in Jayme, E. and Kohler, C., 'Europäisches Kollisionsrecht 2007: Windstille im Erntefeld der Integration' [European Conflict of Laws 2007: All Quiet in the Field of Integration] (2007) 27 *IPRax* 493; see also the same authors in earlier issues.

Enforcement of Foreign Judgments (Brussels I Regulation). Article 2, the general jurisdiction rule, provides that jurisdiction exists in the courts where the defendant is domiciled.[8] Article 4 further clarifies that defendants not domiciled in the EU will not be subject to rules in the Regulation but to traditional pre-Brussels I rules. The claimant's domicile is irrelevant, as is the parties' nationality, thus enabling EU defendants to enjoy the Regulation's benefits even against non-EU claimants. Domicile of private individuals is determined for each Member State by reference to that state's law whereas Article 60 provides an EU-wide definition of corporate domicile. The latter exists where a company has a statutory seat, or central administration, or a principal place of business in a Member State. The criteria are independent, which means that if only one of them exists in a Member State, the defendant can be sued there, irrespective of the fact that others may exist in different Member States.

If the defendant is *not* domiciled in the Member States, the courts will determine jurisdiction using traditional rules, which include exorbitant bases enumerated in Annex I to the Regulation. States vary as to the exact circumstances in which courts can assume jurisdiction over non-present defendants but this is generally possible in common law systems. English courts, for example, assert jurisdiction in defamation cases where no English nationals suffered harm, as long as the claimant can establish a reputation in England. Thus in *Berezovsky v Forbes*[9] an American magazine was sued in England for defamation. Although the Russian claimants were not truly present in England, they alleged that their reputation in England was harmed. The House of Lords refused to decline jurisdiction on the basis of *forum non conveniens*. Somewhat worrying is the possibility that such judgments can be recognized and enforced in other Member States, as the recognizing court is never in the position to question the adjudicating court's jurisdiction (Article 36). The public policy rule, which can normally be used to monitor foreign judgments (Article 34(1)), is interpreted restrictively.

Special jurisdiction rules exist concurrently, in those situations where the defendant is already domiciled as per Article 2, giving the claimant the choice of suing in a court different than the court of the defendant's domicile. In contractual obligations this will be the place of performance of the obligation in question.[10] In tort cases it will be in the courts for the

---

[8]   Article 59 regulates domicile of individuals while Article 60 deals with that of corporations.
[9]   [2000] 1 WLR 104 (HL)
[10]   Article 5(1)(a).

place where the harmful event occurred or may occur.[11] Once the claimant opts for one of the Article 5 bases, courts do not have discretion to decline jurisdiction, a feature inserted for purposes of maintaining certainty and simplicity.

Special jurisdiction gives several other possibilities. Article 5(1) gives jurisdiction to courts of the place of performance of the obligation which is, in the absence of agreement, assumed to be the place of delivery of the goods. In a contract concluded on the Internet, this is the place to which goods ordered online are physically shipped, subject to any exceptions available to consumers.

In the case of provision of services, Article 5(1)(a) gives jurisdiction to the courts for the place of performance of the obligation. Article 5(1)(b) clarifies that, for the sale of goods, this will be the place where the goods were or ought to have been delivered under the contract. For services, this is the place where, under the contract, the services were provided or should have been provided. Where services are provided in several states, the court which has jurisdiction to hear and determine all the claims arising from the contract is the court in whose jurisdiction the place of the main provision of services was situated.[12]

It is not clear if computer programs can be regarded as services for the purposes of Article 5(1). In the early days of the Internet, software was customarily provided on a tangible carrier such as a tape or a disk. Whereas this is still true to some extent, the dominant model is for an IP right/licence to be transferred. This may or may not be accompanied by a carrier disk. In a corporate environment, the two are normally distinct. A typical situation involving a sale of boxed software would fall under Article 5(1)(b), first indent. However, in *Falco and Rebitsch*, the Court said that a contract under which the owner of an intellectual property right grants its contractual partner the right to use that right in return for remuneration is not a contract for the provision of services within the meaning of Article 5(1)(b), second indent.[13] Such contracts fall within the default position of Article 5(1)(a). They will be determined according to the place of performance. According to *GIE Groupe Concorde*,[14] determining the place of performance consists of three steps. First, the contractual obligation in question needs to be classified. Second, the law

---

[11]   Article 5(3).

[12]   C-19/09 *Wood Floor Solutions Andreas Domberger GmbH v Silva Trade SA* [2010] ECR I-02121.

[13]   C-533/07 *Falco Privatstiftung and Thomas Rabitsch v Gisela Weller-Lindhorst* [2009] ECR 03327.

[14]   C-440/97 *Gie Groupe Concorde and Others* [1999] ECR 6308.

applicable to it needs to be applied by reference to the Rome I
Regulation. Third, that law will determine the place of performance.

Similar doubts exist in regard to the provision of audio-visual content
over the Internet. Since there is neither a community-wide definition of
services, nor can the definition from the Single Market area be automatically applied, whether something is a service and therefore under Article
5(1)(b), second indent, or not, and therefore subject to the three-step
discovery of the place of performance is a matter for national courts. As
the Court in *Falco* said, 'a contract under which the owner of an
intellectual property right grants its contractual partner the right to use
that right in return for remuneration' lacks an important feature of a
services contract: 'that the party who provides the service carries out a
particular activity in return for remuneration'. It is safe to say that
contracts concerning the supply of audio-visual material will be scrutinized for a dominant element. Where the transfer of IP rights is determined to be dominant, Article 5(1)(a) would apply.

Special jurisdiction under Article 5(3) gives the claimant an option to
sue in the courts for the place where the harmful event occurred or may
occur.[15] In tort cases, the place where the harmful event occurred was, in
Bier BV v Mines de Potasse D'Alsace SA,[16] said to be both the place
where the event giving rise to the damage occurred and the place where
the damage itself occurred.

In defamation, the European Court of Justice's ruling in *Shevill v
Presse Alliance SA*[17] gave the claimant a wide choice of courts in which
to sue for libel by a newspaper article distributed in several Member
States. The issue for the Court was the appropriate forum for a libel by a
newspaper article circulated in several Member States. The Court ruled
that the claimant may start proceedings in the place of the publisher's
establishment as a place giving rise to the damage, but also in any of the
places where the publication is distributed (as a place where the damage
occurs). The claimant may recover the whole amount in the former case,
and in the latter only the amount suffered for loss of reputation in the
place concerned.

Whereas such jurisdiction cannot be described as exorbitant, its
application to Internet cases depends on the interpretation of 'publication' of web content in national and European contexts. The Regulation
does not overtly require the courts to engage in the measuring of the

---

[15]   Article 5(3). See Hartley, T.C., '"Libel Tourism" and Conflict of Laws' 59
(2010) *ICLQ* 25–38.
[16]   C-21/76 [1978] ECR 1735.
[17]   C-68/93 [1995] ECR I-415.

contacts between the defendant and the Member States in question but such measuring may nevertheless be necessary.

The recently decided *eDate Advertising* case resolves some of the difficulties.[18] The case involved a website operator established in Austria and a German plaintiff whose personal rights were allegedly violated in a publication on that website. The court ruled that:

> Article 5(3) of Council Regulation (EC) No 44/2001 of 22 December 2000 on jurisdiction and the recognition and enforcement of judgments in civil and commercial matters must be interpreted as meaning that, in the event of an alleged infringement of personality rights by means of content placed online on an internet website, the person who considers that his rights have been infringed has the option of bringing an action for liability, in respect of all the damage caused, either before the courts of the Member State in which the publisher of that content is established or before the courts of the Member State in which the centre of his interests is based. That person may also, instead of an action for liability in respect of all the damage caused, bring his action before the courts of each Member State in the territory of which content placed online is or has been accessible. Those courts have jurisdiction only in respect of the damage caused in the territory of the Member State of the court seised.

The approach of this case is largely consistent with the *Shevill* case. The notable difference lies in the addition of the possibility to sue for the whole amount at the place where the person whose personality rights had been infringed has its 'centre of interests'. This place, the Court confirms, largely corresponds with the place where that person has its habitual residence. This need not necessarily always be so and a link may be formed with another state either through the exercise of a professional activity or through other means. The practical consequences of the *eDate* solution may be of some significance. If the Internet publisher, a corporation or an individual, is domiciled in the European Union, it can be summoned in any jurisdiction where the harmful content had been accessed, at least in respect of the damage sustained in that state. The individual states will develop their own versions of the 'Effects Test', in line with these cases, to determine in which cases exactly has forum been 'targeted'. The Effects Test, as interpreted by the court in this case, is based on the defendant *aiming* its activities towards the forum. A subjective element is also necessary, with the defendant having had *knowledge* that harm will result from its actions.

---

[18] C-509/09 *eDate Advertising GmbH v X, Olivier Martinez, Robert Martinez v MGN Limited*, 25 October 2011, not yet reported.

Some doubt remains concerning the use of Article 5(3) in cases involving the violation of intellectual property rights.[19] Whereas disputes involving the registration and validity of IP rights are subject to the exclusive jurisdiction of Article 22(1), the Regulation is silent about other cases involving intellectual property rights. It seems that Article 5(3) has the potential to provide jurisdiction of the court of the place where the infringement took place.[20] This application of Article 5(3) can be used in respect of the restitution of profits and preventive actions.[21]

Article 5(5) gives jurisdiction to courts of the place where a branch, agency or other establishment is situated, provided that the contract arises out of the operations concerning that establishment. As with other headings of Article 5, the effect is simply to add another forum to the one provided in Article 2. This will only be in cases where the dispute arises out of dealings with the branch. As such, this provision is not going to be of particular significance in Internet cases, except in situations where a large corporation, for instance, an e-commerce website, operates through national branches.

2.2 Jurisdiction Agreements

Electronic commerce contracts as well as other types of contracts on the Internet normally contain choice-of-forum clauses. Such clauses will be subject to Brussels I Regulation Article 23, which allows jurisdiction agreements between parties where at least one party is domiciled in a Member State.

Jurisdiction agreements need to be in writing or evidenced in writing or 'in a form which accords with practices which the parties have established between themselves'. Article 23(2) provides that this can also be in 'any communication by electronic means which provides a durable record of the agreement'. An electronically stored copy of a contract will, therefore, be adequate.

---

[19] See Nuyts, A., 'Suing at the Place of Infringement: The Application of Article 5(3) of Regulation 44/2001 to IP Matters and Internet Disputes', in Nuyts, A. (ed.), *International Litigation in Intellectual Property and Information Technology* (Kluwer, The Hague 2008), p. 105.

[20] Which is otherwise available in the Trade Mark Regulation (Council Regulation (EC) 207/2009 of 26 February 2009, OJ L 78/1) and the Design Regulation (Council Regulation (EC) 6/2002 of 12 December 2001, OJ L 3/1).

[21] This in spite of the *GAT* case, C-4/03 *Gesellschaft für Antriebstechnik mbH & Co. KG v Lamellen und Kupplungsbau Beteiligungs KG* [2006] ECR 6509.

The jurisdiction so conferred is exclusive unless agreed otherwise. If the parties agree on non-exclusive jurisdiction, the effect will be to add another forum to those in Articles 2 and 5. The plaintiff will then be able to exercise discretion as to what court to sue in. The effect of an exclusive clause is to confer sole jurisdiction on the chosen court. Such a court has no discretion to decline jurisdiction if the formal conditions have been met.

If proceedings are started in courts other than the chosen ones, such courts must of their own motion declare that they have no jurisdiction. Article 27, however, provides that, where proceedings involving the same cause of action and between the same parties are brought in the courts of different Member States, 'any court other than the court first seised shall of its own motion stay its proceedings until such time as the jurisdiction of the court first seised is established'. If, for example, vexatious proceedings are commenced in another jurisdiction in violation of the jurisdiction agreement, that is, if a court other than the one designated in the exclusive jurisdiction clause is first seized, such court has no possibility of continuing until the court first seized declines jurisdiction.[22] This solution has been extensively criticized due to its potential to reward unconscionable behaviour.[23]

If none of the parties are domiciled in a Member State, the effect of the clause will be to prevent other Member States from taking jurisdiction until the court designated declines jurisdiction under its own national law.

A valid jurisdiction agreement cannot annul the effects of consumer protection law but remains valid if it does not contradict them, that is, if it works in the consumer's favour. Article 17 allows departures from the protective regime applicable to consumers in cases where agreements have been entered into after the dispute has arisen or where such agreements provide forums additional to the ones listed in Section 4 of the Regulation or in cases where both the provider and the consumer are domiciled or habitually resident in the same Member State and the agreement confers jurisdiction on that state. The life of an exclusive jurisdiction clause inserted into a standard consumer contract depends, therefore, on whether it satisfies these conditions. In principle, such a clause will have the effect of a non-exclusive jurisdiction clause in all situations involving a Member State. If an exclusive clause confers jurisdiction on courts of third states, for example, the United States, such

---

[22] See C-116/02 *Erich Gasser GmbH v MISAT Srl* [2003] ECR I-0000.
[23] See, for instance, Fentiman, R., '*Erich Gasser GmbH v. MISAT Srl*' (2005) 42 *Common Market Law Review* 241.

a clause may in the eyes of such a court validly confer jurisdiction but the resulting judgment may be declined recognition and enforcement if it is considered contrary to public policy of the Member State in which recognition is subsequently sought.

3. ENFORCEMENT OF FOREIGN JUDGMENTS

Chapter III of the Brussels I Regulation deals with recognition and enforcement of judgments. The general rule is that the regime will apply to *all* EU judgments, irrespective of the rules of jurisdiction under which they were given.

The most important feature of the regime is the simplified procedure for recognition and enforcement. A judgment from another Member State will be recognized without any special procedure (Article 33), without opening the case on the merits and without questioning the deciding court's jurisdiction. The latter is the case even where the judgment was made on one of the exorbitant bases of jurisdiction normally prohibited under the Regulation.

Article 34 only allows a limited number of defences to recognition which the Court of Justice interprets narrowly. The only general basis that is non-procedural in nature concerns judgments manifestly contrary to the recognizing state's public policy (Article 34(1)). This ground has had very limited and specific use in national courts, which is the interpretation encouraged by the Court. Nothing in the Brussels I Regulation regime indicates that judgments relating to Internet disputes in general or electronic commerce in particular would be accorded special treatment.

From the European perspective, a judgment from a non-EU Member State will be recognized according to each Member State's traditional rules. If a foreign judgment was obtained on the basis of exorbitant jurisdiction of a non-EU court there exists a possibility that such judgment will be recognized and enforced although the ultimate result will depend on national rules.

The principles that govern recognition and enforcement in the United States prevent recognition of judgments that endanger free speech. 'As the First Amendment prevents a state from adopting England's defamation law or France's hate speech law, an American court's enforcement of a foreign judgment based on the English or French law likewise would violate the First Amendment.'[24] Courts in the United States will not enforce a foreign defamation judgment.[25] The leading case in this area is *Matusevich v Telnikoff*,[26] where the District Court for Columbia refused to enforce a British libel judgment. It was said that recognition would violate both the First and Fourteenth Amendments, the basis of the Court's finding being that the libellous speech would have been legal under the First Amendment. The *Matusevich* principle was further applied in the *Yahoo US* case,[27] where Yahoo United States argued that a French injunction is not enforceable in the United States. The court, confirming the *Matusevich* principle for Internet cases, prevented the enforcement of the French judgment. Foreign libel laws thus cannot be applied in US courts whenever this jeopardizes the protection given by the First Amendment.

No similar rule or practice exists in the EU, which stands on politically different grounds regarding free speech. Whereas the First Amendment protection is broad in scope and strong in enforcement, the EU states typically prohibit certain forms of hate speech and would not refuse recognition and enforcement for all but the strongest reasons of procedural or public policy nature. The EU states, under the traditional non-Brussels I regime, would not refuse recognition on the account of protection of free speech. Under the Brussels I regime with its narrow grounds for objection this would be all but impossible. Likewise, an EU court would not, under either regime, refuse recognition of a foreign judgment because of the transient presence of a website or of somebody's reputation.

The Brussels I regime creates certainty and opts for speed. Interested in creating the free flow of judgments between Member States and not designed to police the quality and political values embedded in foreign judgments, it lacks the tools necessary to 'correct' the foreign courts' output. Although this creates an efficient system of recognition, it possibly makes redundant a valuable tool that could have been used in borderline Internet cases.

---

[24] Rosen, M., 'Exporting the Constitution' (2004) 53 *Emory Law Journal* 171.

[25] The basis for that is found is several provisions, including Restatement Third of the Foreign Relations Law of the United States (American Law Institute 1987) para. 482.

[26] 877 F. Supp. 1 (D.D.C. 1995), US District Court for the District of Columbia.

[27] *Yahoo! Inc. v. La Ligue Contre Le Racisme et L'Antisemitisme*, 169 F. Supp. 2d 1181 (N.D. Cal. 2001).

4. APPLICABLE LAW

4.1   Rome I Regulation on the Law Applicable to Contracts

The European Union regime for contracts is found in the Rome Regulation on the Law Applicable to Contractual Obligations,[28] previously the Rome Convention.[29] The Regulation applies to civil and commercial matters involving conflict of laws (Article 1). Article 2 provides that any law which the Regulation specifies is applied whether or not it is the law of a Member State.

The general rule in the Regulation is freedom of choice coupled with default rules applicable in the absence of choice and mandatory rules applicable in special situations, including consumer protection. In a large number of situations, it is precisely the rules on consumer protection that will be relevant for transactions on the Internet.

Article 3 allows the parties to choose the law applicable to their transaction. The choice must be 'expressly or clearly demonstrated by the terms of the contract or the circumstances of the case'. The parties may subject different parts of the contract to different laws and can at any time agree on different applicable law. The existence and validity of their choice will be determined in accordance with Articles 10, 11 and 13 of the Regulation. The parties' choice will be limited by mandatory rules.

Article 4 helps the courts determine the applicable law in the absence of choice. This is done through the concept of the closest connection. The first paragraph introduces assumptions concerning individual types of contract and the corresponding applicable law. For a contract for the sale of goods, this will be the law of the country where the seller has his habitual residence. For the contract for the provision of services, it shall be the law of the country where the service provider has his habitual residence. Where the contract is not covered by any of the headings of paragraph 1, or where the elements of the contract would be covered by more than one of them, the law of the country where the party required to effect the characteristic performance has his habitual residence shall govern the contract (Article 4.2). The laws designated by the first two paragraphs may nevertheless be overridden in cases where it is clear from all the circumstances of the case that the contract is manifestly more closely connected with a country other than that indicated in paragraphs

---

[28]   Regulation (EC) No 593/2008 of the European Parliament and of the Council of 17 June 2008 on the law applicable to contractual obligations (Rome I), OJ L177/6, 4.7.2008.

[29]   OJ C 27/1, 9 10 1980.

1 or 2 (Article 4.3). If it is, however, altogether impossible to determine the applicable law, Article 4.5 provides that the contract will be governed by the law of the country with which it is most closely connected.

Article 6 contains a special regime applicable to consumer contracts. Many transactions on the Internet will be subject to this regime. A consumer is defined in Article 6 as a person who concludes contracts for the purposes that lie outside their profession. The default provision is that such contracts are governed by the law of the place where the consumer has habitual residence provided that the professional either pursues their activities in the country where the consumer is habitually resident or 'by any means, directs such activities to that country or to several countries including that country'. The directing of activities must, by analogy, be understood in light of the *Hotel Alpenhoff* judgment:[30]

> The following matters, the list of which is not exhaustive, are capable of constituting evidence from which it may be concluded that the trader's activity is directed to the Member State of the consumer's domicile, namely the international nature of the activity, mention of itineraries from other Member States for going to the place where the trader is established, use of a language or a currency other than the language or currency generally used in the Member State in which the trader is established with the possibility of making and confirming the reservation in that other language, mention of telephone numbers with an international code, outlay of expenditure on an internet referencing service in order to facilitate access to the trader's site or that of its intermediary by consumers domiciled in other Member States, use of a top-level domain name other than that of the Member State in which the trader is established, and mention of an international clientele composed of customers domiciled in various Member States. It is for the national courts to ascertain whether such evidence exists.

The parties are, as per Article 6(2), allowed to choose the applicable law. No choice that the parties make may have the effect of depriving the consumer of the protection of mandatory rules of the law which would have applied in the absence of choice.

Article 6(4)(a) excludes the consumer regime in cases of contracts for the supply of services where these services are to be supplied to the consumer in a country other than that of his habitual residence. Whereas this targets situations where the consumer cannot reasonably claim protection of the country where they habitually reside, such as tourism, it excludes situations where services were marketed in the consumer's state

---

[30] Joint cases C-585/08 *Peter Pammer v Reederie Karl Schlüter GMBH & CO KG* and C-144/09 *Hotel Alpenhof GESMBH v Oliver Heller*, 7 December 2010, not yet reported. See also section 5.1 in Chapter 7.

but performed entirely out of it. This is neither in accord with Article 15 of Brussels I Regulation nor particularly consistent with the overall aim of EU consumer protection rules.

The Rome I Regulation contains a number of mandatory rules, which are rules whose application cannot be derogated from by the parties' choice and which protect fundamental interests. The Regulation operates with two distinct categories of mandatory rules. The first, broader, refers to rules which cannot be derogated from by contract. This applies to consumer, employee or similar protection rules. The Regulation also introduces a new, narrower category of mandatory rules which Article 9 defines as those 'the respect for which is regarded as crucial by a country for safeguarding its public interests, such as its political, social or economic organisation' and which, under Recital 37, need to be construed more restrictively than ordinary mandatory rules. The first definition corresponds to some extent to the concept of mandatory rules Articles 3 and 7 of the Rome Convention. The second is an attempt to address some of the criticism directed at the Convention.

Articles 3(3) and 3(4) operate with the broader understanding of mandatory rules. Article 3(3) provides that parties' evasive choice of law in situations where the contract has no significant foreign element cannot avoid the application of internal overriding rules of the forum. In other words, this article allows the parties to choose foreign law in a totally domestic situation, but not to override mandatory rules. Article 3(4) provides that choice of law of a third, non-Member State, cannot have as the effect the avoidance of Community mandatory rules. This has the same effect as Article 3(3) but on an EU level. An example of such rules would be, for instance, EU rules on contracts concluded at a distance. A choice of American law, therefore, may be valid but will not achieve the avoidance of Community consumer law or employment laws.

Article 9(2) provides that nothing in the Regulation can restrict the overriding mandatory provisions of the forum. The law chosen by the parties, or arrived at by virtue of Article 4, will be applied to the extent that it does not contradict such mandatory rules. Article 9(3), on the other hand, allows effect to be given to overriding mandatory provisions of the law of the country 'where the obligations arising out of the contract have to be or have been performed, in so far as those overriding mandatory provisions render the performance of the contract unlawful'. This provision addresses the illegality of the contract at the place of its performance only.

4.2 Rome II Regulation on the Law Applicable to Tort[31]

Finding the law applicable to torts committed on the Internet is a difficult and potentially sensitive issue. Many solutions have been proposed in literature and those applied in practice in courts of different states remain controversial. The difficulty lies in the fact that content published on the Internet crosses national borders while potential defendants usually do not. Where both a defamatory statement and the defendant who published it are located in the same Member State, the law applicable will usually be the law of that state. But what happens when the defamatory statement was posted elsewhere or on the Internet? Traditional choice-of-law mechanisms for finding the law applicable may point out to a state with which the tort has the closest connection. But, what law should be applicable in cases where the contents are accessed and read in several states?

The European Union regulates the law applicable to torts in the Rome II Regulation. The history of the Regulation is of some interest concerning the law applicable to Internet torts. In 2002, the European Commission published a preliminary draft Proposal for a Council Regulation on the Law Applicable to Non-Contractual Obligations[32] and amended it in 2006.[33] The Proposal contained several controversial solutions. In relation to the violation of 'private or personal rights or from defamation', Article 7 provided the law applicable to be the 'law of the country where the victim is habitually resident at the time of the tort or delict'. The proposal spurred a debate, with the media lobby expressing concern. This solution, it was argued, would unduly restrict the publishers' freedom and make them liable in the state with markedly lower standards of speech protection.

A later draft, in recognition of the criticism, pointed to the law of the place where 'direct injury' was sustained. This was to be the place where the publication was commercially distributed. Additionally, Article 6 of the Proposal provided that law applicable 'arising out of a violation of

---

[31] Regulation (EC) No 864/2007 of the European Parliament and of the Council of 11 July 2007 on the law applicable to non-contractual obligations (Rome II), OJ L 199, 31.7.2007.

[32] Proposal for a Regulation of the European Parliament and the Council on the law applicable to non-contractual obligations ('ROME II') COM/2003/0427, 22.7.2003.

[33] Amended proposal for a European Parliament and Council Regulation on the law applicable to non-contractual obligations ('Rome II'), COM(2006) 83 final, 21.2.2006.

privacy or rights relating to the personality shall be the law of the forum'
where application of the Host State's laws would be 'contrary to the
fundamental principles of the forum as regards freedom of expression
and information'. In addition, the original proposal had the intention of
giving country of origin rules precedence. Article 23(2) seems to have
been drafted specifically with this purpose in mind.[34] It said that:

> This regulation shall not prejudice the application of Community instruments
> which, in relation to particular matters and in areas coordinated by such
> instruments, subject the supply of services or goods to the laws of the
> Member State where the service-provider is established and, in the area
> coordinated, allow restrictions on freedom to provide services or goods
> originating in another Member State only in limited circumstances.

The provision, as proposed, was insufficiently clear. For, either it
repeated what the first paragraph already said about Community mandatory rules or public policy, or, in the alternative, it invoked a norm which
already had a basis in the TFEU Treaty and therefore did not need a
specific embodiment. For these reasons, the Commission had the provision redrafted, completely removing the second paragraph, and changed
the context of the provision: from one dealing with country of origin rule
to one dealing with other international conventions.

Other interventions came from the Parliament,[35] which expressed
concern that it was not clear what the most significant element of the
damage was in cases concerning media. Thus, in Recital 25a it said that
'the country in which the most significant element or elements of the
damage occur or are likely to occur should be deemed to be the country
to which the publication or broadcasting service is principally directed or,
if this is not apparent, the country in which editorial control is exercised'.

In spite of the original desire to include defamation and violation of
privacy, Article 1(2)(g) of the Regulation excludes non-contractual obligations arising out of violations of privacy and rights relating to
personality, including defamation. It is worth noting that the exclusion
does not relate to other torts committed by the media, such as disclosure
of confidential data or data theft.[36] The former is of increasing relevance,

---

[34]   See Hellner, M., 'The Country of Origin Principle in the E-Commerce
Directive: A Conflict with Conflict of Laws?' (2004) 12 *European Review of
Private Law* 193.
[35]   See footnote 32.
[36]   See Bach, I., 'Comment on Article 1', in Huber, P. (ed.), *Rome II
Regulation: Pocket Commentary* (Sellier, Munich 2011) p. 54.

especially in relation to user-generated websites including social networks, while the latter have an even wider scope.

The general regime in Article 4 is that the law applicable is that of the country in which the damage occurs, irrespective of the country in which the event giving rise to the damage occurs and irrespective of the country in which indirect consequences occur. Where both persons have habitual residence in the same country, the law of that country applies. On the other hand, where it is clear that the tort is manifestly more closely connected with a third country, the law of that country shall apply.

The general regime outlined above is unlikely to apply to Internet torts. This is because torts committed on the Internet relate either to privacy/defamation, to unfair competition or to intellectual property. Whereas the first is excluded from the scope, the latter two are subject to a special regime.

Marketing and advertising through the Internet is subject to an unfair competition conflicts regime in Article 6. The law applicable to a non-contractual obligation arising out of an act of unfair competition is the law of the country 'where competitive relations or the collective interests of consumers are, or are likely to be, affected'. Where, on the other hand, the interests affect one competitor only, the regular regime in Article 4 shall apply. This article covers defamation as an act of unfair competition in spite of the exclusion of Article 1.

According to Article 8(1), the law applicable to non-contractual obligations arising out of infringements of intellectual property rights is the law of the country for which the protection is sought. If the tort arises out of an infringement of a unitary Community intellectual property right,[37] as per Article 8(2), the law applicable is the law of the country in which the infringing act was committed. The Proposal had the general regime (Article 4) apply to IP torts but the present special regime was introduced as a reaction to the criticism received. The regime in Article 8(1) is the law of the place of protection, whereas the one in Article 8(2) is the law of the place of delict.

Since intellectual property rights are territorial, a violation on the Internet by, for example, publishing a copyright-protected material without permission or by violating a trademark, may lead to litigation in several states. Litigation needs to be commenced in each of the states in which the protection is sought, with the law of each of them respectively being applicable. In terms of jurisdiction, the courts of the place where the infringer is domiciled will have jurisdiction as per Article 2 whereas

---

[37] Trade marks, designs, plant varieties and geographical indications.

the courts in each of the states where the infringement took place will have jurisdiction per Article 5(3). For example, a book which has been published in PDF format on the Internet by an individual domiciled in France but also accessed elsewhere in the EU may lead to the jurisdiction of French courts (Article 2) or German courts (Article 5). If litigation is commenced in Germany, the law applicable will be German law.

4.2.1 Privacy and rights relating to personality

As indicated earlier, the Rome II Regulation does not apply to violations of privacy and personality rights. In 2011, the European Parliament proposed adding these rights to the Rome II Regulation.[38] The proposal is based on the developments following the *Shevill* case, namely in *eDate Advertising* as well as in other cases and the comparative study commissioned on the subject.[39] In particular the proposal mentions the phenomenon of 'libel tourism'.[40] The Parliament proposes adding a new article to the Rome II Regulation:

> (1) Without prejudice to Article 4(2) and (3), the law applicable to a non-contractual obligation arising out of violations of privacy and rights relating to personality, including defamation, shall be the law of the country in which the rights of the person seeking compensation for damage are, or are likely to be, directly and substantially affected. However, the law applicable shall be the law of the country in which the person claimed to be liable is habitually resident if he or she could not reasonably have foreseen substantial consequences of his or her act occurring in the country designated by the first sentence.
>
> (2) When the rights of the person seeking compensation for damage are, or are likely to be, affected in more than one country, and that person sues in the court of the domicile of the defendant, the claimant may instead choose to base his or her claim on the law of the court seised.
>
> (3) The law applicable to the right of reply or equivalent measures shall be the law of the country in which the broadcaster or publisher has its habitual residence.

---

[38] European Parliament, Resolution of 10 May 2012 with recommendations to the Commission on the amendment of Regulation (EC) No 864/2007 on the law applicable to non-contractual obligations (Rome II) 2009/2170 (INI), 2.12.2011.

[39] Mainstrat, Comparative study on the situation in the 27 Member States as regards the law applicable to non-contractual obligations arising out of violations of privacy and rights relating to personality, JLS/2007/C47028, Final Report, November 2008.

[40] Hartley, T.C., '"Libel Tourism" and Conflict of Laws', (2010) 59 ICLQ 25.

(4) The law applicable under this Article may be derogated from by an agreement pursuant to Article 14.

The Proposal's main position is that the law applicable should be the law of the state where the injured party's interests are. This reverts to the law of the plaintiff's habitual residence where the plaintiff did not and could not have foreseen the consequences. This provision brings the needed flexibility but opens up the term 'foreseen' to interpretation. Other solutions follow *eDate Advertising*'s logic in opting for the law of the defendant's domicile.

The law of the broadcaster's habitual residence, proposed in paragraph (3) right-of-reply situation, would have to be interpreted for situations involving Internet publishers.

4.3 Country of Origin Principle

In Chapter 2, we have discussed the scope and importance of the country of origin principle. The claim examined here is that home country control has the potential to interfere with the operation of the choice-of-law rules. In spite of the disproportionate amount of interest and legal writing that the principle has generated with conflicts lawyers, much remains ambiguous. Although some scholars believe the impact to be rather dramatic,[41] the settled opinion is now that the principle exercises a limited influence on conflict-of-laws process, ranging from weak, where national judges are obliged to take account of the EU four freedoms without the obligation to do anything in particular to enforce it, to strong, where EU law completely displaces any incompatible national law.

The home country control approach has been used in, among others, the Electronic Commerce Directive,[42] which extends the validity of the 'passport' obtained in one state to other Member States. The Directive concerns nearly all information society services, with exemptions[43]

---

[41] Basedow, J., 'Der kollisionsrechtliche gehalt der Produktfreiheiten im europäischen Binnenmarkt: favor offerentis' [The conflict-of-laws content of the Four Freedoms in the European Single Market: favour offerentis] (1995) 59 RabelsZ 1; or Radicati di Brozolo, L., 'L'influence sur les conflits de lois des principes de droit communautaire en matière de liberté de circulation' [The impact of Community Free Movement principles on conflict of laws] 82 (1993) RCDIP 401.

[42] For more detail, see Chapter 2.

[43] Relating to taxation, data protection, notaries, gambling and representation in court.

enumerated in Article 1(5). It uses the so-called coordinated field[44] to indicate to the Member States the areas in which they are obliged to take action. The purpose is to avoid fragmentation of the market, as only one Member State is in charge of the supervision. Article 3, on the Internal Market, states:

1. Each Member State shall ensure that the information society services provided by a service provider established on its territory comply with the national provisions applicable in the Member State in question which fall within the coordinated field.

2. Member States may not, for reasons falling within the coordinated field, restrict the freedom to provide information society services from another Member State.

This provision is to be read in conjunction with Article 1(4):

This Directive does not establish additional rules on private international law nor does it deal with the jurisdiction of Courts.

The main function of the Directive is to provide that information society services, within the coordinated field, are supervised at the *source* of the activity. Service providers are thus subject to prescriptive jurisdiction and laws of the Member State in which they are established. Host States are not allowed to regulate information services, except those that fall outside the Directive's scope and those that, although within its scope, can be justified in the interests of public policy, public health, public security and/or protection of consumers, provided that they are proportionate to the aim that they wish to achieve.

Recital 22 of the E-Commerce Directive reinforces the importance of subjecting ICT services to the supervision of the country of origin. The recital specifically says that 'information society services should in principle be subject to the law of the Member State in which the service provider is established'.

While Article 3(3) excludes the area outside the coordinated field from the scope of home country control, Article 1(4) of the Directive specifically excludes its application to issues concerning choice of law and jurisdiction. The express exclusion of Article 1(4) is coupled with Recital 23 which emphasizes that the Directive 'neither aims to establish additional rules on private international law relating to conflicts of law

---

[44] Articles 2h and 3, determining the scope of provisions needing harmonization.

nor does it deal with the jurisdiction of Courts'. The Recital mentions only the negative impact of home country control, saying that private international law must not 'restrict the freedom to provide information society services as established in this Directive'.

Article 2, which contains the definition of the coordinated field, says nothing about whether it applies to private law.[45] Certain national implementations limit the scope of the E-Commerce Directive to public law, therefore excluding the private sphere and solving the problem of the potential conflict with e-commerce law.[46]

Looking at Articles 1(4) and 3 of the E-Commerce Directive as well as at Article 23 of the original proposal, it seems that the EU legislator could have had any of the three possibilities in mind.[47] According to the first, the country of origin rule acts as a choice-of-law rule.[48] There can be two interpretations of the first possibility. According to one, Article 3 means *the law of the state of origin is the applicable law*.[49] According to the other, the private international law rules of the country of origin should *determine* the applicable law.[50] Support for this argument in EU law itself is not strong. According to the second possibility, the country of origin rule can be treated as a mandatory rule. In EU law, however, the use of mandatory rules is almost always preceded by specific language[51] and the intention to use the home country principle as a mandatory rule would have been indicated. According to the third possibility, the country of origin rule limits the application of the designated law, in a manner similar to the *ordre public* provision, after choice of law had been allowed to operate.

---

[45]   On the other hand, the proposal does include a wide interpretation and Article 3 excludes specific areas of private law, implying that others are included.

[46]   Thus Article 2(8) of Danish Lov No. 227 of 22 April 2002 om tjenester i informationssamfundet, herunder visse aspekter af elektronisk handel-e-handelsloven [Law on information society services including various aspects of electronic commerce and e-commerce law]. Also Swedish Lag am elektronisk handel och andra informationssamhällets tjänster m.m. [Law on electronic commerce and other infomration society services], Prop. 2001/02:150.

[47]   See Hellner, M., op. cit., p. 109.

[48]   The main proponents of this have been Basedow and Radicati di Brozzolo. See note 41.

[49]   See Waelde, C., 'Article 3 ECD: Internal Market Clause' in Edwards, L. (ed.), *The New Legal Framework for E-Commerce in Europe* (Hart, Oxford and Portland, OR 2005), p. 3, p. 8.

[50]   Waelde, C., op. cit., p. 8.

[51]   Although there may be confusion there as well. See C-381/98 *Ingmar GB Ltd v Eaton Leonard Technologies Inc.* (2000) ECR I-9305.

It is possible to interpret the four freedoms as having no effect on conflict of laws. Primarily, the country of origin principle is not a connecting factor and was not designed to demand the application of the law of the country of origin, or to request the jurisdiction of particular civil courts. And, if the result of the conflict-of-laws process is incompatible with EU law, this is incidental and not connected to the main issues in private international law. There is support for this view in the fact that secondary instruments, such as the E-Commerce Directive, expressly rule out potential effects that they might have on conflict of laws.

The *eDate Advertising* case resolves most of the difficulties of the home country control principle. The referring court asked if Articles 3(1) and (2) of the E-Commerce Directive must be interpreted as having a conflict-of-laws character in the sense that they also require the exclusive application of the law applicable in the country of origin, to the exclusion of national conflict-of-laws rules or only as a corrective at a substantive law level, by means of which the substantive law outcome is altered and adjusted to the requirements of the country of origin.

The Court's decision in the *eDate Advertising* case was that:

> Article 3 of Directive 2000/31/EC of the European Parliament and of the Council of 8 June 2000 on certain legal aspects of information society services, in particular electronic commerce, in the Internal Market ('Directive on electronic commerce'), must be interpreted as not requiring transposition in the form of a specific conflict-of-laws rule. Nevertheless, in relation to the coordinated field, Member States must ensure that, subject to the derogations authorised in accordance with the conditions set out in Article 3(4) of Directive 2000/31, the provider of an electronic commerce service is not made subject to stricter requirements than those provided for by the substantive law applicable in the Member State in which that service provider is established.

This passage must be interpreted to mean that the choice-of-law process needs to be allowed to operate without interference. In paragraph 61, the Court emphasizes that Article 3(1) does impose on a Member State an obligation to ensure that ISS services on their territory comply with the national provisions of that state. The Court proceeds to say that this is not, in nature, a conflicts rule. To the question concerning the clash of such laws with laws of other states in which ISSs operate, the Court, in paragraph 67, says:

> In relation to the mechanism provided for by Article 3 of the Directive, it must be held that the fact of making electronic commerce services subject to the legal system of the Member State in which their providers are established pursuant to Article 3(1) does not allow the free movement of services to be

fully guaranteed if the service providers must ultimately comply, in the host Member State, with stricter requirements than those applicable to them in the Member State in which they are established.

A provider, therefore, cannot be subject to stricter requirements than those in the home state. The solution is phrased differently from that found in Advocate General Cruz Villalón's opinion. On this point the Advocate General insisted that Article 3(1) imposed neither a choice-of-law rule nor a 'corrective at a substantive law level'. The Article, in his view:

> gives concrete legislative expression, in terms of harmonisation, to the freedom to provide services as applied to electronic commerce, while also empowering the Member States, within the margin of discretion granted to them by the directive and by Article 56 TFEU, to lay down measures for the protection of rights which warrant special safeguards, by way of a derogation from the freedom to provide services.

It is difficult to escape the conclusion that the chosen solution treats Article 3(1) as a specific form of an EU mandatory rule which operates as a corrective to substantive law. This is reinforced in paragraph 64 where the Court insists that 'it must be possible to apply mandatory provisions of a directive that are necessary to achieve the objectives of the internal market notwithstanding a choice of different law'. In light of such a solution which clearly contradicts Article 1(4), it is to be expected that the Commission will, in due course, suggest a change to one of the presently contradictory articles.

5. THE INTERNET AND ALTERNATIVE DISPUTE RESOLUTION

Alternative dispute resolution (ADR) is a term that refers to a number of techniques and processes for conflict resolution that do not involve formal litigation. While various forms exist, negotiation, mediation and arbitration are the most widely practised ones. Disputes that arise in relation to the use of the Internet (either in B2B or B2C context) and which can be resolved by reference to an ADR mechanism are conceptually somewhat different from online dispute resolution (ODR),[52] which involves communication, mediation or resolution online.

---

[52] For an overview of ODR, see Kierkegaard, S., 'Online Alternative Dispute Resolution', in Nielssen, R., Jacobsen, S.S. and Trzaskowski, J. (eds), *EU Electronic Commerce Law* (Djøf, Copenhagen 2004), p. 177.

Several EU instruments deal with alternative dispute resolution. Models of alternative dispute settlement have been inserted into the text of the Electronic Commerce Directive under Chapter III, as implementation measures. Article 16, entitled 'Codes of Conduct', provides that Member States and the Commission shall encourage:

(a) The drawing up of codes of conduct at Community level, by trade, professional and consumer associations or organisations, designed to contribute to the proper implementation of Articles 5 to 15;

(b) the voluntary transmission of draft codes of conduct at national or Community level to the Commission;

(c) the accessibility of these codes of conduct in the Community languages by electronic means;

(d) the communication to the Member States and the Commission, by trade, professional and consumer associations or organisations, of their assessment of the application of their codes of conduct and their impact upon practices, habits or customs relating to electronic commerce;

(e) the drawing up of codes of conduct regarding the protection of minors and human dignity.

In addition, Member States and the Commission shall encourage 'the involvement of associations or organisations representing consumers' in the drafting and implementation of codes of conduct affecting their interests and drawn up in accordance with paragraph 1(a). 'Where appropriate, to take account of their specific needs, associations representing the visually impaired and disabled should be consulted.'

Out-of-court dispute settlement is covered in Article 17. The primary obligation is not to hamper the use of out-of-court schemes which are available under national law in any dispute involving an Information Society Services provider and the recipient of services. The addressees of this obligation are the governments and the obligation specifically includes electronic means of dispute resolution. In addition (paragraph 2) Member States have the duty to encourage the bodies responsible for out-of-court settlement to operate in a way which provides adequate procedural guarantees for the parties concerned. This specifically includes consumer disputes. Finally (paragraph 3), Member States must encourage the same out-of-court dispute settlement bodies to inform the Commission of the significant decisions they take regarding information society services and to transmit any other information on the practices, usages or customs relating to electronic commerce.

The Mediation Directive[53] encourages the use of mediation as a means of settling disputes. The Directive applies to cross-border civil and commercial matters, with certain exclusions. Its main task is to compel Member States to authorize courts to suggest mediation, without making it mandatory. As such, the Directive does not contain detailed rules on mediation but provides guidelines concerning ensuring quality of mediation (Article 4), appropriateness of a court's call to mediation (Article 5), enforceability (Article 6), confidentiality (Article 7) and effect of mediation (Article 8).

In terms of consumer protection, mandatory EU rules apply. Directive 93/13 on unfair terms in consumer contracts[54] prohibits clauses which are:

> excluding or hindering the consumer's right to take legal action or exercise any other legal remedy, particularly by requiring the consumer to take disputes exclusively to arbitration not covered by legal provisions, unduly restricting the evidence available to him or imposing on him a burden of proof which, according to the applicable law, should lie with another party to the contract.

Alternative and online dispute resolution have recently been the target of additional efforts. The draft directive on ADR in consumer disputes[55] is meant to improve redress for consumers in the context of the internal market. Drafted at the same time and meant to complement the former is a regulation on consumer online dispute resolution,[56] which aims to create a dispute resolution system for consumers.

---

[53]   Directive 2008/52/EC of the European Parliament and of the Council of 21 May 2008 on certain aspects of mediation in civil and commercial matters, OJ L 136/3, 24.5.2008.

[54]   OJ L 095, 21.4.1993, (Unfair Terms in Consumer Contracts Directive).

[55]   Proposal for a Directive on alternative dispute resolution for consumer disputes and amending Regulation (EC) No 2006/2004 and Directive 2009/22/EC (Directive on consumer ADR), COM(2011) 793 final, 29.11.2011.

[56]   Proposal for a Regulation on online dispute resolution for consumer disputes (Regulation on consumer ODR), COM(2011) 794 final, 29.11.2011.

6. THE APPROACH IN THE UNITED STATES AND THE EU

Two general features distinguish the European rules-based system from the American discretion-based system.[57] First, the European system is more rigid than the American. National courts acting under Brussels I Regulation are *obliged* to take jurisdiction and have no discretion to act otherwise. This means less flexibility but more certainty. Second, the European Regulation is not activated unless the defendant is domiciled in the Member State. If the defendant *is* domiciled in a Member State, traditional rules of jurisdiction do not operate at all and the use of the Regulation is mandatory.

American rules on jurisdiction *in personam* are complex, but can be described in outline as follows: a court is allowed to exercise jurisdiction *in personam* on the basis of presence, domicile, consent or activities having effect in the forum, the latter existing where the defendant's contacts with a jurisdiction were 'continuous or systematic'.[58] Sporadic or casual activity does not justify assertion of jurisdiction. General jurisdiction is based on a continuous activity or presence of a non-resident defendant. Formally, general international civil jurisdiction exists in the United States if the service of process can be effected. If the defendant is not resident in the jurisdiction, to comply with due process principles in terms of exercising jurisdiction over non-resident defendants, the defendant must have substantial or continuous and systematic contacts with the forum state. If there is no general jurisdiction, specific jurisdiction may exist, where the action relates to a single activity or relationship between the defendant and the forum, if it falls within the 'minimum contacts' framework and the jurisdiction is exercised reasonably.

In Internet disputes, American courts have experimented with various approaches. In *Inset Systems Inc. v Instruction Set*,[59] a Connecticut district court said that purposefully directing web advertising activities towards Connecticut on a continuous basis satisfies the minimum contacts test. This meant that a simple creation of a web page amounted to

---

[57]   In detail see Borchers, P., 'Tort and Contract Jurisdiction via the Internet: The "Minimum Contacts" Test and the Brussels Regulation Compared' (2003) 50 *Netherlands International Law Review* 401.

[58]   *International Shoe Co. v Washington*, 326 U.S. 310, 316 (1945), US Supreme Court. See also *World-Wide Volkswagen Corp. v Woodson*, 444 U.S. 286, 291–92 (1980), US Supreme Court.

[59]   937 F. Supp. 161.

'purposeful availment' and that the web was equated to ordinary advertising.[60] An alternative approach was developed in *Bensusan*.[61] In that case, a New York district court looked at specific circumstances of the case and introduced a difference between active and passive websites. The former actively target persons in the forum, by virtue of advertising, promotion or otherwise, the latter do not.

An important publishing case, *Calder v Jones*,[62] involved a libellous article published in one but accessed in another state. Here the United States Supreme Court held that a state could assert personal jurisdiction over the author and editor of a national magazine, which published an allegedly libellous article about a resident of that state, where the magazine had wide circulation in that state. The activities here (newspaper publishing) were intentionally directed at a California resident and could constitute jurisdiction.

A new Internet-specific approach to jurisdiction was adopted in 1997 in *Zippo Manufacturing Co. v Zippo Dot Com Inc.* (the 'Zippo Test').[63] The court there distinguished the cases where the defendant does business over the Internet from situations where information is simply posted on the website. The former are active, the latter passive, but there are a number of situations in between where some form of interaction takes place. In the latter case, the court should examine the exercise of the existing level of interactivity:

> This sliding scale is consistent with well developed personal jurisdiction principles. At one end of the spectrum are situations where a defendant clearly does business over the Internet. If the defendant enters into contracts with residents of a foreign jurisdiction that involve the knowing and repeated transmission of computer files over the Internet, personal jurisdiction is proper. At the opposite end are situations where a defendant has simply posted information on an Internet Web site which is accessible to users in foreign jurisdictions. A passive Web site that does little more than make information available to those who are interested in it is not grounds for the exercise [of] personal jurisdiction. The middle ground is occupied by interactive Web sites where a user can exchange information with the host computer. In these cases, the exercise of jurisdiction is determined by

---

[60]   See Geist, M., 'The Shift Toward "Targeting" for Internet Jurisdiction', in Thierer, A. and Crewds, C. (eds), *Who Rules the Net?* (Cato Institute, Washington D.C. 2003), p. 95.

[61]   *Bensusan Restaurant Corp. v King*, 126 F.3d 25, 29 (2d Cir. 1997).

[62]   465 U.S. 783 (1984).

[63]   952 F. Supp. 1119, 1126 (W.D. Pa. 1997), the United States District Court for the Western District of Pennsylvania.

examining the level of interactivity and commercial nature of the exchange of information that occurs on the Web site.

For a while, the Zippo Test was dominant. But, in the first years of this century, American courts shifted towards a more sophisticated approach originally developed in *Calder v Jones*.[64] The question asked was: may a state court exercise jurisdiction over a non-resident newspaper, editor and its reporters in a libel action filed by a forum resident when the newspaper has a substantial circulation in the forum state and the newspaper, its editors and reporters aimed the article at the complaining forum resident knowing it was likely to cause harm against the forum resident? This approach, called the Effects Test, is based on a simple idea that personal jurisdiction exists where the defendant's tort is aimed towards the forum. At the same time, the defendant must have had knowledge that harm will result from its actions. A strong confirmation of the targeting doctrine happened in May 2003 when the Supreme Court rejected an application for leave to appeal against a decision of the US Court of Appeal in *Young v New Haven Advocate*.[65] The court held that defamation proceedings relating to material published online in Connecticut cannot be commenced in Virginia. The court held that courts in Virginia have no jurisdiction where the newspapers in question did not 'manifest an intent to aim their websites or the posted articles at a Virginian audience'.

Courts in the United States, unlike European and common law courts, will not recognize and enforce foreign defamation judgments.[66] The Internet as a 'brave new world of free speech'[67] requires that information and ideas published be protected robustly and the First Amendment has so far successfully provided that protection. While freedom of speech is a basic human right which enjoys considerable protection in many jurisdictions, no other state provides such extensive protection as the United States.

Finally, criteria for choice of law rules (choice of choice-of-law rules) are different in the United States and in Europe. Whereas the US relies

---

[64]   465 U.S. 783 (1984).

[65]   315 F 3d 256 (4th Cir. 2002), United States Court of Appeals, Fourth Circuit. See also *Revell v Lidov*, No. 01–10521 (5th Cir. Dec, 2002), United States Court of Appeals, Fifth Circuit.

[66]   *Yahoo! v LICRA*, 169 F. Supp. 2d 1181 (N.D:Cal. 2001), United States District Court, Northern District of California.

[67]   *Blumenthal v Drudge*, 992 F. Supp. 44 (D.D.C. 1998), United States District Court, District of Columbia.

on issue-selective approaches,[68] Europe uses a rule-selection method. The result is more flexibility and less certainty in the former and the opposite in the latter. In the United States, there has never been much consensus on appropriate laws for multistate defamation[69] and it now seems that traditional rules, based on the plaintiff's domicile and contacts may be out of date. It has been suggested[70] that specific rules for the Internet should be developed, but this suggestion remains doubtful.[71]

---

[68] Such as those listed in para. 6 of Restatement Second of Conflict of Laws.

[69] See Pielemeier, J., 'Choice of Law for Multistate Defamation' 35 *Arizona State Law Journal* 55, p. 42.

[70] Johnson, D. and Post, D., 'Law and Borders – The Rise of Law in Cyberspace' (1996) 48 *Stanford Law Review* 1367, p. 1378.

[71] For other views, see Lessig, L., *Free Culture* (Penguin, London 2004), pp. 277–87.

4.   Speech and content regulation

The Internet was born with a promise of bringing a world without national boundaries, where content is supplied and consumed at a low cost from the periphery. Such an Internet was supposed to be free of national control as it was assumed that content placed on it either cannot or will not be regulated.[1] Although this proved to be illusory the exact extent to which the Internet is controlled remains controversial.[2]

By content regulation we understand various state-initiated efforts to control the substance of the Internet rather than its technical aspects. In other words, content control may be defined as an effort to ensure that certain types of information on the Internet are not seen, or are seen by certain groups of users only or under certain circumstances. In broadest terms, this is simply the question of whether a particular content can legally be put on the Internet in a jurisdiction, the circumstances under which this can be done, the regime for enforcing it and the consequences of breach. The measures through which content is controlled may involve public law, such as criminal or administrative, or private law, such as the law of defamation or intellectual property law, or hybrid branches, such as media and telecommunications law. In this chapter, content regulation is looked at through a number of issues which are conceptually connected and which are chosen for their practical importance. The first is control of illegal and harmful content. The second is free speech and defamation. The third is copyright infringement. The final two are sexually explicit speech and hate speech.

1.   CONSTITUTIONAL PRINCIPLES

The legal framework for content protection is constitutionally divided between the EU and Member States. Unlike the Single Market, where

---

[1]   On this, see Chapter 1.

[2]   For an overview of filtering across the Globe, see Deibert, R., et al. (eds), *Access Denied: The Practice and Policy of Global Internet Filtering* (The MIT Press, Cambridge, MA 2008).

EU competence is clear, the majority of areas concerning content regulation fall within national competence with the EU being on the periphery. Nevertheless, certain constitutional principles govern the area. Among these, general free movement principles and principles governing freedom of expression are of particular relevance.

Articles 49, 54 and 114 TFEU, the standard sources for regulating electronic commerce, do not have a direct impact on the type of regulated content. On the other hand, they do ensure that free movement of goods and services are EU-protected values. The goods and services, which may be carriers of content, are therefore free to move between Member States. Where a limitation on Internet content is imposed at national level but the situation involves free movement of goods or services across EU borders, the principles can be invoked to protect the content. In that case, a discriminatory limitation can only be defended by invoking a specific exception, such as public policy, and other exceptions in Article 36 TFEU. A non-discriminatory limitation can also rely on a Court-created list of mandatory exceptions. A putative national law prohibiting the distribution of obscene material which would include particular kinds of pornography would be scrutinized for its validity in light of free movement provisions but would likely be justified.

Freedom of speech is constitutionally protected in Article 10 of the 1950 European Convention of Human Rights:

1. Everyone has the right to freedom of expression. This right shall include freedom to hold opinions and to receive and impart information and ideas without interference by public authority and regardless of frontiers. This article shall not prevent States from requiring the licensing of broadcasting, television or cinema enterprises.
2. The exercise of these freedoms, since it carries with it duties and responsibilities, may be subject to such formalities, conditions, restrictions or penalties as are prescribed by law and are necessary in a democratic society, in the interests of national security, territorial integrity or public safety, for the prevention of disorder or crime, for the protection of health or morals, for the protection of the reputation or rights of others, for preventing the disclosure of information received in confidence, or for maintaining the authority and impartiality of the judiciary.

This constitutional protection is repeated in the constitutions of the Member States, including the formalities and conditions mentioned in Section 2. Government actions which limit free speech on the Internet are subject to regular challenges for violation on freedom of expression grounds.[3]

Article 11 of the 2000 Charter of Fundamental Rights of the European Union provides similar protection:

1. Everyone has the right to freedom of expression. This right shall include freedom to hold opinions and to receive and impart information and ideas without interference by public authority and regardless of frontiers.
2. The freedom and pluralism of the media shall be respected.

The EU declares itself committed to opening up access, although it does not constitutionally protect it. In the Digital Agenda 2010–2020,[4] for example, it lists a number of required actions which can be interpreted as an effort to reduce national content control and open up access to content. Among them, the first key action is to 'simplify copyright clearance, management and cross-border licensing' while key action 5 introduces a review of EU standardization policy.

The constitutional framework of the EU, while protecting content through free movement, freedom of expression and other constitutional provisions, stops short of proclaiming absolute freedom of speech akin to the First Amendment to the US Constitution. A number of Member States have express provisions against speech that incites racial hatred.

2. ILLEGAL AND HARMFUL CONTENT

2.1 The EU Approach to Content Regulation

The EU has no laws which directly regulate illegal and harmful content[5] but engages instead in a number of initiatives and self-regulatory policy documents which are meant to have an impact on Internet content.

The Safer Internet Action Plan 1999–2004[6] forms part of a set of policies at EU level designed to fight illegal and harmful content on the

---

[3] UN General Assembly, 'Report of the Special Rapporteur on the promotion and protection of the right to freedom of opinion and expression', 20 April 2010, A/HRC/14/23.

[4] COM(2010) 245, 19.5.2010.

[5] The exception is found in limited efforts to regulate child pornography, see Child Pornography Directive, OJ L 335, 17.12.2011.

[6] Decision No 276/1999/EC of the European Parliament and of the Council of 25 January 1999 adopting a multiannual Community action plan on promoting

Internet. A number of the initiatives target children and young users. The European Framework for Safer Mobile use by Young Teenagers and Children[7] was created in 2007. It introduces principles and measures designed to improve safety of the young on mobile platforms. Another example is found in The Safer Social Networking Principles for the EU,[8] which is a self-regulatory agreement. The agreement contains guidelines for the use of social networking sites by children and has been adopted by a number of players in the industry.

2.2 Audiovisual Media

The Audiovisual Media Services Directive (AVMSD)[9] amended the Television Without Frontiers Directive. The Directive now regulates both traditional television (linear services) and video-on-demand (non-linear services). Recital 22 is clear about the Internet falling within the scope of the Directive as it talks of all websites except those where 'the principal purpose of which is not the provision of programmes, that is where any audio-visual content is merely incidental to the service and not its principal purpose'. A website such as YouTube would, therefore, fall within the scope of the Directive but a website containing short clips or animations would not. Nevertheless, defining non-linear services may be increasingly complex as websites use video content in a variety of situations.

Article 2 of the Directive introduces the country of origin principle and subjects service providers to the law of their own country, defined in paragraph 2 of that Article, with the exception for broadcasters from third states using an up-link in an EU country. The latter are to be subject to the law whose up-link they use or, if that is not the case, the law of the state whose satellite capacity they use.

The relevant content control rules are found in Article 3, which provides that:

---

safer use of the Internet by combating illegal and harmful content on global networks, OJ L033/1, 6.2.1999.

[7] SIPMC 07 26, February 2007; see also the Commission's Press Release IP/10/704, 9 June 2010.

[8] See Donoso, V. (2011), 'Assessment of the implementation of the Safer Social Networking Principles for the EU on 9 services: Summary Report', European Commission, Safer Internet Programme, Luxembourg, August 2011.

[9] Audiovisual Media Services Directive, OJ L 95/1, 15.4.2010.

Member States shall ensure freedom of reception and shall not restrict
retransmissions on their territory of audiovisual media services from other
Member States for reasons which fall within the fields coordinated by this
Directive.

Member States are allowed to derogate from Article 3(1) in special cases
concerning on-demand services. Article 3(4) provides that measures: (i)
must be necessary; (ii) must be taken against services which 'prejudice'
the objectives mentioned in paragraph (i); and (iii) must be proportionate.
Article 3(4)(i) clarifies that the objectives for which derogations can be
obtained relate to public policy and, in particular:

- public policy, in particular the prevention, investigation, detection
  and prosecution of criminal offences, including the protection of
  minors and the fight against any incitement to hatred on grounds of
  race, sex, religion or nationality, and violations of human dignity
  concerning individual persons;
- the protection of public health;
- public security, including the safeguarding of national security and
  defence;
- the protection of consumers, including investors.

Article 4 allows Member States to introduce more stringent and detailed
rules. Where a broadcaster establishes itself in another Member State to
circumvent stricter rules in the second state, the first state has jurisdiction
to apply the appropriate measures.

Article 6 prohibits 'incitement to hatred based on race, sex, religion or
nationality'. Article 9 addresses audiovisual commercial communications
and provides that they must not use 'subliminal' techniques which, in this
context, must be understood as those that appeal to the consumer's
subconscious. Additionally, commercial communications must not prejudice respect for 'human dignity' or incite discrimination based on 'sex,
racial or ethnic origin, nationality, religion or belief, disability, age or
sexual orientation', encourage behaviour prejudicial to health and safety
or to the protection of the environment. The advertising of tobacco
products is banned and that of alcohol products must not be directed at
minors, while commercials for medicaments only available on prescrip-
tion are prohibited. Commercial communications must not cause 'physical or moral detriment' to minors.

Special rules apply to on-demand services. Article 12 protects minors,
stating that services which may 'impair the physical, mental or moral
development of minors' must be delivered in such a way as to ensure that

minors will not be able to see them. Article 13 requires that on-demand services promote, 'where practicable', the production of and access to European works.

While the extension of the Directive to on-demand services is to be congratulated, a number of questions remain. One of them relates to the status of services provided mainly and exclusively on the Internet which are subject both to the general electronic commerce regime and the regime created under AVMSD. Video distribution sites such as YouTube or Vimeo are available both as traditional websites (and thus clearly under the scope of the E-Commerce Directive) and as on-demand services through television and video sets which are increasingly connected to the Internet. Such sites should be able to avail themselves of the home country control principle of Article 3 of the E-Commerce Directive but may also be subject to the circumvention control regime of Article 4 AVMSD.

2.3 Liability for Illegal Content

Liability for illegal and harmful content posted on the Internet may arise in parts of the world where legal subjects do not expect it. There may be potentially numerous situations of such extraterritorial reach. Liability, from the viewpoint of the defendant, is territorially indeterminable or difficult to localize, and therefore costly. A statement published on a French website may have effects in England, where the claimant has an interest which English courts will be prepared to protect. A person accessing and storing photos containing child pornography or illegally sharing movies may be located in the Cayman Islands but will easily be subject to the jurisdiction of the American courts on the ground of business contacts there. What is criminally punishable hate speech in Germany is constitutionally protected in the United States.

Liability in such cases may be criminal, in cases such as child pornography or counterfeiting and piracy, or it may be civil, in cases where the injured party sues for damages or restitution. The problem of liability arises, in case of individuals, out of illegal acts performed on or with the aid of the Internet. Internet service providers as intermediaries may also be subject to legal action where unlawful and illegal content is posted by others but transmitted through or stored on their servers.

For purposes of determining liability, the actors on the Internet can be distinguished based on the *capacity* in which they come in touch with the information, that is, whether they create, transmit or receive it. The first category involves posters of illicit content. A pirate who illegally obtains a copy of a movie and posts it on the Internet is primarily liable for copyright infringement. The second involves those who illegally access them. A user accessing and storing child pornography, for example, may be liable under these provisions. The third category involves intermediaries: this liability concerns Internet service providers understood in the wide sense of the word (i.e., including universities, internet cafes or other entities that make the internet available). Whereas the third category is insulated from liability under conditions which will be discussed in the next chapter, most categories of illegality on the Internet apply to the first two. Thus a copyright infringement action may hit both the original poster of a link to a pirated movie and the end user. The same is true of other categories of illicit content, for example, content harmful to minors or content inciting racial hatred.

The same phenomenon can be looked at either from the perspective of the *source* of liability, or the *act* that gives rise to it. The first mentioned form of liability is the direct liability of individuals based on *information content*. This is liability that arises from material posted on the Internet and concerns individual posters and recipients (users). The typical categories here include defamation (libel), intellectual property infringements or the distribution of pornography. This is the liability of somebody who posts or accesses illegal content on the Internet and not of persons who transmit or distribute it through technological means. In Benkler's division of the Internet into layers, discussed in Chapter 1,[10] this liability concerns actions on the content layer.

The second is the liability of *intermediaries* such as internet service providers, whose liability arises not because they originated the content itself, but because they transmitted it. The existence of this category is intuitively understandable, as the anonymity that arises from the architecture of the Internet shields the individual users. It is in this context inevitable and financially viable to target the intermediaries.[11] Postings on the Internet are identifiable by their IP numbers but the practical accessibility of Internet users may be limited or, alternatively, it may be economically more efficient to target the Internet service providers. The idea behind this is that the ISPs, much like publishers, should bear the responsibility for content that is placed on their servers.

In spite of these classifications, the actors on the Internet are difficult to classify and therefore difficult to make liable. In the EU, the 'hosts' are not the same as ISPs. The E-Commerce Directive takes a broad

---

[10]   See footnote 6, Chapter 1.

[11]   This has been, until Recording Industry Association of America (RIAA) started individual lawsuits against file-sharers in 2004, the accepted route in the United States.

definition of services for remuneration, as it specifies in Article 2 that these are 'Information Society Services', thus extending the application of the Directive well beyond simple ISPs. Web pages hosted on private computers or those belonging to universities may therefore fall within this category. In such cases, the internet service need not be provided for remuneration, as is currently required under, for example, the E-Commerce Directive.

Finally, the last category includes liability that cannot be included in either of the first two categories as it is triggered neither by posting material nor by transmitting. Tentatively, this category covers acts against the security of computer systems. These are typically hacking attacks perpetrated by third parties on illegally hijacked computers. The essence of the problem is in the fact that the party in question, either an ISP or an individual, unknowingly acts as a host for the attack that affects a third party. Does the third party, then, have recourse against the host? The benefit of such an approach is in the accessibility of hosts, as the actual attacker may be and usually is anonymous. The justification for making hosts liable is in the fact that hosts ought to have effective security measures in place, in the same way a proprietor of a dangerous manufacturing facility ought to secure it against attacks from the outside that may result in injury to passers-by. This may also be economically the most effective solution but no case law has emerged yet. It is to be expected that future attempts may be made in the law of torts.

More widely, the last category can be described as comprising acts that take place on the web and result in some form of disruption and damage to the affected party. Potentially, a whole range of acts may result in this kind of liability, such as: breaking or hacking into computer systems that results in damage to, loss or theft of data, hacking into others' web pages and defacing them or changing their content, denial of service attacks, invasion of privacy, transmission of viruses or other malware and threats to release confidential information.

In spite of the above provisional categorization, it appears difficult to summarize liability for acts taken on the Internet in the EU. The liability based on information content is not separately regulated in the EU but is affected by national criminal, civil and administrative law and a number of EU instruments, including the Brussels I Regulation. The most obvious forms of liability arise from defaming others, from infringing copyright, from circulating obscene material and from hate speech. These will be analysed in turn.

3. DEFAMATION

3.1   Some Regulatory Models: United States, Australia and the UK

The law of defamation plays a vital role in attempting to 'reconcile the
competing interests of freedom of expression and the protection of
individual reputation'.[12] The regulation of defamation on the Internet
varies widely across the globe. The most important disagreement is about
the place where the defaming material was 'published'. The first question
raised is: who is considered to be a 'publisher', and the second: in which
jurisdiction will the publisher be liable? In principle, in the UK and in
Australia, the publisher is anyone who posts or transmits the material and
the liability will arise where the material is accessed. In the United
States, however, liability arises only in cases where the material was
directed or targeted towards a particular jurisdiction.

In 2002 the Australian High Court decided *Gutnick v Dow Jones*.[13] The
case concerned defamation proceedings brought in Australia by Mr
Gutnick against Dow Jones, a USA company owner of *Barron's* magazine, where allegedly defamatory statements concerning Mr Gutnick
were published. Most of the readership of that magazine was located in
the USA, but a minority also existed in Australia. The offending article
was published in the print version of the magazine but also in its online
version. In the proceedings, Dow Jones claimed that publication occurred
where the material was placed on the Internet – in the United States –
and that a single publication rule, which provides that publication occurs
only when material is placed in circulation for the first time and not on
subsequent occasions, should apply to subsequent dissemination. Mr
Gutnick claimed that publication occurs every time an item is read and
comprehended – in this case Australia. The Australian High Court took
the view that an Internet article is published where it is *accessed and
comprehended*, that is, downloaded, therefore potentially opening the
gates to litigation in all cases where the material is accessible in another
country.

In the United Kingdom, the position is underlined by several cases. In
Godfrey v Demon,[14] a statement defamatory of the plaintiff was posted on
an internet bulletin board in the United States. It appeared in the UK
through Godfrey's own Internet service provider, Demon, and Godfrey

---

[12]   Collins, M., *The Law of Defamation* (3rd ed., Oxford University Press,
Oxford 2010), p. 4.

[13]   [2002] HCA 56.

[14]   [1999] 4 All ER 342.

sued in defamation. The ISP defended itself by claiming that it is only a passive distributor and should, therefore, not be held liable for publication. The court held that transmitting and/or hosting the material amounts to publication. Similar reasoning was seen in *Loutchensky v Times*,[15] where a Russian businessman brought a libel case against *The Times*. The Court of Appeal accepted the defence of qualified privilege, which provides immunity from damages for material published in the public interest the truth of which cannot be proved in court, but rejected the contention that the same defence should apply to the archived parts of *The Times* newspaper. *Harrods v Dow Jones*[16] rested on similar facts as the Australian *Gutnick* case. Dow Jones sought a stay of English proceedings claiming that England was not the proper forum to hear the case. The High Court refused to stay, saying that publication took place where the material was downloaded and read – in England. Therefore, two separate publications took place – one in the USA, where the magazine was distributed, and one in England, where the website was accessible. Finally, in *Don King v Lennox Lewis*,[17] a defamatory statement was made in the USA and both the defendant and the plaintiffs were based there. An application was made to serve out of jurisdiction, which the defendants sought to set aside. This was rejected, with the Court emphasizing that Don King enjoyed a substantial reputation in England and that English law regards Internet publication to have occurred where the material was accessed.

The position in the United States is markedly different from that in both Australia and the United Kingdom. The two important early cases are *Cubby, Inc. v CompuServe Inc.*[18] and *Stratton Oakmont, Inc. v Prodigy Services Company*.[19] *Cubby* revolved around an online forum on journalism, owned by CompuServe, but independently managed by another firm, Cameron Communications. The latter had a contract with a third firm, Don Fitzpatrick Associates, for the provision of a gossip newsletter named Rumorville USA. Under that contract, Don Fitzpatrick accepted full responsibility for the content. The plaintiffs, publishers of a rival service, claimed that they were defamed in several editions of Rumorville USA. The judge equated Compuserve's status to that of a public library or a news-stand. The former has as much control over the

---

[15] [2002] QB 321 and [2002] QB 783.
[16] [2003] EWHC 1162 (QB).
[17] [2004] EWHC 168 (QB).
[18] 776 F. Supp. 135 (SD NY, 1991), US District Court, Southern District of New York.
[19] 1995 WL 323710, New York Supreme Court.

content of the publication as the latter, and to make it liable as a publisher would be to seriously hamper the freedom of speech protected by the First Amendment of the US Constitution. It would be observed here that the result under the limitation of liability provisions of the E-Commerce Directive would have been the same, provided that the ISP had no actual knowledge of the information or activity.

In *Stratton Oakmont*, Prodigy was hosting a financial bulletin called Money Talk. The plaintiffs alleged that they have been defamed by statements posted on the board. It was held that Prodigy was a publisher, not a distributor, under the law of the state of New York. Prodigy, unlike CompuServe in the previous case, had exercised editorial control over the content and also used automatic screening software and content guidelines.

On 19 May 2003, the Supreme Court confirmed a case decided by a Court of Appeal in *Young v New Heaven Advocate*.[20] In that case, it was held that defamation proceedings for material published in Connecticut could not be commenced in Virginia simply because defamatory statements were accessible there. It was held that the alleged defaming newspapers did not target their websites towards a Virginian audience.

Zeran v AOL,[21] involved defamatory statements posted on AOL's bulletin board. The poster was unidentified, but Zeran notified AOL, which assured Zeran that postings would be removed, but subsequently failed to act. Zeran filed a lawsuit against AOL, claiming that AOL was liable for defamation. The court rejected this argument, saying that, pursuant to Section 230 of the Communication Decency Act 1996 (CDA), the Internet service provider is never liable for defamatory material posted by third parties, even where the ISP has been previously notified.[22] The court, defending the vigour of Internet communication, said that to impose tort liability in cases concerning ISPs would force the latter to constantly monitor the traffic on their networks. This would have a negative impact both on their business and, more importantly, on the freedom of speech. But, this case also highlights the problematic implications of encouraging the ISPs to have editorial control, which was also evident in the *Prodigy* case (above). Put in different terms, it seems that the price that the ISPs have paid for this effective insulation from liability is the loss of it in all cases where they have exercised editorial

---

[20]   315 F 3d 256 (4th Cir. 2002).

[21]   129 F 3d 327 (4th Cir. 1997), US Court of Appeals, Fourth Circuit.

[22]   For this line of reasoning, see also *Blumenthal v Drudge*, 992 F. Supp. 44 (DDC 1998) and *Doe v America Online*, 718 So 2d 385 (4th Cir. 1999), US Court of Appeals, Fourth Circuit.

control, placed adequate filtering or have done anything else to insulate themselves.

3.2 Defamation in the EU

The described provisions of the previous three jurisdictions relate to situations where national courts (Australian, English, American) take jurisdiction for material accessible on their territory and apply their defamation law. The EU has not harmonized substantive law on defamation, but it has dealt to a considerable extent with jurisdiction and choice-of-law issues. There are three European sources that have an impact on domestic defamation law in general, and on defamation on the Internet specifically. The first is the Brussels I Regulation. That regulation contains jurisdiction rules that determine which courts will hear the case concerning defamation online.[23] Together with this may be considered the Rome II Regulation on law applicable to tort.[24] Another source is the European Convention on Human Rights. The final source is the E-Commerce Directive and its provisions on Internet service provider liability. The last of these, it has to be remarked, concerns only the liability of ISPs as intermediaries and normally has a very limited impact on national defamation cases involving subjects which are not transmitters (see below).

When will courts of Member State A take jurisdiction for a defamatory article posted on the Internet in Member State B? Article 5(3) of the European Regulation on jurisdiction and judgments provides that 'A Person domiciled in a Member State may, in another Member State, be sued … in matters relating to tort, delict or quasi-delict, in the courts for the place where the harmful event occurred or may occur'. The Court of Justice has in *Shevill v Presse Alliance*[25] ruled that the victim of libel by a newspaper article distributed in several Member States may bring an action in damages against the publisher either in the court of a Member State where the publisher is established or before the courts of each Member State in which the publication was distributed. In the case of the former, the court has jurisdiction to award damages for all the harm caused by defamation. In respect of latter, only in respect of the harm caused in the Member State of the court seized.

---

[23] Notably Article 5(3) on tort. See Chapter 3.
[24] See Chapter 3.
[25] C-68/93 [1995] ECR I-415.

In light of *eDate* jurisprudence,[26] an action can be brought 'in respect of all the damage caused, either before the courts of the Member State in which the publisher of that content is established or before the courts of the Member State in which the centre of his interests is based'. Additionally, in respect of the damage caused in the territory of the Member State only, an action can be brought before the courts of that state if the content was placed online or has been accessible there. This decision is important as it makes the claimant's position more certain. Instead of suing in a number of Member States, only one suffices, but where the plaintiff is interested in covering one state only, this will also be possible. The general problem, however, may be to locate the defendant. A statement published on an Internet blog, for instance, may be signed with a pseudonym, making identification difficult and requiring a further action to reveal the identity of the publisher. More importantly, the claimant may not have the financial and legal resources to bring an action in a state other than the home state in which he is located. In that respect, the other option – to sue in the state where the content has been distributed – may not be better.

Rights and freedoms of the European Convention of Human Rights (ECHR) form part of the laws of Member States. Of primary importance here is Article 10[27] of the ECHR which can potentially come into conflict with defamation verdicts in favour of claimants. The greatest protection in the ECHR is afforded by the court to political speech.[28] Similar levels of protection are afforded to other matters of public concern. On the other hand, commercial and artistic speech, while also deserving protection, are not accorded the same level of protection. There are, as yet, no direct cases that deal with this problem but the general jurisprudence of the court can be extrapolated onto Internet cases.[29] In *Times v UK*,[30] the court said that the publisher's Article 10 ECHR right could be interfered with in cases where a defamation action was brought against it for material *archived* on the Internet. Article 8 ECHR, which protects private and family life, may be an element in a defamation action where a severe

---

[26]   C-509/09 and C-161/10 *eDate Advertising GmbH v X, Olivier Martinez, Robert Martinez v MGN Limited*, 25 October 2011, not yet reported.

[27]   Also of some importance may be other Articles, such as Article 6 (right to a fair and public hearing) or Article 8 (privacy and family rights).

[28]   See Collins, M., *The Law of Defamation and the Internet* (2nd ed., OUP, Oxford 2005), Chapter 30.

[29]   Collins, M., op. cit., pp. 461–3.

[30]   [2009] EMLR 14.

attack on the personal integrity of the applicant exists.[31] In such cases, Articles 8 and 10 may have to be weighed and balanced.

4. COPYRIGHT INFRINGEMENT AS A TOOL FOR CONTENT CONTROL

Copyright protection is the subject of a separate analysis in this book. In this section we look at copyright rules from the prism of content control only. The idea is that copyright protection serves as a tool for monitoring which groups of users access the material over and above what is normal in cases of the regular exercise of IP rights. A copyright holder has rights defined and assigned by law which are exercised under defined circumstances. When these rights are defined and enforced broadly, copyright has the capacity to be used as a tool for content control.

Liability for violation of intellectual property rights arises from Directive 2001/29/EC (Copyright, or InfoSoc) and Directive 2004/48/EC[32] on enforcement.[33] The InfoSoc Directive, Article 8(2), obliges Member States to have an effective system of remedies:

> Each Member State shall take the measures necessary to ensure that rightholders whose interests are affected by an infringing activity carried out on its territory can bring an action for damages and/or apply for an injunction and, where appropriate, for the seizure of infringing material as well as of devices, products or components referred to in Article 6(2).

Injunctions exist against intermediaries whose services are used by third parties.

The crucial provision of the Copyright Enforcement Directive is found in Article 13, which provides that damages are due for infringements committed with knowledge or with reasonable grounds for it, on application by the injured party to the appropriate judicial authorities. These damages shall be appropriate to the actual injustice suffered as a result of the infringement. The Article also includes the rules for setting the amount of damages. These provide that the courts shall take into account all aspects of the case, including negative economic consequences, lost profits, unfair profits made by the infringer and other, non-economic, factors. As an alternative to such a way of measuring damages, the courts

---

[31] Collins, M., op. cit., p. 464.
[32] Copyright Enforcement Directive, OJ L 195, 2.6.2004, pp. 16–25.
[33] For more details on the IP regime, see Chapter 6.

can, in appropriate cases, set a lump sum which shall be no less than the
amount of royalties which would have been due, had the infringer
requested authorization. If the infringement was committed without
knowledge, a Member State may provide either the recovery of profits or
payment of pre-established damages.

The provisions on damages are poorly drafted. Even though the article
provides that the amount of damages ought to be appropriate to the
injustice suffered, it allows the courts to take into account negative
economic consequences and lost profits. There is no indication as to how
the courts might measure these. Typically, the entertainment industry
declares lost profits in terms of the total number of pirated songs/CDs
multiplied by the regular commercial price. This rests on the assumption
that all those who have downloaded a song or an album would have
purchased it at full price. This is not so. In fact, if the vast majority of
file-swappers are in a lower age bracket (16–25), then their budgets are
limited and, as a consequence, they would not have purchased the music
at full price. This gives a distorted measure of actual profit loss and may
lead to disproportionately high damages.[34]

The Enforcement Directive in its draft form caused a positive reaction
from the entertainment industry but strong opposition from the telecommunications companies, part of the computer industry, most of the
national press and the public, on account of the draconian ways in which
infringements were to be treated. In terms of liability, the draft Directive
introduced criminal liability for deliberate violations of intellectual
property conducted in the course of business. The provision on criminal
liability in the draft Directive was replaced with Article 16, allowing the
Member States to apply 'other appropriate sanctions' where IP rights
have been infringed, without prejudice to the civil and administrative
measures. This, in effect, turns the Enforcement Directive into a civil
enforcement instrument.

Criminal liability was subsequently addressed in a 'Proposal for a
European Parliament and Council Directive on Criminal Measures Aimed
at Ensuring the Enforcement of Intellectual Property Rights'.[35] This is
accompanied by a 'Council Framework Decision to Strengthen the
Criminal Law Framework to Combat Intellectual Property Offences'.[36]
The key provision is Article 3, which provides that 'Member States shall

---

[34]   On the problem of measuring loss, see Rob, R. and Waldfogel, J., 'Piracy
on the High C's: Music Downloading, Sales Displacement, and Social Welfare in
a Sample of College Students' (2006) 49 *Journal of Law and Economics* 29.
[35]   COM(2005) 276 final, 12.7.2005.
[36]   [SEC(2005)848], COM(2005) 276 final, 12.7.2005.

ensure that all intentional infringements of an intellectual property right on a commercial scale, and attempting, aiding or abetting and inciting such infringements, are treated as criminal offences'. The introduction of criminal offences is, in itself, very likely an ineffective measure, unlikely to deter large-scale pirates and inefficient with small-scale file-swappers.[37] Particularly worrying is the incrimination of attempting, aiding, abetting or inciting infringements. This latter has been raised as a concern at the introduction of the stalled INDUCE[38] and SOPA acts[39] in the US Congress. The particular worry is that producers of new technology devices, such as the iPad, would discontinue their research and production, fearful of the possible outlawing of the devices they are producing.

The penalties are set out in Article 4. Custodial sentences are provided for natural persons. Fine and confiscation are provided for both natural and legal persons. A selection of penalties is made available for in Section 2 of Article 4, to be applied at Member States' discretion. This includes destruction of goods, permanent or temporary closure of establishments or a ban on engaging in commercial activities, placing under judicial supervision, winding-up, a ban on access to public assistance and publication of judgments. The introduction of criminal penalties for natural persons seems a particularly harsh measure, especially given the lack of proof that their introduction has a significant effect on the level of infringement.

The 'commercial scale' criterion is originally contained in Article 61 of the 1995 Agreement on Trade-Related Aspects of Intellectual Property Rights (TRIPS Agreement). That Article obliges WTO Members to 'provide for criminal procedures and penalties to be applied at least in cases of wilful trademark counterfeiting or copyright piracy on a commercial scale'. Remedies available are supposed to include imprisonment and/or monetary fines which are sufficient to provide a deterrent, consistent with the level of penalties applied to corresponding crimes. In appropriate cases, the available remedies must also include the 'seizure, forfeiture and destruction of the infringing goods and of any materials and implements the predominant use of which has been in the commission of the offence'. The Member States have freedom to provide for

---

[37] For an analysis of the American experience, see Bhattacharjee, S., et al., 'Impact of Legal Threats on Online Music Sharing Activity: An Analysis of Music Industry Legal Actions' (2006) 49 *Journal of Law and Economics* 91.

[38] Introduced as S. 2560 by Senator Orrin Hatch on 22 June 2004.

[39] H.R.3261 – Stop Online Piracy Act; House Judiciary Committee; 26 October 2011.

criminal procedures and penalties to be applied in other cases of infringement of intellectual property rights, especially where they are committed wilfully and on a commercial scale.

The TRIPS provision is, on the surface, an unremarkable one. Criminal sanctions for counterfeiting have existed for some time in a number of WTO member states. What makes the transposition of this obligation into EU law questionable is the lack of proper definition of a 'commercial scale'. It should, in principle, include larger scale operations conducted for significant profit but it could, in fact, include rather small one-man operations that attract a negligible profit. In practice, this would depend on the interpretation of the national courts.

5. SEXUALLY EXPLICIT SPEECH

In terms of its capacity to distribute harmful material, the Internet is possibly more powerful than any media before it. But, what is considered to be pornography in one part of the world would hardly deserve notice in the other. Different standards may not easily be reconciled and actors from more liberal legal regimes may find themselves on the receiving end in more stringent jurisdictions. The freedom of speech protection in such cases may be overruled by other interests. The problem of liability for obscene material is twofold. First, criminal liability may arise out of providing illegal material, with individual posters, hosts and transmitters all being affected. Secondly, civil liability may arise out of removing the material deemed to be offensive that turns out not to be, by ISPs acting out of their own accord.

The American history of regulating obscenity is of interest. The first attempt to tackle the problem was the Communication Decency Act 1996 (CDA)[40] which set out to limit the distribution of indecent speech in cases where it can be accessed by a minor. Effectively, it made all manner of speech illegal. In *Reno v ACLU*[41] the Supreme Court struck down the indecency provisions, saying that they are an unconstitutional abridgement of the right to free speech as guaranteed in the First Amendment. In reality, what the Act did is to limit the acceptability of speech on the Internet to that of a minor where this restriction does not exist for other forms of communication. Two later attempts to deal with the same issue were equally unsuccessful: the Federal Government was

---

[40]   47 USC (USA), s 230(c) (1996), Title V of the Telecommunications Acts 1996 (USA).
[41]   *Reno v American Civil Liberties Union*, 521 U.S. 844 (1997).

enjoined from enforcing the Child Online Protection Act 1998 (COPA)[42] and the Children's Internet Protection Act 2000 (CIPA) was challenged.

Importantly, however, Article 230(c) of the Communication Decency Act says that providers and users of computer services shall not be treated as publishers or speakers of information given by another information content provider. Also, they will not be held liable for action to restrict access to or availability of material considered to be obscene. The first part of the Article, in other words, insulates ISPs from liability while the second part enables intermediaries to remove offensive material without fear of being sued. Although parts of the CDA were declared unconstitutional in *Reno v ACLU*, this Article has not. As for the first part of the Article, it will be observed that the said defence is considerably more specific (if not wider) than the defences in Articles 12–15 of the E-Commerce Directive (see below). It applies to all providers/users, not just to conduits/intermediaries. Second, the article protects the subjects even where they are fully aware of the content.[43]

The European Union did not attempt to regulate obscenity on a general level. It does not have measures to fight adult pornography and only limited ones to fight child pornography. Concerning the latter, the first measure of some importance is the Council Decision of 29 May 2000 to combat child pornography on the Internet.[44] It logically continues the 1997 Joint Action to combat trafficking in human beings and sexual exploitation of children,[45] the Recommendation on protection of minors and human dignity[46] and the Safer Internet Action Plan (1999–2005).[47]

---

[42] In *Ashcroft v American Civil Liberties Union* 542 U.S. 656 (2004), the Supreme Court affirmed the injunction. The actual law only concerned commercial speech by US providers.

[43] For how the Article is applied by the courts, see *Zeran v AOL*, 958 F. Supp. 1124 (ED Va, 1997), Eastern District Court of Virginia.

[44] See footnote 5.

[45] Joint Action 97/154/JHA of 24 February 1997 adopted by the Council on the basis of Article K.3 of the Treaty on European Union concerning action to combat trafficking in human beings and sexual exploitation of children, OJ L 63, 4.3.1997, amended by Council Framework Decision 2002/629/JHA of 19 July 2002 concerning trafficking in human beings, OJ L 203, 1.8.2002.

[46] 98/560/EC, October 1998, which provides national legislative guidelines regarding illegal and harmful content over electronic media, OJ L 270, 7.10.1998.

[47] Decision No 276/1999/EC of the European Parliament and of the Council of 25 January 1999 adopting a multiannual Community action plan on promoting safer use of the Internet by combating illegal and harmful content on global networks, OJ L 108, 27.4.1999, pp. 52–6. Extended by Decision No 1151/

The 1997 Joint Action aimed to establish common rules for action to combat human trafficking and the sexual exploitation of children, to fight against certain forms of unauthorized immigration and to improve judicial cooperation in criminal matters.[48] Member States undertook the obligation to review their national legislation with a view to eliminating human trafficking and the sexual exploitation of children. Although the measure did not specifically address the Internet, it does have some importance for it. One of the three behaviours specifically identified is 'sexual exploitation' which, in relation to a child, means:

> the inducement or coercion of a child to engage in any unlawful sexual activity; the exploitative use of a child in prostitution or other unlawful sexual practices; the exploitative use of children in pornographic performances and materials, including the production, sale and distribution or other forms of trafficking in such materials, and the possession of such materials.

Most of this can be mediated through the use of emails, chat rooms, portals, real-time text messaging services, and so on. The Action Plan did not introduce specific criminal measures. Its main areas of activity were: establishing a safer environment through a network of hotlines and the encouragement of self-regulation and rules of conduct; filtering technologies; awareness campaigns; and support activities.

While it is possible that different standards in different Member States may lead to cases alleging violation of the Single Market provisions of the TFEU, such cases would be defendable under Treaty provisions or mandatory requirements. In *Henn and Derby*[49] the European Court ruled that:

> a Member State may, in principle, lawfully impose prohibitions on the importation from any other member-State of articles which are of an indecent or obscene character as understood by its domestic laws and that such prohibitions may lawfully be applied to the whole of its national territory even

---

2003/EC of 16 June 2003, OJ L 162, 1.7.2003. The new action plan, New 'Safer Internet Plus' (2005–2008): Decision No 854/2005/EC of the European Parliament and of the Council of 11 May 2005 establishing a multiannual Community Programme on promoting safer use of the Internet and new online technologies, OJ L 149, 11.6.2005.

[48] At present, Directive 2011/36/EU of the European Parliament and of the Council of 5 April 2011 on preventing and combating trafficking in human beings and protecting its victims, and replacing Council Framework Decision 2002/629/JHA, OJ L 101, 15.4.2011.

[49] C-34/79 *Regina v Maurice Donald Henn and John Frederick Ernest Darby* [1979] ECR 3795.

if, in regard to the field in question, variations exist between the laws in force in the different constituent parts of the member-State concerned.

Such a prohibition cannot be arbitrary and presupposes the absence, on the territory of the Member State in question, of the trade in the said goods.

6. HATE SPEECH

Hate speech is a synonym for written or oral communication or public behaviour that invites prejudice based on ethnicity, race, gender or religious, sexual, political, social or other characteristics. Defining it properly is difficult, as it can extend well beyond the most commonly found forms (such as racial hatred) and cover the territory that some label as 'controversial' although legal speech. The most important feature, however, is that it is based on publicly expressed judgment which is not based on evidence and which invites discrimination towards a group of people individualized by one of their common features.

A marked difference exists between the United States, where the First Amendment protects freedom of speech, including hate speech, and Europe, where hate speech attracts criminal and/or civil liability. Various Member States have regulated it differently. Holocaust denial, for example, is illegal in a number of EU states, including Germany, Austria and France, but not in others. Incitement of hatred based on racial or ethnic origins is illegal in all EU states.

The regulation of hate speech has considerable importance for the Internet. If speech is legally placed on the Internet in Member State A it will be accessible in Member State B where it might be illegal. Liability arising out of this action may be both criminal (as, for example, in the case of Holocaust denial) and civil (as in the case where damages are obtainable for something that is also considered defamatory).

From the viewpoint of certainty, the desirable situation is either complete lack of regulation of hate speech, which is the American model, or unified regulation, which is the European model.[50] To put it simply, American society believes that hate speech can best be eliminated by allowing all opinions to be voiced and letting the public choose.

---

[50] The United States have joined in the European Cybercrime Convention effective from 1 January 2007 but not the Additional Protocol. Concerns were voiced by the US government during negotiations that the final Protocol would not be compatible with the US Constitution.

Europeans, on the other hand, derive their views from different political traditions and their experience during the two world wars.

The European Convention on Cybercrime, adopted by the Council of Europe,[51] in its amended version,[52] prohibits:

> any written material, any image or any other representation of ideas or theories, which advocates, promotes or incites hatred, discrimination or violence, against any individual or group of individuals, based on race, colour, descent or national or ethnic origin, as well as religion if used as pretext for any of these factors.[53]

The first main provision of the amending Protocol is Article 3, which deals with dissemination of racist and xenophobic material on computer systems. It places an obligation on Member States to criminalize intentional 'distributing, or otherwise making available of racist and xenophobic material to the public through a computer system'. If other effective remedies are available, a party may choose not to attach criminal liability to the described conduct, provided other effective remedies are available and where the material promotes or incites discrimination that is not associated with violence. Irrespective of this exception, a party may reserve the right not to apply the Article to those cases of discrimination for which there are, due to the national system of freedom of expression, no effective remedy.[54] This latter has been inserted to address the concerns of those Member States which constitutionally protect free speech.

Article 4 criminalizes racial and xenophobic threats. The offence consists of threatening, through a computer system, the commission of a serious criminal offence as defined under domestic law. The threat has to relate to a group, distinguished by race, colour, descent or national or ethnic origin, as well as religion, if used as a pretext for any of these factors, or a group of persons which is distinguished by any of these characteristics.

Furthermore, Article 5 deals with intentional racially motivated insult. This consists of insulting publicly, through a computer system, persons belonging to a group distinguished by race, colour, descent or national or ethnic origin, as well as religion, if used as a pretext for any of these

---

[51]   And, strictly speaking, falling outside the scope of the EU. For more on these issues, see Chapter 10 on Cybercrime.

[52]   Additional Protocol to the Convention on Cybercrime Concerning the Criminalisation of Acts of a Racist and Xenophobic Nature Committed Through Computer Systems, Strasbourg, 7 November 2002, PC-RX (2002) 24.

[53]   Article 2 of the Additional Protocol.

[54]   Paragraph 3 of the Article.

factors, or a group of persons which is distinguished by any of these characteristics. A party may additionally require that the person or group in question is exposed to hatred, contempt or ridicule or reserve the right not to apply the Article whatsoever.

Article 6 covers what is colloquially referred to as 'Holocaust denial' but in fact encompasses denial, gross minimization, approval or justification of genocide or crimes against humanity and is therefore much wider in scope, both in terms of historical periods covered and the geographical extent. The criminal offence consists of:

> distributing or otherwise making available, through a computer system to the public, material which denies, grossly minimises, approves or justifies acts constituting genocide or crimes against humanity, as defined by international law and recognised as such by final and binding decisions of the International Military Tribunal, established by the London Agreement of 8 April 1945, or of any other international court established by relevant international instruments and whose jurisdiction is recognised by that Party.

The party may require that the denial be committed with intent to incite hatred discrimination or violence or, otherwise, decide not to apply the Article at all.

Intentional aiding or abetting in any of the acts in Articles 3 to 7 is criminalized in Article 7 of the Protocol.

A number of European countries already have laws that cover racial hatred. The changes, from their perspective, may not look revolutionary. More importantly, though, a proportion of racist sites are also hosted in the United States, which is not bound by the Protocol. This is further complicated by the consequences of the US position in the American *Yahoo!* case,[55] which can be summarized as protecting freedom of speech in the First Amendment through refusing recognition and enforcement of judgments that do not respect it.

7. CONCLUSION

The EU, unlike most of its Member States, does not have a consistent policy on regulating Internet content. Most of its regulatory efforts are sector specific. Where such a policy exists, it is limited to specific issues. This is true of the EU's work on protecting minors, which has resulted in efforts to combat child pornography and harmful advertising.

---

[55] See Chapter 3.

5.   Liability of intermediaries

1. INTERMEDIARIES AND THE INTERNET

The Internet's unique layered structure[1] creates three separate relevant categories of actors or subjects. The first are those who create or post information. The second are those who this information targets – the recipients. Although the two roles can be blurred in real life (e.g., a home user can post information on a blog and read other users' blogs), legally the roles are distinct in that legal action would normally target a subject in one of its roles only.

The third actor, the intermediaries, plays an essential role which revolves around three points. First, they enable the flow of information between the two other subjects without contributing to the content. Second, they act as guardians of the users' identity and anonymity. Third, they are in a unique position to prevent or mitigate the damage that may be inflicted by the other two categories' illegal activity. As such, they may, under certain circumstances, be liable as contributors.

Internet service providers are commercial entities guided by commercial logic. Their operation, however, is not solely determined by market forces but is influenced by groups who desire to control the Internet. In the first place, these are the federal and regional governments[2] who exercise force on ISPs to control undesirable behaviour on the Internet. The ISP actions, their cooperation or the lack thereof, can influence a whole range of government policies concerning, among other things, defamation, sexually explicit speech or copyright infringement. For corporations, the intermediaries who possess knowledge of possibly illegal downloading patterns are valuable holders of information concerning potential end-users and their behaviour. This information can be

---

[1]   See Chapter 1.
[2]   In the United States, for instance, some states have enacted child protecting legislation. See *Center for Democracy and Technology v Pappert*, 337 F. Supp. 606, US District Court for the Eastern District of Pennsylvania.

extracted with relative ease, depending on the court system.[3] For individual users, the intermediaries are guardians of their privacy, without which it would be difficult to trace them, but also guarantors of their ability to meaningfully exercise free speech.

The choice of the regulatory model applied to the intermediaries may have important consequences for the development of the Internet. Economically, there is a direct relationship between regulatory burden and development. The more exposed the intermediaries are to liability, the less likely they will invest in the Internet's development. The stricter the regulation, the more restraint it will place on the development of the medium. Strict liability of providers will result in their withdrawal from the market and the limitation of the type and range of the services they provide. Dragging file posters into jurisdictions based on a generously treated reputation in defamation will cripple the content to the level of the lowest common denominator as long as there are assets that can be attached.

This objective is specifically recognized in the preamble of the American Communication Decency Act 1996, Section 230, the aim of which is, among other things:

(1) to promote the continued development of the Internet and other interactive computer services and other interactive media;
(2) to preserve the vibrant and competitive free market that presently exists for the Internet and other interactive computer services, unfettered by Federal or State regulation;
(3) to encourage the development of technologies which maximize user control over what information is received by individuals, families, and schools who use the Internet and other interactive computer services.

The question concerning liability deals with the legal responsibility for actions on the Internet that cause harm to others. By exposing our actions worldwide, the borderless instantly accessible Internet poses a challenge to the traditional notion of civil liability.[4] In 'real life', we are liable for harm we cause to others. Mostly, this kind of liability is easy to localize: it happens on the territory of a determined or determinable state(s) and results from conscious actions of particular individuals or corporations (such as driving negligently or violating the terms of a contract).

---

[3] The Court of Justice affirmed that rightholders may seek injunctions against ISPs in file-sharing cases. See C-557/07 *LSG-Gesellschaft zur Wahrnehmung von Leistungsschutzrechten* [2009] ECR I-01227.

[4] See Smith, G., *Internet Law and Regulation* (Sweet & Maxwell, London 2003).

Sometimes, the liability is objective (as in the case of faulty equipment). In that situation, one is liable because one has done something that a particular law system proscribes. The standard is set by the state, in the form of private and public laws, and its violation leads to liability.

This can tentatively be called the standard model of regulation. Previous chapters have highlighted some of the difficulties of the standard model in the digital age and occasionally looked at the alternative solutions. On the Internet, the intermediaries are in the unique position of power, with the ability to introduce private control, in the form of filtering or self-censoring measures. Here we will look at how EU liability regimes reflect their position. Liability of such intermediaries is widely accepted today: those who store or transmit data can and are made liable for the damage arising from data even when they are not posters.

There are two important points that need to be considered. First, under what circumstances will liability be imposed on intermediaries? The second is: under what circumstances can intermediaries be requested to submit information they hold about users?

1.1   Choice of Regulatory Regime

Hosting, transmitting and publishing form the main, revenue-generating part of the ISPs' business. The problem concerning liability, which is contemporary with the popular spread of the Internet in the mid 1990s, is caused by the ISPs' fear of civil liability for the material they host, transmit or publish. Conceptually, the regulators distinguish these activities. Hosting involves keeping and/or managing websites for end-users. All web pages require hosting on a computer from which other users will access them. This can be performed on a local computer (i.e., a university, a corporation or a tech-savvy user will host their own web pages) or it can be hosted on the ISP's equipment, usually for a monthly or yearly fee. Transmitting involves providing access to the Internet (normally for a subscription) and sending and receiving signals from other computers. Publishing involves making content available on a web page hosted or controlled by the ISP. A typical example is a web forum or a chat group generally open not only to ISP members but to third parties as well.[5]

---

[5]   Most such forums today are open. AOL is a typical example of a provider which until recently charged a subscription fee for the content and services it provided.

In a contractual relationship between the end-user and the ISP, possible breaches are anticipated and usually addressed in contractual provisions. This may give redress to an ISP in cases where the infringing material originates with the other contracting party (i.e., a hosted web page or file-sharing site in breach of the terms) but does not help if third parties are involved. The very nature of the Internet means that the users who access the web through their ISPs as intermediaries identify themselves to other users, but are not limited to posting content on pages owned or operated by their ISPs. Thus a group hosted on Yahoo! may be accessed by anyone, not just those with a Yahoo! broadband contract, making contractual protection of little use. On top of this, Internet service providers like not to be involved in disputes between the injured party and the end-user and prefer the regime where they are completely exempt from liability.

Clearly, the regime where there is no liability for ISPs satisfies the providers but very few other parties. Alternatively, the regime which puts the entire burden on the ISPs introduces self-censorship, limits their capacity to introduce new services and exposes them to risk from transmitting material by third parties. The appropriate regime, therefore, needs to strike the right balance between the interests of the injured parties and those of the transmitters.

Some states have recently introduced legislation which invites a more active role from ISPs without introducing the obligation to monitor, otherwise prohibited in Article 15 of the Electronic Commerce Directive. The French HADOPI-1 bill[6] invites copyright owners to report potential infringements to a specially created authority which, in turn, consults other parties involved including the ISPs. While the law does not introduce extra liability on ISPs nor does it demand that they 'police' the Internet, it encourages them to cooperate with the authorities, raising questions about collaboration. Similar efforts have been extended in the UK with the Digital Economy Act 2010 (DEA),[7] which not only requires ISPs' cooperation but imposes heavy fines where that cooperation is not given without good reason.

---

[6] Loi favorisant la diffusion et la protection de la création sur Internet [Creation and Internet Law], Loi no. 2009–669 du 12 juin 2009, JO no. 135 du 13 juin 2009.

[7] 2010 c 24.

Currently, there exist three regimes for liability of intermediaries on the Internet based on the degree of control imposed on the providers.[8] The first of these involves direct application of criminal sanctions on Internet service providers for noncompliance with the imposed regime. Under this regime, ISPs are to be liable criminally for material that is hosted on or transmitted through their computers and can also be liable civilly. Even though it might have a limited effect in the case of obscene material, for which it was designed, it has little or no effect on other material. For reasons mainly to do with the ability to implement it, this regime has been abandoned in all but a handful of countries.[9]

The second regime insulates ISPs from liability almost completely by granting them immunity and encouraging them to self-regulate. The ISP liability regime in the United States belongs to this model.

The third regime limits the liability of ISPs, normally on the condition that any infringing material is removed upon notification. The EU Electronic Commerce Directive takes this approach.

1.2 The American Approach

The American approach to Internet liability has its foundation in the First Amendment which guarantees freedom of speech and freedom of the press, values which American courts have repeatedly protected. As a result, the model developed in the United States was never based on strict but on limited liability, with the main idea being that a distributor or deliverer that is considered a passive conduit would not be found liable unless there is fault on its part.[10]

The American statutory response to the Internet was robust and involved two separate statutes. The first of these is Section 230 of the Communication Decency Act 1996 which deals with the problem of intermediaries' liability *in general*. The second is the 1998 Digital Millennium Copyright Act which only deals with providers' liability *for copyright infringement*. Section 230 CDA stipulates:

---

[8]   For a detailed discussion of these regimes, see Edwards, L., 'Articles 12 – 15 ECD: ISP Liability', in Edwards, L. (ed.), *The New Legal Framework for E-Commerce in Europe* (Hart: Oxford and Portland, OR 2005), p. 106 et seq.

[9]   For example, the Australian Broadcasting Services Amendment (Online Services) Act 1999 that was eventually watered down to a point where ISPs in Australia had immunity.

[10]   See Ludbrook, T., 'Defamation and the Internet, Part 2' (2004) 15 *Entertainment Law Review* 105.

No provider or user of an interactive computer service shall be treated as the publisher or speaker of any information provided by another information content provider.

Here, an 'interactive computer service' specifically includes the Internet, and an 'information content provider' is taken to mean anybody who is responsible for the creation of information provided through the Internet. Although the broad immunity which is evident from this section may sound excessive, in practice it is counterbalanced by a more aggressive role reserved for ISPs, who are supposed to self-regulate the dissemination of material.[11]

Liability for IP violation is regulated by the DMCA.[12] This act introduces in Section 512 limitations of liability in respect of online material and says that a provider shall not be liable for intermediate storage or transmission of material through the Internet if:

- the transmission was initiated by another person;
- the storage and transmission is carried out through an automatic technological process, without any selection of that material by the provider;
- no copy of the material thereby made by the provider is maintained on the provider's system or network in a manner ordinarily accessible to anyone other than the recipients anticipated by the person who initiated the transmission, and no such copy is maintained on the system or network in a manner ordinarily accessible to such recipients for a longer period than is reasonably necessary for the transmission.

Unlike Europe, the DMCA introduces a special standard of liability for non-profit educational institutions.[13]

One of the earliest cases to examine ISP liability in the defamatory context was *Cubby*.[14] CompuServe was an ISP that provided access to the Internet in addition to a variety of special services only available on CompuServe, such as various forums. One of these was Journalism Forum and part of it was a daily newsletter called Rumorville USA.

---

[11] See comments on *Zeran*, below.
[12] Bill Number H.R.2281 for the 105th Congress.
[13] Section 512(e). For a wider comparison, see Tiberi, L. and Zamboni, M., 'Liability of Service Providers' (2003) 9 *Computer and Telecommunications Law Review* 49.
[14] *Cubby, Inc. v CompuServe, Inc.* 776 F. Supp. 135, United States District Court for the Southern District of New York.

CompuServe was not reviewing the contents of the newsletter nor was it in any way in charge of the publication as it was uploaded. The plaintiffs were Cubby, Inc. and Robert Blanchard, publishers of Skuttlebut, a gossip column intended to compete with Rumorville. The plaintiffs claimed that the defendant published defamatory statements on separate occasions. CompuServe's defence was that it was a distributor and not a publisher and it did not know and had no reason to know of them. The court took the view that 'CompuServe, as a news distributor, may not be held liable if it neither knew nor had reason to know of the allegedly defamatory Rumorville statements'. In other words, the court took the view that CompuServe is more like a distributor than like a publisher.

In another case, *Stratton Oakmont*,[15] defamatory statements were made against the defendants in a bulletin board in 1994. Prodigy was 'the owner and operator' of the computer network on which these statements appeared. At the time, Prodigy had two million subscribers and the bulletin in question, Money Talk, was possibly the most widely read such publication on the Internet. The plaintiffs alleged that Prodigy should be considered a publisher and not a distributor. In claiming this, they relied on Prodigy's stated policy which stated that it was a family oriented network. This policy was widely advertised by its executives who repeated on many occasions that they exercised editorial control over the contents on the network.

Zeran v AOL[16] confirms that Section 230 'creates a federal immunity to any cause of action that would make service providers liable for information originating with a third-party user of the service'.

In the context of copyright infringement, a number of cases have come through the American courts. The US Supreme Court case *Grokster*,[17] which held that point-to-point sharing companies could be sued for inducing copyright infringement, was held in *Viacom*[18] not to apply to situations involving ISPs, which are normally not aware of infringements until they receive notice. An ISP which responds to a notice will, therefore, not be liable.

---

[15]   *Stratton Oakmont, Inc. v Prodigy Services Co.*, New York Supreme Court 1995, 1995 WL 323710.
[16]   *Zeran v America Online, Inc.* 129 F.3d 327, US Court of Appeals, Fourth Circuit.
[17]   *MGM Studios, Inc. v Grokster, Ltd.* 545 U.S. 913 (2005).
[18]   *Viacom International Inc. v YouTube, Inc. and Google, Inc.*, No. 07 Civ. 2103, US District Court for the Southern District of New York. See also the appeal judgment of the Court of Appeals (Second Circuit), 10 Civ 3270.

2. THE EUROPEAN APPROACH

2.1 Information Society Services

The E-Commerce Directive provisions on ISP liability are relatively wide in scope. The Directive operates with the concept of 'information society services'. Information society services (ISSs) are defined as those provided for remuneration and at a distance, by means of electronic equipment, for the processing and storage of data, and at the individual request of a service recipient.[19] Remuneration does not normally mean that the services need to be directly paid for by the end users. It is sufficient that they are economic in nature. A website which is funded through advertising is, therefore, included. The fact that services need to be provided at a request excludes services where the recipient plays little or no role in selecting individualized content, such as television or radio.

Information society services defined in this manner encompass a broad range of activities as long as they take place online and as long as one of the sides in the transaction reaps economic benefits. As emphasized in Recital 18 of the E-Commerce Directive, these roughly fall in three categories: transmission of information, access to communication networks and hosting of information content. Such a definition also includes ISPs, which typically provide access to communication networks but can also provide hosting and other services.

Recital 18 of the E-Commerce Directive explains that ISSs include not only economic activities relating to online contracting but any activities which are not remunerated by those who receive them. This distinction is of importance, as it extends the scope of possible insulation from liability to a great number of actors. Television broadcasting is excluded but audiovisual services which are provided on-demand are presumably within the scope. Thus, television signal provided through a regular broadband connection is out of the scope of the Directive but on-demand streaming or extra content provided through the same network is not.

In early American case law, there has been some doubt as to the circumstances at which access providers ought to be treated as intermediaries. The doubt arises because access providers typically engage in a number of activities which involve some degree of providing primary

---

[19]   The definition has been taken from, among others, Directive 98/34/EC of the European Parliament and of the Council of 22 June 1998 laying down a procedure for the provision of information in the field of technical standards and regulations and on rules on information society services, OJ L 204, 21.7.1998, p. 37 (Technical Standards Directive).

content or editing. This is typically the case where they exercise a degree of editorial control. The Court confirmed in the *LSG* case that access providers 'which merely provide users with Internet access, without offering other services such as email, FTP or file sharing services or exercising any control ... must be regarded as "intermediaries"'.[20] In other words, as long as the access provider does not engage in controlling the content, it retains its status as an access provider. That distinction is crucial, taking into consideration the fact that many intermediaries give the users much more than pure access.

Articles 12–15 of the E-Commerce Directive, together with some provisions of the Copyright Directive, establish an EU regime for the liability of intermediary service providers. The disparities that existed between Member States in this area were seen as a burden to the smooth functioning of the Internal Market and removing them was put as one of the priorities. More importantly, however, insulating the providers from liability was seen as an encouragement to the development of services which would otherwise be lacking for fear of legal reprisals. The absence of the limitation would either prevent the providers from entering the market or would severely reduce the content they were offering.

It is important to understand which situations Articles 12–15 of the Directive exactly apply to. These Articles cover the liability of intermediaries in their role as *intermediaries*, not as primary publishers. The First Report on the application of the E-Commerce Directive[21] throws light on the original intentions of the draftsmen:

> The Directive does not affect the liability of the person who is at the source of the content nor does it affect the liability of intermediaries in cases which are not covered by the limitations defined in the Directive. Furthermore, the Directive does not affect the possibility of a national court or administrative authority to require a service provider to terminate or prevent an infringement. These questions are subject to the national law of the Member States.

Put in other words, the Directive envisages limitations on civil and criminal liability within its sphere of application, but does not influence

---

[20] C-557/07 *LSG-Gesellschaft zur Wahrnehmung von Leistungsschutzrechten GmbH* [2009] ECR I-1227.

[21] Report from the Commission to the European Parliament, the Council and the European Economic and Social Committee, First Report on the application of Directive 2000/31/EC of the European Parliament and of the Council of 8 June 2000 on certain legal aspects of information society services, in particular electronic commerce, in the Internal Market, COM/2003/0702, 8.6.2003.

the liability of the primary infringer nor does it prevent Member States from introducing measures to stop the infringement.

2.2 Mere Conduits

Article 12 covers the liability of passive intermediaries. This refers to the situation where the Information Society Service Provider (ISSP) has not produced the information or chosen the intended recipient but acts as a mere transmitter of the information. Article 12(1) stipulates that the provider will not be liable where it:

- does not initiate the transmission;
- does not select the receiver; and
- does not select or modify the transmission in transit.

The conditions imposed describe the passive status of the transmitter. The first condition, that the ISP did not initiate the transmission, relates to the fact that it is always the users who request information in an Internet context. The second condition refers to the fact that the intermediary must not filter the recipients, that is, it must not restrict access to some but not to others. The final condition describes editorial control, which must be absent. Any of the actions mentioned in Article 12(1), however, would equate the intermediary with the creator/poster of information and expose it to liability.

Transmissions here include temporary storage for the sole purpose of carrying out the transmission and under the condition that the information is not stored for periods longer than is reasonably necessary. Such storage is normally automatic and takes place in the course of the transmission and not for other, data gathering, purposes. A further condition is the temporary nature of the storage.

The transmission consists of communication of information to a recipient of the service, defined in Recital 20. The recipients are defined in that Recital as anybody who seeks information either for private or professional uses, irrespective of the nature of that information.

The liability in question must be understood to comprise both civil and criminal liability. The possibility exists[22] for courts or administrative authorities to terminate or prevent the infringement, which is normally achieved through an interlocutory measure.

---

[22] Article 12(3) of the Directive.

The crucial element of this provision is that the transmitter is passive. It does not create the information, has no knowledge of it and does not control it. This solution is necessary and understandable and the alternative regime would require the intermediary to constantly monitor the traffic on its network for any potential infringements – a prospect that is as difficult as it is ineffective. The experience of other jurisdictions confirms this view.

It is not clear from the wording of Article 12 whether ISSPs need to act on information that infringing content is passing through their network. Unlike Articles 13 and 14, no such obligation is imposed in the Article itself. On the other hand, both Articles 12(1) and Recital 42 would seem to indicate that knowledge and control removes insulation from liability. Additionally, Article 12(3) allows action for prevention and termination of infringement which would seem that, although a *bona fide* ISSP is not liable, the one who learns of an infringement is exposed to regular legal action and liability after the moment where the infringement had been communicated.

A separate question arises in situations where a mobile operator enters into a contract with a content provider, controlling the applications and/or the content available on its network or in its 'app store'. Whereas there is no clear answer to this question due to the lack of a definition of 'selecting or modifying information' under Article 12(1), it would seem that an intervention of that kind would remove the protection of Article 12.[23]

2.3 Caching

A further exemption from liability exists in Article 13 which deals with caching. Caching is defined as automatic, intermediate and temporary storage of computer data for later faster and easier access. It can take place not only at ISP level, but at any point between them and the end-user and also at the end-user's computer. It was mentioned that Article 12 exempts providers from liability for temporary storage. Article 13 has a similar purpose as Article 12, the difference being in the length and nature of the storage. In terms of the length of storage, caching is storage on a temporary basis that is meant to speed up access to content by keeping it stored on a local server, rather than retrieving it constantly for every transaction.

---

[23]   See Jakobsen, S.S., 'Mobile commerce and ISP liability in the EU' (2010) 18 *International Journal of Law and Information Technology* 1, p. 12.

The transmissions covered in this article are automatic, intermediate and temporary. The automatic element refers to the absence of a deliberate and targeted human intervention. For example, the operator may initiate the taking of a 'snapshot' of the system, but this cannot be for the purpose of storing specific information from a specific email or web page. The intermediate nature of the transmission refers to the fact that the ISSP is neither the initial poster nor the intended recipient. The temporary nature refers to the fact that information cannot be retained indefinitely. In any case, the sole purpose of the storage must be to facilitate the flow of information to the intended recipient.

To insulate itself from liability, the provider would have to refrain from modifying the information (for this prevents it from being treated as an intermediary), would have to comply with any conditions on access to information (the cached page should follow the same conditions that exist for the main page, if the latter is available in different versions depending on access privileges, the former cannot ignore that), with rules regarding the updating of information (for only updated information guarantees that a cached page is the same as the original). The provider is not allowed to interfere with the lawful use of technology used to obtain usage statistics. Finally, the information should be as accurate as possible.

It is currently unclear whether caching which mainstream search engines (such as Google) provide as part of their service qualifies as caching under Article 13. The said cached copies typically appear as part of search results, in the form of a link or a button. The problem is that the cached copies, although automatic and temporary, do not seem to be intermediate but rather a permanent, albeit updated, feature. It is also possible to envisage a service where the search engine provides several copies, taken at different times.

As in Article 12, courts or administrative authorities can require ISPs to terminate or prevent an infringement. Also, as in that Article, interlocutory measures can be used as well as regular actions.

2.4 Hosting

Article 14 of the Directive regulates hosting. Hosting, unlike transmitting or caching, is the act of methodical and permanent storage of information, based on a contract between a provider and the user. Under this contract, the information is placed on the host's servers wherefrom it is made available to the general public. In modern times, hosting can take more complex and more ambiguous forms.[24] User-generated content sites (UGC sites) allow users to store information they created independently (photos, videos, music, text, etc.) and typically use a particular structure to display these files. File hosting sites allow users to store their files in general without structuring the content. A number of websites share links only, often of infringing content (movies, software) which can be obtained from file hosting sites. Other sites manipulate the links, aggregating them and making indexes available to users. The status of some of these will be tested in the courts in the years to come.

Article 14 stipulates that the provider will not be liable for the information if either of two conditions has been met. The first is that the provider must not have actual knowledge of illegal activity or information and 'as regards claims for damages, is not aware of facts or circumstances from which the illegal activity or information is apparent'. This condition will not be fulfilled where the provider is aware that a significant proportion of the activity on its servers is illegal in nature (such as in the case of popular file-sharing websites).

The second condition is that the provider who has obtained knowledge or awareness of the illegality must act quickly to remove or disable access to information. This is the case where the rightholder informs the ISSP of the alleged infringement. The second condition may lead to considerable difficulties in cases where a provider is notified by a third party that the information put on the web by the recipient is illegal. The provider may act quickly, fearing exposure to liability. This may lead it to effectively censor content on the Internet at a mere notice from the affected party. At the same time, the provider is concerned that removing the material prematurely may expose it to action by the recipient. In practice, the evidence has shown that providers are prepared to remove content after just a notice from the affected party.

Article 14(3) allows Member States to terminate or prevent an infringement. Importantly, it also allows Member States to establish procedures governing the removal or disabling of access to information.

In a case involving the sale of L'Oréal products without its consent on the eBay marketplace, the European Court ruled that the E-Commerce Directive:

---

[24] For classification of hosting business models, see Nordeman, J.B., 'Liability for Copyright Infringements on the Internet: Host Providers (Content Providers) – The German Approach', (2011) 2 *Journal of Intellectual Property, Information Technology and E Commerce Law* 37, p. 38.

must be interpreted as applying to the operator of an online marketplace where that operator has not played an active role allowing it to have knowledge or control of the data stored.[25]

The operator of the website, eBay, plays such a role when it optimizes the presentation of the offers for sale in question or promotes them. eBay, the Court ruled, is not a passive host but one that arranges the offers and actively profits from them.

Where the operator of the online marketplace has not played an active role as explained above, the service provided will fall within the scope of Article 14(1) of Directive 2000/31. In such cases, the Court ruled, the operator nevertheless cannot rely on the exemption from liability:

> if it was aware of facts or circumstances on the basis of which a diligent economic operator should have realised that the offers for sale in question were unlawful and, in the event of it being so aware, failed to act expeditiously in accordance with Article 14(1)(b) of Directive 2000/31.

The preceding paragraph seems to suggest that an operator well aware of the illegality of operations should not be able to benefit from the protective regime. In practice, this will be difficult to determine. A very stringent interpretation of Article 14 may force the operators to monitor, an obligation which is clearly excluded in Article 15. Complete insulation from liability, on the other hand, encourages illegal content, as only operators who have been specifically notified by the rightholders cease to be protected.

2.5 Monitoring

Internet service providers have no general obligation to monitor contents that pass on their servers.[26] This is a very important exemption, as some early case law in Member States seemed to suggest the opposite.[27] An obligation to monitor traffic would have been extremely costly and difficult to enforce as the volume in Internet traffic increases yearly, particularly on user-generated sites. Although some Internet sites are edited or moderated, in the sense that an ISP-approved individual or

---

[25] C-324/09 *L'Oréal SA, Lancôme parfums et beauté & Cie SNC, Laboratoire Garnier & Cie, L'Oréal (UK) Ltd v eBay International AG et al.*, 12 July 2011, not yet reported.

[26] Article 15 of the Electronic Commerce Directive.

[27] For instance, the 1998 *Somm (Compuserve)* case in Germany, File No: 8340 Ds 465 Js 173158/95, Local Court Munich.

individuals are overseeing the traffic and editing or deleting potentially illegal content, the majority are not.

Article 15(1) stipulates that no general obligation to monitor information which the providers transmit or store exists. Additionally, no obligation exists 'actively to seek facts or circumstances indicating illegal activity'. The difference between the two formulations is in the nature of the activity. While the former excludes the obligation to observe the traffic, the latter excludes the obligation to 'hunt down' suspected lawbreakers. In the former case, an ISSP would not be liable for not knowing what was being stored on its servers, in the latter for not taking active action against a suspected infringer. On the contrary, Article 15(1) seems to allow ISSPs to remain passive until the moment when they receive relevant information from rightholders.

On the other hand, Article 15(2) suggests that Member States may establish an obligation to inform the authorities of any alleged illegal activities or information, provided by recipients, or, crucially, the obligation to communicate to the authorities, at their request, information enabling the identification of recipients with whom they have storage agreements. In other words, the ISSPs may be required by Member States to facilitate the governments' spying on users.

The European Court, however, ruled in the *Promusicae* case[28] that Article 15(2) does not require Member States to lay down an *obligation* to communicate personal data of suspected copyright violators to rightholders. It further ruled that other EU directives do not do so either.

Analysing the provisions of the E-Commerce Directive, it would seem that ISS providers cannot be made liable for violations committed by end-users as long as they remain passive and as long as they promptly remove infringing material upon receiving notification. The *L'Oreal* case suggests that simple knowledge of the incriminating facts may remove the protection of the E-Commerce Directive. In the United States, the options have been somewhat extended in the *MGM v Grokster* case,[29] where the Supreme Court held that 'one who distributes a device with the object of promoting its use to infringe copyright ... is liable for the resulting acts of infringement by third parties'. In a manner practically similar to the *L'Oreal* case, but conceptually different, the Supreme Court confirmed that Grokster and others induced the copyright infringement by marketing the file-sharing software. It would, therefore, seem unlikely

---

[28]   Case C-275/06 *Productores de Música de España (Promusicae) v Tele-fónica de España SAU* [2008] ECR I-271.
[29]   See footnote 17.

that a website mainly used for illegal activity could avail itself of the protection available in Articles 12–15.

In *Google France v Louis Vuitton*, the issue was whether the use of a registered trade mark in an Adword link within the Google search system constituted an infringement of that registered trade mark.[30] The European Court ruled that search engines must be treated as hosts:

> where that service provider has not played an active role of such a kind as to give it knowledge of, or control over, the data stored.

Where, on the contrary, it has played an active role, it will still be protected for the data which it has stored at the request of an advertiser. Liability comes only where, having obtained the knowledge of the illegal nature of the advertiser's activity, it 'failed to act expeditiously to remove or to disable access to the data concerned'.

2.6 Injunctive Relief and Requests for Information

The intermediaries are unique among the actors on the Internet in that they hold the information about the users' surfing habits. This information includes times of access, websites visited, the duration and the actual content. On its own, this information is of limited relevance. Aggregated, it can have damaging effects and is deserving of separate protection. For that reason, it is very important that access to confidential information is under strict control.

The obvious avenue for a plaintiff alleging an infringement is to seek to obtain the details of the alleged primary infringer or, in the alternative, to prevent the ISSP from facilitating the infringement. Two separate issues arise. The first is the right of a third party to request the ISSP to release information about the alleged infringer's identity. This is a situation concerning an ISSP which holds the accounts of the alleged infringers. The second is the right of the rightholders to obtain injunctive relief against an ISSP rather than the actual infringer. This will typically be the case because it is easier to identify and begin action against the ISSP than individual violators.

Injunctive relief is available under the TRIPS Agreement, Article 50, as well as under other international and national instruments, including the Brussels I Regulation, Article 31. In the EU, in copyright cases, Article

---

[30] Joined cases C-236/08 and C-238/08 *Google France SARL and Google Inc. v Louis Vuitton Malletier SA and Others* [2010] ECR I-0000.

8(3) of the Copyright Directive[31] provides that Member States shall 'ensure that rightholders are in a position to apply for an injunction against intermediaries whose services are used by a third party to infringe a copyright or related right'. A similar right exists in Article 9 of the Copyright Enforcement Directive which regulates provisional and pre-cautionary measures. Article 9 of that Directive provides:

> an interlocutory injunction may also be issued, under the same conditions, against an intermediary whose services are being used by a third party to infringe an intellectual property right; injunctions against intermediaries whose services are used by a third party to infringe a copyright or a related right are covered by Directive 2001/29/EC;

The Copyright Enforcement Directive, Article 8, also allows a 'justified and proportionate' request for information concerning the 'origin and distribution networks' of the infringing goods and services. The subject of the obligation is not only an infringer but also any other person who was, among other cases, 'found to be providing on a commercial scale services used in infringing activities' or was indicated by the main infringer as 'being involved in production, manufacture or distribution' of the said goods and services. Either of these two possibilities may include an ISSP which actively promotes infringement or, although not behind it, is aware of and profits directly from it. In any case, safeguards inserted in Article 8(3) serve to prevent abuse.

In the *LSG* case,[32] the Court held that the E-Privacy and Copyright Enforcement Directives do not:

> preclude Member States from imposing an obligation to disclose to private third parties personal data relating to Internet traffic in order to enable them to bring civil proceedings for copyright infringements.

Nevertheless, the Court said that, when interpreting and applying the Copyright Enforcement and the Electronic Privacy Directives, national courts must not rely on an interpretation which would conflict with fundamental rights.

This interpretation, which confirms the earlier *Promusicae* case,[33] clearly puts a significant responsibility on national courts. The EU law does not oblige Member States to release data. They may or may not

---

[31] For Copyright and Copyright Enforcement Directives, see Chapter 6.
[32] See footnote 20.
[33] See footnote 28.

allow this in their national law but, if they do, this must not be contrary to EU and international fundamental rights. The question which the Court had avoided in this case, however, is the legal status of data released in cases where this does *not* violate fundamental rights.

An important dilemma concerning the obligation to install filtering was resolved in the *SABAM* case.[34] There, the European Court ruled that the E-Commerce Directive, the Copyright Directive, the Copyright Enforcement Directive, the Data Protection Directive and the E-Privacy Directive, read together in light of protection of fundamental rights:

> must be interpreted as precluding an injunction made against an internet service provider which requires it to install a system for filtering:
> – all electronic communications passing via its services, in particular those involving the use of peer-to-peer software;
> – which applies indiscriminately to all its customers;
> – as a preventive measure;
> – exclusively at its expense; and
> – for an unlimited period.

Restraining injunctions against ISPs in the context of the Electronic Commerce Directive remain possible at the national level in those legal systems which allow them. Thus, the Danish courts allowed a restraining injunction in several cases. One of these[35] was a Supreme Court case and the other[36] was a lower court injunction against the service provider who acted as a gateway for the server where files violating the applicant's copyright had been held.[37]

Many areas other than intellectual property are out of the scope of EU law but, in principle, are still subject to injunctive relief in civil proceedings. Article 31 of the Brussels I Regulation specifically allows provisional measures even in cases where other courts have jurisdiction as to the substance of the matter. Thus an application can be made to

---

[34] C-70/10 *Scarlet Extended SA, SABAM*, 24 November 2011, not yet reported.

[35] Supreme Court decision 49/2005, 10 February 2006, *TDC v IFPI*, The Danish Weekly Law Report (U.) 2006.1474 H.

[36] Sheriff's Court Copenhagen, Order F1–15124/2006, 25 October 2006, *IFPI v Tele2*.

[37] See Frost, K., 'Denmark: Restraining Injunction against Internet Providers' (2007) 2 *Computer Law Review International* 50 and (2007) 3 *Computer Law Review International* 87.

courts in France to eliminate the advertising of Nazi memorabilia on auction sites.[38]

Governments may also hold significant information relating to potential infringements. Under normal circumstances, national law regulates access to information the government holds about the citizens. These citizens have the right to know what data is being held about them and this right is exercised under the conditions set out in national law. Additionally, the government limits the recourse of others to information that it holds, so that only interested parties (e.g., other departments of the government) may access it under strictly controlled conditions. This area is largely out of the scope of EU competence.[39]

In the *Bonnier Audio* case,[40] which involved a request to a Swedish ISP to release the identities of the alleged infringer, the Court ruled that the Data Retention Directive[41] must be interpreted as not precluding the application of national legislation based on Article 8 of the Copyright Enforcement Directive (right of information). The ruling simply confirms that Member States may introduce legislation obliging ISPs to release data (under the safeguards mentioned above).

---

[38] *Ligue contre le racisme et l'antisémitisme et Union des étudiants juifs de France c. Yahoo! Inc. et Société Yahoo! France (LICRA v Yahoo!),* Tribunal de Grand Instance de Paris, 20 November 2000.

[39] With the exception of data retention, see Chapter 8 on privacy and data protection.

[40] C-461/10 *Bonnier Audio AB v Perfect Communication Sweden AB,* 19 April 2012, not yet reported.

[41] See Chapter 9.

6.   Intellectual property

Two features determine the EU regulation of intellectual property rights. The first feature is the comprehensiveness of that regulation.[1] Most of the areas traditionally included in IP law are addressed in various IP-related policies and documents, covered by one or more regulations or directives and frequently addressed in the Court of Justice. The EU law affects national IP rights in two ways. First, it harmonizes various IP rights or establishes unitary EU-wide IP rights. Second, it subjects national IP regimes to free movement provisions.[2] While these approaches are conceptually different, together they produce a very wide coverage of various IP rights.[3]

The second feature is that the EU's international obligations significantly influence its regulatory model. The EU member states individually and the EU as a whole are party to the 1995 Agreement on Trade-Related Aspects of Intellectual Property Rights (TRIPS). Although the agreement does not have direct effect, it can and is interpreted and applied at EU level.[4] Similarly, and of equal importance for the present subject, the EU and the Member States are parties to the World Intellectual Property Organization (WIPO) Copyright Treaty 1996 and the WIPO Performances and Phonograms Treaty 1996.[5]

This chapter analyses the application of the EU intellectual property regime to the digital world. Two directives will be analysed in detail: the Copyright Directive (also known as Information Society, or InfoSoc, Directive) and the Copyright Enforcement Directive. Both have direct application to the Internet and have been tested in national courts and in the European Court. Other selected harmonized IP laws *specifically* address the digital world while most are written in a technology-neutral

---

[1]   For an overview of the field, see Cook, T., *EU Intellectual Property Law* (OUP, Oxford 2010).

[2]   On the different effect of these two influences, see Cook, T., op. cit., especially Chapters 1 and 2.

[3]   The Single Market aspect of the question, while of considerable interest, is only of limited importance for the Internet.

[4]   C-53/96 *Hérmes* [1998] ECR I-03603.

[5]   Council Decision of 16 March 2000, OJ L 89/6, 11.4.2000.

manner, leaving scope for their application to the Internet. Some of these will also be looked at.

1. COPYRIGHT IN THE INFORMATION SOCIETY DIRECTIVE[6]

The InfoSoc Directive implements the provisions of the WIPO Copyright Treaty 1996 and WIPO Performances and Phonograms Treaty 1996 into European law. It lays the foundations for modern copyright law in the digital age by harmonizing disparate laws of Member States.[7] While meant as a copyright instrument for the digital age, the Directive also implements the four freedoms in copyright regulation. In other words, it fine-tunes copyright law to the demands of the digital economy while maintaining the Single Market context.[8]

The Directive is not an entirely new instrument, but is based on previous Community legislation, such as the Software Directive (Original Version) for the protection of computer programs,[9] the Rental and Lending Rights Directive (Original Version)[10] and the Database Directive.[11] The first proposal for the Copyright Directive dates back to 1997.[12] The amendments were approved by the European Parliament in 1999[13] and the final support came in 2000. The Directive was not approved until 2001, with the final implementation date in 2002.

Several important points need to be mentioned at the outset. First, the Directive starts from the premise that disparities in copyright laws and related rights harm the competition and the development of the Internal Market.[14] This puts it in line with other IP EU instruments, giving it focus but limiting its scope. The Single Market dimension informs the

---

[6]   Directive 2001/29/EC on the harmonisation of certain aspects of copyright and related rights in the information society, OJ L 167/10, 22.6.2001.

[7]   See Recital 15 of the Directive.

[8]   See Recitals 5–8.

[9]   Council Directive 91/250/EEC of 14 May 1991 on the legal protection of computer programs, OJ L 122, 17.5.1991.

[10]   Council Directive 92/100/EEC of 19 November 1992 on rental rights and lending right and on certain rights related to copyright in the field of intellectual property, OJ L 346, 27.11.1992.

[11]   Directive 96/9/EC of the European parliament and of the Council of 11 March 1996 on the legal protection of databases, OJ L 77, 27.3.1996.

[12]   OJ C 108/6, 7.4.1998.

[13]   OJ C 150/171, 28.5.1999.

[14]   For example, Recitals 1, 6 and 8.

Directive's objectives as well as its approach. Second, the Directive, which has 'a high level of protection' as a basis (Recital 9), is strongly economically oriented, having as its goal increased growth.[15] Recital 4 says:

A harmonised legal framework on copyright and related rights, through increased legal certainty and while providing for a high level of protection of intellectual property, will foster substantial investment in creativity and innovation, including network infrastructure, and lead in turn to growth and increased competitiveness of European industry, both in the area of content provision and information technology and more generally across a wide range of industrial and cultural sectors. This will safeguard employment and encourage new job creation.

Finally, although the Directive implements the WIPO Treaty and largely follows the American regulatory model, it deviates from both in some important aspects.[16] The Directive is a minimal and targeted harmonization of copyright law which does not replace national laws.

The scope of the Directive is set out in Article 1, which highlights its Internal Market aspect but also puts an emphasis on the information society services. The Directive covers the whole field of copyright, being in that sense a comprehensive harmonization measure. However, the Directive is not an overarching harmonization of the whole area, but rather one that puts a 'particular emphasis on the information society'. The exceptions are set out in Article 1(2) and they include: legal protection of computer programs;[17] rental right, lending right and certain rights related to copyright;[18] copyright and related rights applicable to

---

[15] For more on the Directive's objectives, see its Preamble, Recitals (1) to (19).

[16] Especially in relation to the protection of technological measures.

[17] Covered in Directive 2009/24/EC of the European Parliament and of the Council of 23 April 2009 on the legal protection of computer programs (Codified version), OJ L 111/16, 5.5.2009, (Software Directive (Codified)). On abortive attempts to protect software with patents, see Park, J., 'Has Patentable Subject Matter Been Expanded?: A Comparative Study on Software Patent Practices in the European Patent Office, the United States Patent and Trademark Office and the Japanese Patent Office' (2005) 13 *International Journal of Law and Information Technology* 336.

[18] Covered in Directive 2006/115/EC of the European Parliament and of the Council of 12 December 2006 on rental right and lending right and on certain rights related to copyright in the field of intellectual property (codified version), OJ L 376, 27.12.2006 (Rental and Lending Rights Directive (Codified)).

broadcasting;[19] term of protection;[20] and legal protection of databases.[21] The Directive covers 'copyright and related rights'. This is an acknowledgment of the existence of two systems: the continental and the common law one.

The Internal Market dimension of the Directive is emphasized in the general way in the Preamble,[22] which talks of ensuring that competition and marketing and distribution of new products is not distorted. Of more direct relevance, however, is the idea set out in Recital 6 that national action responding to 'technological challenges', already initiated in a number of Member States at the time of drafting, might lead to uncertainty and hinder free movement of goods and services or economies of scale for new products. In other words, one of the aims was to pre-empt Member States from legislating in this important field.

The new information society dimension is recognized and emphasized explicitly throughout the document. The current law 'should be adapted and supplemented to respond adequately to economic realities such as new forms of exploitation'.[23] In this chapter, we are only concerned with the information society aspect of the Directive.

Article 2 deals with reproduction rights. It obliges Member States to provide for the exclusive right to authorize or prohibit 'direct or indirect, temporary or permanent' reproduction 'by any means or in any form, in whole or in part' to authors, performers, phonogram producers, producers of first fixations of films, and broadcasting organizations. The Directive, in Recital 21, calls for a broad definition, in conformity with *acquis communautaire*, of acts covered by the reproduction right of Article 2.

In terms of content, Article 2 provides a broad protection of copyright. The exclusive right to authorize reproduction extends to 'direct or indirect, temporary or permanent reproduction by any means and in any form, in whole or in part'. While temporary reproduction is included, a special exception exists in Article 5(1) for reproductions which are only

---

[19]   Covered in Council Directive 93/83/EEC of 27 September 1993 on the coordination of certain rules concerning copyright and rights related to copyright applicable to satellite broadcasting and cable retransmission, OJ L 248, 6.10.1993, (Satellite and Cable Broadcasting Directive).

[20]   Covered in Directive 2011/77/EU of the European Parliament and of the Council amending Directive 2006/116/EC on the term of protection of copyright and certain related rights, OJ L 265/1, 11.10.2011 (Copyright Term Directive).

[21]   Covered in Directive 96/9/EC of the European Parliament and of the Council of 11 March 1996 on the legal protection of databases, OJ L 077, 27.03.1996 (Database Directive).

[22]   Recitals 1–4

[23]   Recital 5.

part of a technological process. This would cover most instances where temporary electronic copies are made to enable IT functionality. The subjects are defined according to the scope of exploitation specific for the group in question. Authors are covered in general, performers in relation to their performances, phonogram producers in relation to their phonograms and film producers and broadcasting organizations in the scope of their respective businesses.

Although the protection is broad, it is surprising how little in terms of explanation the Directive offers for the scope of protection offered in Article 2. It entails the right to authorize or prohibit both the direct and indirect reproduction of both a temporary or a permanent nature, which covers total or partial reproduction in any form and by any means. This approach provides very wide protection without proper consideration of the technical aspects of the Internet. It is clear that by its very nature, the Internet involves making indirect, temporary or partial reproductions even when the exception from Article 5(1) is applied. For example, providing snippets of information from news websites on a commercial web page would amount to partial reproduction and fall under Article 2.[24] In light of the rapid development that the Internet had witnessed in recent years, the Article may be in need of a revision.

Article 3 covers the right of communication to the public. The right applies to 'wired or wireless means' and includes on-demand uses, 'from a place and at a time individually chosen'. Paragraph 3 specifically provides that the right of communication is not exhausted by communication or other acts of making works available. The distinction made in the Article between 'communication' and 'making available' of 'other subject matter' refers to the disparity in Member States' laws between those systems that recognize a general right of communication and those which do not. The authors retain, in paragraph 1, an exclusive right to control the communication to the public, by 'wire or wireless means'. Importantly, as paragraph 2 provides, this includes the right by 'members of the public' to access the works 'from a place and at a time individually chosen by them'. This latter feature is then specifically regulated in the next paragraph, which obliges Member States to introduce this right in respect of performers, phonogram producers and broadcasting organizations. This Article simply extends the right of communication, itself

---

[24] In *Infopaq*, the Court ruled that storing an 11-word extract from a news website and allowing it to be printed constitutes a violation of copyright within the meaning of Article 2. C-5/08 *Infopaq International A/S v Danske Daglades Forening* [2009] ECR I-6569.

well known and protected throughout the Member States, to the new digital subject matter.

Article 4 covers distribution right, which is different from communication in Article 3 and relates to tangible objects. The right applies only to authors and not to holders of related rights. The former have the exclusive right of distribution which is only exhausted in the EU at the first sale or transfer of ownership in the EU. Article 4 obliges Member States to provide an exclusive right to authorize distribution 'in respect of the originals of their work or copies thereof'. Member States are obliged to grant the authors the exclusive right to authorize or prohibit 'any form of distribution to the public by sale or otherwise'. This is a comprehensive distribution control which is not exhausted except where the first sale is made by the rightholder himself.

This Article may cause some confusion. First, it relates only to authors and not to other rightholders. Second, it does not relate to the distribution channels mentioned in Article 3 but, as Recital 28 explains, only to the distribution of works previously incorporated in a tangible form. This should be taken to mean that authors have the right to control distribution of a physical object which incorporates the creation until the first sale is made which would then exhaust the right. It is not clear what exactly the authors of the Directive were trying to achieve. In respect of the information society, there is no doubt that the transmission of physical objects plays a minor role. On the contrary, on the Internet at least, intellectual property mostly relates to digital copies.

1.1 Exceptions

Achieving the balance between the rights of various rightholders on one side and users on the other is one of the key tasks that a copyright regime needs to fulfil. A system of exceptions obtains that balance by allowing limited use of copyrighted material in specific situations.

The Copyright Directive contains a somewhat peculiar regime of copyright exceptions in Article 5. This peculiarity arises out of a combination of two factors. First, the Directive opts for an exhaustive list of exceptions, limiting Member States' ability to introduce new ones. Second, only one exception is mandatory while the others are left at Member States' discretion.

The list of exceptions begins with an important one relating to temporary acts of reproduction in Article 5(1). Those acts must be a 'transient or incidental and integral and essential part of a technological process'. Their sole purpose must either be (a) to enable 'a transmission in a network between third parties and an intermediary', or (b) a 'lawful use of a work without independent economic significance'. The first refers to acts of making copies in the normal functioning of transmission on IT systems. This will be the case when data is moving between different computers/servers on its way from the provider to the recipient. The second refers to acts of making copies for regular and lawful acts of use for both private individuals and corporations. Thus, downloading a purchased copy or making a local hard copy from an external device would fall into this category. It is to expect that new technological solutions, as long as they are lawful and without 'independent economic significance', would also fall under this Article. An act of maintaining a back-up copy on a private external server would probably fall under this definition.

The exception, although phrased somewhat inelegantly, is necessary, as it refers to the process of saving copies locally that enable faster access to content. The exceptions of Article 5(1) are the only mandatory ones in the list. Their aim and spirit is mirrored in Articles 12–14 of the E-Commerce Directive.

Other exceptions to the reproduction right in Article 2 only are provided in Article 5(2). Unlike the previous Article, these are optional, which is reflected in the phrasing of the Article ('may provide'). The first, Article 5(2)(a), relates to reproduction on paper made by photographic equipment, except for sheet music, in cases where the rightholders receive compensation. This is simply a right to be compensated for photocopying. It may have a significance in the digital world in situations where the reproduction originates on the Internet but where the output is a paper copy.

The second, Article 5(2)(b), includes reproductions made by natural persons for private use. This exception allows reproductions on any medium 'made by a natural person for private use' and for non-commercial means provided that rightholders are compensated and that the technological protection of Article 6 is taken into account. This exception relates to personal non-commercial use only. This excludes corporate use including works which a person can use at home but which are provided by the corporation. It is not clear from the language of the Article and the preamble whether commercial character should be determined by reference to potential markets in a particular product. Whereas the user may argue that making a digital copy of a CD, for instance, is personal non-commercial use, the rightholder will maintain that this limits the potential of developing an independent product solely based on digital content. The commercial character can be determined by reference to direct or indirect criteria, which may also limit the scope of the Article. If national courts, for instance, decide that downloading a small number of copyright-protected songs from the Internet amounts to indirect commercial use, this would significantly limit the usefulness of the exception, provided that a Member State adopts it in the first place.

In any case, Article 5(2)(b) requires fair compensation to be paid to the rightholder. In *Padawan*,[25] the Court held that fair compensation is an autonomous concept in EU law. It further said:

> fair compensation must be calculated on the basis of the criterion of the harm caused to authors of protected works by the introduction of the private copying exception. It is consistent with the requirements of that 'fair balance' to provide that persons who have digital reproduction equipment, devices and media and who on that basis, in law or in fact, make that equipment available to private users or provide them with copying services are the persons liable to finance the fair compensation, inasmuch as they are able to pass on to private users the actual burden of financing it.

The third exception, Article 5(2)(c), relates to 'specific acts of reproduction' for public libraries, educational institutions, museums or archives, provided that they do not lead to an 'economic or commercial advantage'. Specific acts of reproduction refer to reproduction of individual works for specific purposes rather than general copying. The latter should be interpreted to mean that a library cannot make a copy of a work which is otherwise commercially available in a digital form, neither can it profit from the copies it made (by selling, for instance, extra subscriptions or charging for access). This should be interpreted to mean that a library can only make a general online database of works which are both commercially exploitable and under copyright with the express permission of the rightholder. Works outside of copyright protection, such as ancient manuscripts, collections of old letters, and so on, can freely be put online, including for commercial exploitation (e.g., subscriptions). Article 5(2)(c) has special importance for furthering research, innovation and development. In the absence of a collective licence or a similar arrangement under national law, individual acts of copying would otherwise have been illegal under the provisions of the Directive.

The fourth exception, Article 5(2)(d), relates to ephemeral recordings for broadcasting purposes and includes recordings made for preservation in the broadcasters' archives. This means that the broadcaster can make a copy for broadcasting purposes *only* and preserve that copy for reuse, but not commercially exploit it or give it away. Broadcasters who wish to make archives of their own works publicly and commercially available

25   C-467/08 *Padawan SL v SGAE*, 21 October 2010, not yet reported.

(such as the popular BBC iPlayer service) may do so under various national copyright regimes.

The fifth exception, Article 5(2)(e), relates to reproductions made by social institutions (such as hospitals) which pursue non-commercial aims. Reproductions are made under the condition on fair compensation.

In summary, Article 5(2) does not bring surprises. The exceptions are well known and uncontroversial. The case is somewhat different only with Article 5(2)(b), which is remarkable for its treatment of technological measures of protection. The wording, which links these measures to fair compensation, would suggest that any application of these measures would either exclude compensation to the rightholder altogether or reduce the amount received by them.[26] This seems to be an economic approach, balancing the costs to society and the benefits received by the rightholders. As such, it may prove to be successful in the long term.

Exceptions to *both* the reproduction right of Article 2 and the right of communication to the public of Article 3 are regulated in Article 5(3). The exceptions of Article 5(3) are not mandatory, and implementation varies considerably across Member States, which decreases legal certainty.[27] Article 5(3) allows Member States to make exceptions to Articles 2 and 3 based on the special status of the beneficiary (as in Article 5(3)(b) or (3)(n)) or on the privileges of the public, as in Article 5(3)(a) or (3)(c).

The first exception, Article 5(3)(a) involves the right to use an illustration for teaching or scientific purposes, provided the source and name are quoted. The purpose must remain non-commercial. This should be interpreted to mean that displaying the item for teaching must not substitute legitimate commercial acquisition. Thus a teacher displaying material from a commercial repository based on the Internet cannot make a copy and make it available for students irrespective of whether the latter have the opportunity to acquire the work commercially or not.

Furthermore, the exclusion in Article 5(3)(b) includes reproductions made for the benefit of disabled person(s), as much as necessary in respect of a specific disability and of 'non-commercial nature'. This

---

[26] See Koelman, K., 'The Levitation of Copyright: An Economic View of Digital Home Copying, Levies and DRM' (2005) 16 *Entertainment Law Review* 75.

[27] More on this in Ernst, S. and Haeusermann, D., 'Teaching Exceptions in European Copyright Law – Important Policy Questions Remain' Berkman Center Research Publication No. 2006–10, accessed 1.8.2012 at http://ssrn.com/abstract=925950.

would include the right to make a digital audio copy of a book that can then be read aloud, or implementing a device that can put captions on videos. The exception covers only specific disabilities, which is probably meant to apply to individual users. It is not clear what status the copies made by associations of disabled people would have but it should be taken that these also fall within the exception as long as they satisfy the conditions. It is not clear how the exception would work in terms of the obligation not to remove the technical measures of protection in Article 6.

The exception in Article 5(3)(c) relates to reproductions in the act of communication to the public of 'current economic, political or religious topics' or the 'reporting of current events' unless reserved. In such a case, the source and the author must be named.

Further exemptions, in Articles 5(3)(d) to 5(3)(m), relate to quotations for purposes of criticism or review (d), public security or reporting of administrative or judicial proceedings (e), political speeches (f), publicly organized religious or official celebrations (g), public displays of architecture or sculpture (h), incidental inclusion (i), advertising of public exhibitions (j), caricature or parody (k), demonstration or repair of equipment (l), reconstruction of buildings (m).

The exception in Article 5(3)(m) allows 'use by communication or making available' of electronic services in libraries or universities on 'dedicated terminals' only and 'on the premises' of works not otherwise subject to purchase or licensing terms. The works are the same as in Article 5(2)(c), namely works not otherwise covered by a licensing agreement which enables other kinds of distribution. The Article does not apply to online distribution in any form, for which a special licence under national copyright law must be obtained.

A further exception in Article 5(3)(o) exists in cases of minor importance, regulated under national law, that involve analogue uses.

Member States who maintain their discretion under Article 5, paragraphs 2 and 3, may decide to extend the exceptions to the right of distribution of Article 4.

Possible limitations and exceptions are restricted by international obligation expressed in the form of the 'Berne three step test'. The TRIPS formulation of that test is found in Article 13:

> Members shall confine limitations and exceptions to exclusive rights to certain special cases which do not conflict with a normal exploitation of the work and do not unreasonably prejudice the legitimate interests of the rights holder.

Article 5(5) contains the InfoSoc (Copyright) Directive version of the three-step test. It was first introduced in Article 9(2) of the Berne Convention for the Protection of Literary and Artistic works of 1887 but found its way into a number of other international instruments and national laws. The test says that limitations and exceptions to exclusive rights: (a) will only be applied in certain special cases; (b) will not conflict with normal exploitation of the work or other subject-matter; and (c) will not unreasonably prejudice the legitimate interests of the right-holder. The test is of considerable importance as it determines whether exceptions, enumerated in Article 5, can be applied to beneficiaries but its vagueness can mean only that courts will have to determine its exact scope. The Court of Justice has not yet had the opportunity to rule on it and it is only hoped that its interpretation would not be too narrow.[28]

It has often been emphasized that the balance between various interests in society has largely been maintained through the system of broad exceptions to very wide rights.[29] The presence of the exceptions in Articles 5(3)(c) to (m) is thus both understandable and desirable. The exceptions protect certain freedoms, such as the freedom to conduct scientific research or the freedom of speech, which outweigh the right of copyright holders. On the other hand, Article 5 speaks of exceptions 'and limitations'. Although this difference is probably without any practical consequence, it could be taken to mean that there are certain points beyond which copyright protection cannot go.[30] Recital 32 provides, on the other hand, that Article 5 contains an *exhaustive* list of exceptions. In other words, Member States are not free to introduce new ones but may adopt some or all of the optional ones listed in Articles 5(2) and 5(3).

Article 5 contains two sections – mandatory and discretionary. Somewhat surprisingly, most exceptions have been placed in the voluntary part[31] and this is easily the main weakness of the Directive. The fact that the European Union has chosen to make these important exceptions

---

[28] See Koelman, K., 'Fixing the Three-Step Test' (2006) 28 *European Intellectual Property Review* 407. Also Gervais, D., 'Towards a New Core International Copyright Norm: The Reverse Three-Step Test' (2005) 9 *Marquette Intellectual Property Law Review* 1.

[29] On how this works in the United States, see Litman, J., *Digital Copyright* (Prometheus, New York 2001), Ch. 3 'Copyright and Compromise'.

[30] Cf. Vivant, M., 'Directive 2001/29/EC', in Lodder, A. and Kaspersen, H., *eDirectives: Guide to European Union Law on E-Commerce* (Kluwer, The Hague 2002), p. 95, at p. 106.

[31] See Articles 5(2), 5(3) and 5(4).

optional signals indifference to the interests of the public and a certain
regulatory disorder not normally characteristic for electronic commerce
instruments. There is little doubt that the character of Article 5 will be a
further source of legal disparity between Member States. Indeed, the
Directive itself recognizes so in Recital 31, where it expressly acknow-
ledges the existence of disparities in 'exceptions and limitations'.

The question of whether and how the EU could respond to changes
brought about by the advance in the 'knowledge economy' was raised in
the Green Paper published in 2008.[32] In that document, the Commission
sought answers from stakeholders on a number of issues relating to the
operation of the directive and its exceptions. The Communication on
Copyright in the Knowledge Economy[33] is based on the material
submitted in response to the Green Paper and summarizes the Commission's views on future steps.

The Communication identifies five areas which are fundamental for the
development of the digital economy: libraries and archives, orphan
works, teaching and research, disabilities and user-created content.

In terms of libraries and archives, item 3.1 confirms that the current
regime does not allow massive digitization of material (which is already
being undertaken by many commercial and non-profit organizations). The
current exceptions only allow digitization upon prior authorization, which
is a cumbersome and expensive process. The Commission concludes that
a new approach, possibly based on collective licensing, may solve some
of the problems.

In terms of orphan works in item 3.2, which are works that are in
copyright but whose rightholders cannot be identified or located, the
Commission recognizes that the present non-binding instruments[34] do not
address the problem of mass digitization. The Commission adopted a
Proposal for a Directive on certain permitted uses of orphan works.[35] The
proposed Directive would apply to 'publicly accessible libraries, educational establishments or museums as well as to archives, film heritage
institutions and public service broadcasting organizations'. The proposal
aims to establish common rules on digitization and online display. It

---

[32]   Green Paper: Copyright in the Knowledge Economy, COM(2008) 466/3,
16.7.2008.
[33]   COM(2009) 532 final, 19.10.2009.
[34]   Commission Recommendation 2006/585/EC on the digitisation and online
accessibility of cultural material and digital preservation, OJ L 236/28,
31.8.2006; and the 2008 Memorandum of Understanding on Orphan Works and
the related diligent search, 4 June 2008, OJ L 236, 31.8.2006
[35]   Brussels, COM(2011) 289 final, 24.5.2011.

covers the diligent search criteria necessary to be fulfilled in order to identify something as an orphan work (proposed Article 3), and permitted and authorized uses (Articles 6 and 7). In other words, it clarifies when a work will be treated as an orphan work and states under which conditions it may then be used. Article 7, which is optional, allows commercial use by public libraries under some conditions. This responds to the reality of scanning efforts in the commercial world (such as Google Books) but may prove controversial.

Item 3.3 applies to teaching and research. The core difficulty is the fragmented status of the licensing regime between institutions and publishers. The former are required to enter into many different licensing arrangements, all of different scope and effect, and the agreements are most often territorial. The Commission signalled its willingness to explore different options, including open access arrangements.

Item 3.4 concerns equal access under the 2006 UN Convention on the Rights of Persons with Disabilities, Articles 4, 9, 21 and 30. The reported difficulties relate to only a fraction of the EU's cultural output being accessible in alternative formats. The Commission obliged itself to look into alternative solutions while, at the same time, encouraging the publishers to participate.

Item 3.5 concerns user-generated content. This is simply content which the users create themselves, often relying on copyright-protected material. The resulting works are important and have societal value but violate copyright. No concrete proposals have been suggested.

Similar to the Copyright Communication is the 2011 Green Paper on the online distribution of audio-visual works,[36] which looks into the effect of technological developments on audio-visual works. The paper explores three avenues: it looks at the rights clearance mechanism for online distribution, explores the problem of remuneration for online works and looks into possible legislative measures. The paper seeks a better understanding of the reasons behind market fragmentation and the methodologies that can maximize the development of the 'digital internal market'. Significantly, the paper explores the facilitation of the collective rights management as one of the possible strategies for addressing the issues, seeing 'Cross-border and pan-European licences' as playing a significant role.[37]

---

[36] Brussels, COM(2011) 427 final, 13.7.2011.

[37] This is consistent both with the Digital Agenda for Europe, COM(2010) 245, 19.05.2010, and with the Single Market Act – Twelve levers to boost growth and strengthen confidence; Working together to create new growth, COM(2011) 0206 final, 13.4.2011.

1.2 Protection of Technological Measures

The Infosoc Directive takes as a basis a high level of protection.[38] Recital 10 leaves no doubt that the purpose of the Directive is to further enhance the existing protection in this field. Moreover, and in the view of the author more problematic, is the insistence on the protection afforded by technical measures.[39] Thus, Recital 47 emphasizes that technological developments allow the rightholders to better control the market for the works in question. It warns, however, that the measures can be circumvented and proposes to harmonize the regulation of technological measures in order to avoid possible discrepancies.

Technological measures are those measures introduced by rightsowners, usually companies, to prevent illegal access or copying of works. There are two types of such measures: access-protection measures prevent unauthorized access to protected works while copy-protected measures prevent acts of reproduction. Examples of the latter are measures on video discs that prevent them from playing in any region but the one they were marketed for or Digital Rights Management (DRM) measures that prevent free copying of MP3 files legally purchased in an online store. An example of the former are password/activation measures for software protection.

Article 11 of WIPO Copyright Treaty 1996 requires contracting parties to:

> provide adequate legal protection and effective legal remedies against the circumvention of effective technological measures that are used by authors in connection with the exercise of their rights under this Treaty or the Berne Convention and that restrict acts, in respect of their works, which are not authorized by the authors concerned or permitted by law.

The United States has introduced such protection in the Digital Millennium Copyright Act 1998 Anticircumvention Provision.[40] The Act prohibits circumvention of *access control* measures:

> No person shall circumvent a technological measure that effectively controls access to a work protected under this title.

In addition to this, the Act prohibits distribution of tools that circumvent either *access control* or *copy control*:

---

[38] Recital 9.
[39] Recitals 13 and 47.
[40] Section 103 (17 U.S.C Sec. 1201(a)(1)).

No person shall manufacture, import, offer to the public, provide, or otherwise traffic in any technology, product, service, device, component, or part thereof, that –

(A) is primarily designed or produced for the purpose of circumventing a technological measure that effectively controls access to a work protected under this title;

(B) has only limited commercially significant purpose or use other than to circumvent a technological measure that effectively controls access to a work protected under this title; or

(C) is marketed by that person or another acting in concert with that person with that person's knowledge for use in circumventing a technological measure that effectively controls access to a work protected under this title.

Section 1201(b)(1) DMCA prohibits the trafficking in tools that circumvent technologies that effectively protect a right of a copyright owner in a work – this is copy control as opposed to the access control of the previous paragraph. The Article also provides that the Librarian of Congress shall have the power to determine what the non-infringing uses are and introduces criteria on which these decisions shall be made. In the past, the Librarian has included audio-visual works in university libraries, obsolete video games, computer programs protected with dongles, read-aloud functions of e-books, wireless telephone handsets or audio CD protection measures that can damage the computers they are played on.

The provision has been extensively analysed by the American and global academic community. Among many criticisms, it was said that it stifles innovation and research by subjecting new technology to legal scrutiny, that it significantly reduces the right to fair-use by the public, that it limits free speech and has a negative effect on competition.[41] The wording was described as awkward and incomprehensible and the administrative procedure as cumbersome. Contrary to these views, Ginsburg has concluded:[42]

---

[41] See Litman, J., 'Electronic Commerce and Free Speech' (1999) 1 *Journal of Ethics and Information Technology* 213. See also Electronic Frontier Foundation, 'Unintended Consequences: Seven Years under the DMCA', March 2010, accessed 1.8.2012 at www.eff.org.

[42] Ginsburg, J., 'Legal Protection of Technological Measures Protecting Works of Authorship: International Obligations and the US Experience', Columbia Public Law & Legal Theory Working Papers, No. 0593, 1 August 2005, accessed 1.8.2012 at http://lsr.nellco.org/columbia/pllt/papers/0593. This paper also contains an overview of the Act's effects vis-à-vis international obligations and a summary of the most relevant literature on the technology versus law debate.

The US experience to date indicates that legal protection for technological measures has helped foster new business models that make works available to the public at a variety of price points and enjoyment options, without engendering the 'digital lockup' and other copyright owner abuses that many had feared. This is not to say that the US legislation and its judicial interpretation represent the most preferable means to making the internet a hospitable place for authors while continuing to enable lawful user conduct. But brooding forecasts and legitimate continuing concerns notwithstanding, the overall equilibrium so far appears to be a reasonable one.

Article 6 of the Copyright Directive establishes and regulates the system of technological protection very similar to the one described above. It consists of anti-circumvention and anti-trafficking provisions.

Article 6(1) is the anti-circumvention provision. It provides that Member States shall give adequate legal protection against the circumvention of 'effective technological measures', which the person concerned carries out with the knowledge, or with knowledge on reasonable grounds. Two questions present themselves. First, what is the significance of the subjective element, and second, when can a measure be considered to be 'effective'? As to the first question, the knowledge required does not relate to actual copyright violation but only to the technological measures. The person must know that he is tampering with a protected device. That is all that is needed to trigger the protection of this Article. It is irrelevant if the person believes that he may be entitled to copy the work or if he really is entitled.

The requirement of effectiveness is of uncertain reach, in spite of the attempt to define it in Article 6(3). That definition provides that a technological measure is effective where the use of the work is controlled by the rightholders through application of an access control or protection process. The examples given are encryption, scrambling or others that achieve the protection objective. In reality, effective means any measure that completely prevents circumvention or copying, that is, the one which either cannot be removed or can be so with great difficulty or considerable knowledge. Ineffective means a measure that can be circumvented with relative ease. It would seem that, once the protection had been removed, the measure becomes ineffective and the requirement of Article 6(1) becomes superfluous, in spite of the standard which the Directive purports to introduce. In addition to that, the definition of effectiveness in Article 6(3) in reality provides that any measure is effective that gives the rightholders the ability to control access. This definition does not take into account the technical effectiveness of the measure.

Access control devices prevent access to copyrighted content, while copy control, by preventing duplication, protects actual rights.[43] The ability to copy exists independently of the ability to access. One usually has the ability to access a video disc such as Blu-ray without the immediate ability to copy it. The DMCA distinguishes between the two in parts 2 and 3 of Section 1201. This distinction consists of the ban on circumvention of access control but not copy control, the latter being allowed under fair use.[44] The InfoSoc Directive does not. It follows from Article 6(3) specifically and from other parts of the Directive that the same protection is given to technologies controlling access and technologies which protect content, with the only allowed circumvention being the one authorized by the copyright holder. This inclusion of copy control, in addition to access control, is in stark contrast with digital media prior to the advance of the Internet.

It is worth noting here that mandatory exceptions, introduced in Article 5(1) for temporary acts of reproduction, and optional exceptions, listed in Article 5(2) and (3), also apply to prohibition under Article 6. Additionally, Article 6(4) provides help to the beneficiaries of exceptions. In the absence of voluntary measures taken by the rightholder, Member States are entitled to provide that beneficiaries can enjoy the exceptions and limitations of Articles 5(2) and 5(3) where they have legal access to the work. The protection of Articles 6(1) and 6(3) do not apply to remote access provided to the public.

Article 6(2) is the Directive's anti-trafficking provision. It obliges Member States to provide adequate legal protection against the 'manufacture, import, distribution, sale, rental, advertisement for sale or rental, or possession for commercial purposes' of devices, products or components or the provision of services which:

(a) are promoted, advertised or marketed for the purpose of circumvention of, or

(b) have only a limited commercially significant purpose or use other than to circumvent, or

---

[43] More on this difference in Ginsburg, J., 'From Having Copies to Experiencing Works: The Development of an Access Right in U.S. Copyright Law' (2003) 50 *Journal of the Copyright Society of the USA* 113.

[44] The ban on trafficking applies to both. On this and other differences between the US and EU regime, see Foged, T., 'US v EU Anticircumvention Legislation: Preserving the Public's Privileges in the Digital Age' (2002) 24 *European Intellectual Property Review* 525.

(c) are primarily designed, produced, adapted or performed for the purpose of enabling or facilitating the circumvention of any effective technological measures.

No knowledge requirement exists under this provision and the action becomes illegal without the subjective element. The purpose of the measure is to prevent the trafficking of any technological devices which serve the purpose of violating digital copyright.

Article 6(4) is designed to enable the beneficiaries of exceptions and limitations of Article 5 to avail themselves of the benefits in spite of the technological protection introduced through Article 6. The Article says that if voluntary measures are not taken by the rightholders, Member States shall step in. There are two categories of such exceptions: public and private.[45] The public exception relates to specifically enumerated sections of Article 5 and is mandatory. The private exception, on the other hand, relates only to Article 5(2)(b) and is optional. The Article says that it may be given 'unless reproduction for private use has already been made possible by rightholders to the extent necessary to benefit from the exception or limitation concerned'. This must be in accordance with Articles 5(2)(b) and 5(5) (three-step test) and must not prevent the rightholder from adopting adequate measures to control the number of copies. Finally, voluntary measures by rightholders also enjoy protection.

In conclusion, the anti-circumvention provisions are problematic for a number of reasons. First and most important, it is unclear how a radical protection of technical measures can be squared with the drive for innovation. Circumvention cannot be equated with piracy. Furthermore, there is no economic data on its effectiveness. Second, equally important, a number of unresolved issues from Article 6 will eventually have to be decided by the national courts. These include the definition of technological measures, the issue of effectiveness and the scope and mode of application of any exceptions.

Under Article 7 of the Directive, Member States are under an obligation to provide adequate legal protection[46] against anyone who knowingly removes or alters any electronic rights-management information, distributes, imports, broadcasts or makes available to the public protected works

---

[45] Gasser, U., Girsberger, M., 'Transposing the Copyright Directive: Legal Protection of Technological Measures in EU-Member States', Berkman Working Paper No. 2004–10, November 2004, accessed 1.8.2012 at http://ssrn.com/abstract=628007, p. 10.

[46] This does not have to be criminal, although it may be. See also section 2 on Copyright Enforcement.

from which rights-management information has been removed or altered without authorization. Rights-management information is understood to be any information provided by the rightholder which identifies the work.

Sanctions and remedies are covered in Article 8. This Article says that adequate sanctions and remedies shall be provided for the infringements set out in the Directive. The sanctions shall be 'effective, proportionate and dissuasive'. These terms are not properly defined in the Directive, leaving them to national authorities. The rightholders are, furthermore, granted the right to bring an action for damages or seek an injunction. They can apply not only for the seizure of the infringing material but also for the seizure of devices, products or components used for circumvention (referred to in Article 6(2)). Finally, rightholders are granted the possibility to apply for an injunction against intermediaries whose services are used to infringe copyright. The last provision, in particular, causes concern. The disparity in the system of interlocutory measures in the Member States may lead to serious difficulties to ISPs in some Member States, where these measures are known, and no action in others where they are not.

1.3 Assessment

In spite of objections that have been heard about the Directive and the draftsmen's apparent desire to follow the American model, the main copyright instrument for the digital age survives. This shows that its technology-neutral approach has had some success. The cautious calls for reform seen in the Commission's policy documents demonstrate that there is space for reform rather than hasty replacement.

The difficulties outlined in the policy documents quoted and which relate to adjusting the Directive to modern technologies exists in spite of the technology-neutral approach. In fact, they are partially caused by the somewhat inflexible approach of Articles 5 and 6. The Information Society Directive potentially makes a number of activities illegal: multi-region DVD and Blu-ray players, copying of music for research purposes or parody and criticism. 'Fencing off' targets authorized as well as unauthorized use. Also, it has previously been possible to challenge the *legality* of copyright protection in courts. But now that *technology* protects the content, and anti-circumvention per se is made illegal, those who might otherwise have relied on an exception may seek alternative ways.

2. THE INTELLECTUAL PROPERTY RIGHTS ENFORCEMENT DIRECTIVE[47]

The Intellectual Property Rights Enforcement Directive (IPRED)[48] finds
its basis in various international instruments, such as TRIPS, Part III, or
WIPO Copyright Treaty 1996, Article 14(2), which deal with important
aspects of copyright enforcement. The Commission was motivated by
what it perceived as 'major disparities'[49] which existed in spite of the
obligations imposed in the mentioned international instruments.

The Directive requires all Member States to apply effective, dissuasive
and proportionate remedies and penalties against those engaged in
counterfeiting and piracy.[50] Thus, the purpose of the instrument is to
regulate *enforcement* of intellectual property rights, not the rights
themselves. The Directive does not aim to harmonize rules of private
international law (Recital 11) nor does it affect competition law
(Recital 12).

The subject matter of the Directive is defined in Article 1. It applies to
enforcement of intellectual property rights which include industrial
property rights. The scope of the Directive is defined in Article 2: it
applies to all infringements of IP rights in Community and national law,
without precluding more stringent protection that Community or national
law may otherwise grant. On the other hand, it excludes specific
enforcement provisions of the Software Directive on the protection of
computer programs[51] and of the Information Society Directive. In respect
of the latter, specifically excluded are provisions of Articles 6 and 8 on
circumvention of technical protection measures. Finally, the Directive
leaves unaffected the substantive provisions on intellectual property,
international obligations of the Member States and national provisions
relating to criminal procedure and criminal enforcement. In short, the
Directive adds extra measures on enforcement of digital copyright while
leaving national law in other areas largely unaffected.

---

[47]   Directive 2004/48/EC of the European Parliament and of the Council on
the enforcement of intellectual property rights; Communication on the management of copyright, OJ L 195/16, 2.6.2004.

[48]   Original Proposal for a Directive of the European Parliament and of the
Council on measures and procedures to ensure the enforcement of intellectual
property rights, COM(2003) 46, 30.1.2003.

[49]   Recital 7.

[50]   Article 3(2).

[51]   Directive 91/250/EEC, now Directive 2009/24/EC on the legal protection
of computer programs, OJ L 111/16, 5.5.2009 (Software Directive(Codified)).

The general obligation in the Directive, Article 3, is to provide for remedies necessary to enforce intellectual property rights. These shall be 'fair and equitable' and must not be 'complicated or costly, or entail unreasonable time-limits or unwarranted delays'. They must furthermore be effective, proportionate and dissuasive and must not act as barriers to trade.

The persons who are entitled to apply for the remedies (Article 4) are primarily the holder of the intellectual property right, but also any person authorized to use it, such as licensees. Collective rights management bodies and professional defence bodies also have this right, provided that they are 'regularly recognized' as having a right of representation and provided they have the permission. A presumption of authorship is introduced in Article 5 for people whose name appears on the work.

Section 2 of the Directive deals with obtaining evidence. Article 6 gives the power to the interested party to apply for evidence regarding an infringement that lies in the hands of the other party. The only requirement is for that party to present 'reasonably available evidence sufficient to support its claim' to the court. Confidentiality will be respected. Optionally, Member States may provide that such evidence will only be presented if the applicant gives a 'substantial number of copies' of the protected work. In case of an infringement on a commercial scale, Member States must also take steps to ensure that 'banking, financial or commercial documents' of the opposing party are presented. In both cases confidential information shall be protected.

Measures for preserving evidence are available even before the proceedings commence. Article 7 provides that such measures may be granted under the same conditions as under Article 6 and include provisional measures such as physical seizure not only of the infringing goods (for instance, hard drives) but also materials used in the production and distribution.

Particularly worrying is the provision in that Article that such measures may be taken 'without the other party having been heard, in particular where any delay is likely to cause irreparable harm to the rightholder or where there is a demonstrable risk of evidence being destroyed'. These are interlocutory, *ex parte* and *in personam* orders known in English law as 'Anton Piller orders'.[52] They give the right to search the premises in order to seize the evidence where there is a risk of its disappearance. Since such orders are made on application, without the knowledge of the

---

[52] *Anton Piller KG v Manufacturing Processes Limited* [1976] Ch 55; [1976] 1 All ER 779.

other party, the safeguards introduced in the *Anton Piller* case were rather strict. First, there has to be a strong prima facie case against the respondent. Second, the actual or potential damage must be serious. Third, evidence must exist that the respondents possess the incriminating evidence and that they may dispose of it before proper court proceedings are initiated. There is now, in the place of this order, a statutory search order under the Civil Procedure Rules 1998.[53]

Anton Piller orders were applied with caution by the courts before the Civil Procedure Act 1997 came into force and they are even more so since then. There is little reason to believe that this common law instrument will be properly applied by the continental courts. There is even less reason to believe that they will be effective. Although used in trade mark and intellectual property cases, the ability to acquire evidence in disputes on the Internet is dramatically increased with the presence of intermediaries. The evidence may be obtained and secured through the ISP, by means of getting an order to produce records of electronic transactions. This is often the path that has been chosen in the United States. Arguably, in spite of the privacy issues and concerns, it is fairer and more effective, at least when properly supervised by a court. Moreover, Article 7 orders have the capacity to be combined with the freezing injunctions of Articles 9 and 11.

Article 8 covers the 'right of information'. This is a sensitive procedure by which the courts can order, on application by the claimant, that the 'information on the origin and distribution networks of the goods and services which infringe an intellectual property right' be produced. For the information to be provided, the infringer must have been found in possession of or have been using the goods on a commercial scale, or have been commercially providing services or was otherwise involved in manufacture, production or distribution. The information concerned consists of names and addresses of people involved in the production/distribution chain and information on the goods themselves. This applies irrespective of any other statutory provision which may have the same or similar aim.

Article 9 regulates provisional and precautionary measures. At the request of an applicant, the judicial authorities may issue an interlocutory injunction to prevent an 'imminent infringement' of intellectual property rights or to prevent a continuing infringement. In the latter case, the order may be followed with a recurring penalty payment or lodging of a

---

[53]   See Sections 7(1), 23 and 25.

guarantee intended to compensate the rightholder. The court may also order seizure or delivery of the infringing goods.

More problematic than the ordinary injunctions of the previous paragraph are the so-called *Mareva* injunctions of paragraph 2 of Article 9. In common law, these are *ex parte* and *in personam* orders used to freeze assets to prevent abuses of process.[54] They can be issued as worldwide injunctions, preventing worldwide dispersal. In that case, their effectiveness depends on their *in personam* character, as a party who is found to be guilty of disposing of assets will be in contempt of court. Article 9(2) provides that, in the case of an infringement on a commercial scale, judicial authorities may order a precautionary seizure of 'movable and immovable property', which includes freezing the bank accounts and other assets. This may only be done if the applicant demonstrates that it is likely that recovery of damages will be endangered. Further to that, documents relating to banking and other financial transactions may be communicated.

The effects of this provision may prove to be negative for all parties involved. First, Mareva injunctions are highly specialized instruments used in English courts. As such, they do not have an equivalent in continental Europe, with the exception of the Netherlands. Their introduction is a poorly investigated novelty. Second, the use of Mareva injunctions in English courts is subject to strict tests. The applicant must demonstrate that there is a good arguable case on the merits and that the refusal of an injunction would involve a risk that assets will be removed or dissipated. The standard of 'good arguable case' is not required in Article 9(2). Third, the possibility to disclose financial information introduced in Article 9(2) is unreasonable and unjustified. Finally, the potential to combine the injunctions with *Anton Piller* orders may have negative effects on the business of the party against which these are used. The disclosure of trade secrets in poorly documented cases may shift the balance in favour of the claimants.

Also resulting from the merits of the case, 'corrective measures' may be taken on application and pursuant to Article 10 to recall temporarily or definitely remove the infringing goods from channels of commerce or to destroy them. This decision is without prejudice to any damages that may follow from the main proceedings. The same measures are available for disposal of materials used in creation of the infringing goods. The Article

---

[54] *Mareva Compania Naviera SA v International Bulkcarriers SA* [1975] 2 Lloyd's Rep 509.

demands that the requirement of proportionality between the infringement and the remedies be kept in mind when determining whether this
measure will be used.

Article 11 provides that an injunction preventing further infringements
can be issued in cases where a decision has already been taken. The
substance of the injunction consists of the prohibition of further infringement, and non-compliance may be subject to punitive damages under
national law. An injunction can also be issued, under the same conditions,
against an intermediary, but these are covered in Article 8(2) of the
Information Society Directive and are, in principle, subject to national
law. This addition is unfortunate, as the intermediaries' role for the
proper functioning of the Internet is vital and the information in question
may affect a large number of actors not parties in the original dispute.

Although not specifically confirmed, injunctive relief of Article 9-type
could be used against ISPs in cases where they are 'infringers'. This
would be in situations falling under Section 4 of the E-Commerce
Directive. For example, an ISP host which is notified of an infringement
and does nothing to remove the infringing content may then be subject to
intermediary relief in the national courts. Indeed, Article 18 of that
Directive specifically allows interim relief. However, as confirmed in the
SABAM case,[55] the ISPs have no obligation to install filtering mechanisms and an injunction cannot be used for this purpose. The decision
specifically confirms that this transpires from, among other instruments,
the Copyright Enforcement Directive. In the earlier *Promusicae* case,[56]
the Court ruled that no ISP obligation to communicate personal data to
rightholders arises from, among others, the Copyright Enforcement
Directive and injunctive relief could not be used here.

Instead of the corrective measures of Article 10 and injunctions of
Article 11, the national court may, under Article 12, impose pecuniary
compensation for the injured party, provided that the persons 'acted
unintentionally and without negligence' and if the execution of these
measures would cause disproportionate harm.

The result of an infringement is the payment of damages. Article 13
obliges Member States to introduce adequate damages for wilful or
negligent infringements. In setting the damages, the judicial authorities,
under Article 13(1)(a), may take into consideration such effects as
negative economic consequences and lost profits and any unfair profits

---

[55] See Chapter 5.
[56] C-275/06 *Productores de Música de España (Promusicae) v Telefónica de
España SAU* [2008] ECR I-271.

made by the infringer and, 'in appropriate cases' only, elements other than economic factors, such as 'moral prejudice'. In the alternative, that is, at their discretion, under Article 13(1)(b), they may set lump sum damages based on 'at least' the royalties or fees which would have been due had the infringer requested authorization.

Putting aside for the moment the complex question of the economics of copyright infringement, it may be observed that the Directive allows the alternative application of two incompatible regimes. One regime, embodied in letter b), bases damages on the sum that would have been due had the legal path been followed from the start. This regime is rational at least in its ability not to prejudice the actual economic loss. Or, in other words, it bases the economic loss on measurable elements and then adds to them the punitive component which results from the wilful or negligent behaviour. On the other hand, there is little merit in basing damages on putative royalties.

The other regime starts from a different premise. It takes 'all appropriate aspects' into consideration. Such aspects include, primarily, 'negative economic consequences' and 'lost profits'. The first is a vague category that is impossible or at least very difficult to measure. The second is known as 'economic damage' in tort law and is either not awarded or is very rarely so and under special circumstances. The fact that the Directive bases damages on 'lost profits' shows lack of understanding of the principles on which tort law operates.

But, in reality, neither approach necessarily gives an accurate picture of the cost involved. A thought experiment with an example of a CD downloaded from the Internet can be made. If such a CD contains 15 songs, what is the appropriate amount of damages under Article 13? If one took the second option first, namely Article 13(1)(b), one would add up the cost of each of the individual songs as sold on the nearest legal alternative, such as iTunes store or a similar e-outlet, and add to it a punitive amount. If we accept a different path, that of Article 13(1)(a), we could take the full price of a retail CD as a basis, even if only one or two songs were taken from each CD. Therefore, this version seems significantly less fair than the previous one. In reality, however, neither may provide adequate compensation. The person who downloaded the songs in the first example need not have purchased them at their full price even if they had opted for the cheaper and more flexible version involving downloading an electronic copy. In addition, digital songs may be sold at different price levels, with different rights management systems, at different bit-rates, increasing the confusion. Had the infringing party in the case of small-scale copying faced a choice between legal and no purchase at all, the applicant may not have suffered any loss.

In the draft, the infringements targeted by the Copyright Enforcement Directive were those 'for commercial purposes or causing significant harm'.[57] This requirement was deleted in the final document and the text now refers to 'any infringement of intellectual property rights'. Effectively, the change of direction has potentially proscribed everyday practices and very significantly extended the scope of the Directive, which now does not concentrate purely on piracy and counterfeiting but leaves scope for individual infringements.[58] Very few parts of the Directive are *strictly* applicable to commercial matters,[59] with the majority of provisions potentially deployable against individuals. Since the enforcement measures proposed are draconian, this is unreasonable and not supported by any evidence that such measures may be effective.[60]

Furthermore, there is no definition of 'intellectual property rights' in the Directive or elsewhere in EU law, which further opens up the scope of application of this instrument. At least two examples spring to mind. The first concerns patents, which are complicated and technical enough not to be subject to provisional and precautionary measures. The second concerns trade secrets, which are treated as intellectual property rights under the law of certain states. The questions concerning the Directive's legality and legitimacy are also serious. 'Does the draft satisfy the constitutional basis for action, i.e. that it contains harmonising provisions "which have as their object the establishment and functioning of the internal market". Is it proportional? Does it respect the principle of subsidiarity?'[61] The draft speaks of 'infringements carried out for commercial purposes or causing significant harm to the right holder'. The problem will arise where private behaviour falls foul of the provisions, which will be in any case where there is a transfer of material without the copyright holder's consent. Thus a simple file-swap would fall under 'significant harm' – a vague term left undefined in the proposal.

The Directive contains a host of provisional and protective measures from the arsenal of private international law. One such measure is contained in Article 7 and relates to *Anton Piller*-type measures for

---

57   See Article 2 of the Draft, footnote 45 above.
58   Cf., for example, Article 13(1)(a).
59   Such as Articles 6(2), 8(1)(a) and (c) or 9(2).
60   Issues of compatibility with the Human Rights Act 1998 have been raised in the UK. See Birnhack, M., 'Acknowledging the Conflict between Copyright Law and Freedom of Expression under the Human Rights Act', (2003) 14 *Entertainment Law Review* 24.
61   See Cornish, W., et al., 'Procedures and Remedies for Enforcing IPRS: The European Commission's Proposed Directive' (2003) 25 EIPR 447, p. 448.

protecting evidence. The harmful potential of these 'search and seize' orders, which may be used against universities or other places where file-swapping forms part of the daily routine, is considerable. Furthermore, Articles 9–11 introduce other provisional measures, including the *Mareva* freezing injunctions.[62] Putting aside the necessity of these and the logic behind them, the main difficulty arises from the fact that only English courts are familiar with interlocutory measures of this kind and have, over the years, developed the necessary safeguards for their deployment. The same cannot be said of most of the other Member States which do not know or use these measures, yet might be tempted to experiment with them on this example.

Problems do not end there. A number of provisions in the Directive can be used against intermediaries, and ISPs have voiced concern over this. The right to obtain information is introduced in Section 3, although even the United States rejects such an approach as unconstitutional.[63] The original draft, now amended, in Article 20 introduced criminal law provisions – with 'serious infringements' criminalized as well as 'attempts'. These have been deleted after a public outcry. A subsequent attempt to introduce a Criminal Enforcement Directive has failed[64] but may yet be revived.

2.1 Anti-Counterfeiting Trade Agreement

On an international level, the Anti-Counterfeiting Trade Agreement (ACTA),[65] a secretly negotiated multinational treaty, aims to improve enforcement of intellectual property rights in signatory states. The EU as well as most of the Member States signed the Agreement, although its controversial nature puts its ratification in doubt.

The Agreement's main task is to create a framework for enforcing IP rights. In that sense, it introduces general obligations in respect of IP enforcement (Article 6), civil enforcement measures (section 2), border measures (section 3), criminal measures (section 4) and contains a special section on enforcement in the digital environment (section 5).

---

[62] Article 10(2) of the draft; Articles 9 and 11 of the Directive.

[63] *RIAA v Verizon Internet Services,* 351 F.3d 1229, 1233 (D.C. Cir. 2003), US Court of Appeals, District of Columbia Circuit.

[64] Amended proposal for a Directive of the European Parliament and of the Council on criminal measures aimed at ensuring the enforcement of intellectual property rights, COM(2006) 168 final, 27.4.2006.

[65] Council of the European Union, 23.8.2011, 12196/11.

Article 27 obliges the parties to make civil and criminal enforcement measures available in the digital environment. The parties may introduce measures obliging the ISPs to disclose information about potential infringers (paragraph 4). The parties are obliged to provide comprehensive protection against the circumvention of technological measures (paragraphs 5 and 6) but also against the circumvention of digital rights management (including pure inducement).

The Agreement has been criticized extensively both in the public press and in the academic world.[66] The criticism concentrates on the non-democratic nature of the voting process, on the fact that the Agreement covers not only large- but also small-scale infringements, that it potentially violates fundamental rights, that it lacks the usual safeguards, that it is incompatible with the existing EU legal framework and would require additional legislation and that it bypasses the WTO framework.

3.   REVIEW OF EU LEGAL FRAMEWORK ON COPYRIGHT[67]

There is no doubt that the more-than-a-decade-old InfoSoc Directive proved robust and adequate, in spite of the problems associated with it. Its technology-neutral framework proved flexible and able to accommodate new technologies, while its narrow interpretation of exceptions and robust protection of technological measures appeals to industry and acts as an incentive to bring about new technologies. At the same time, it is true that the exceptions regime is the bottleneck in the current system, at least in respect of copyright on the Internet. That regime is under scrutiny and will be adjusted in future revisions of the Directive, which can be expected to be incremental.

Recently, calls have been heard for the constitutionalization of intellectual property rights,[68] an enterprise which would bring it into the sphere

---

[66]   For a comprehensive legal review, see Metzger, A. et al. 'Opinion of European Academics on ACTA', accessed 1.8.2012 at http://www.iri.uni-hannover.de/acta-1668.html.

[67]   Some general recommendations can be found in Van Eechound, M. et al., *Harmonizing European Copyright Law: The Challenges of Better Lawmaking*, Information Law Series (Kluwer, The Hague 2009).

[68]   Geiger, C., '"Constitutionalizing" Intellectual Property Law? The Influence of Fundamental Rights on Intellectual Property in the European Union?' (2006) 37 *International Review of Intellectual Property and Competition Law* 371.

of fundamental principles and therefore resolve some of the serious dilemmas that courts currently face. There is no doubt that the Court has already showed sensitivity for the issue in cases such as *Promusicae* or *SABAM*.

A common objection to copyright law at EU level is the lack of transparency and uniformity in law-making as well as the inability to properly balance the interests of the public against those of the right-holders. Projects such as the European Copyright Code,[69] strive to bring about more understanding and minimize the difficulties which arise from lack of transparency and uniformity.[70] The Commission's steady work on reforming the directives, through a review process involving Green Papers is also addressing this issue.

The second key copyright instrument, the Copyright Enforcement Directive, in its attempt to bring about harmonization of the enforcement regime, overlooks the larger difficulties concerning the resources available for copyright enforcement. This main difficulty with the Copyright Enforcement Directive was aptly summed by Cornish et al.:

> Can it be seriously maintained that current differences over the extent of remedial relief (largely in civil process) is exercising pirates in choosing where to do their buccaneering business? Do they sit down with their lawyers and say 'Let's concentrate on Softland – no double damages there!' 'No, no, Secretland would be better – can't be required to reveal our source there!' The Commission produces no evidence that they do. Of course not. What they want to know is how much time and money is available for their pursuit by the police, customs and consumer protection agencies, as well as enforcement bodies set up by interest groups; and how effective these operations tend to be. The proposed Directive does not deal with such hard-line questions of resources in any significant way. It is hard to imagine that a Directive to Member States could ever do so.[71]

---

[69] Accessed 1.8.2012 at http://www.copyrightcode.eu.

[70] See also Ginsburg, J., *European Copyright Code – Back to First Principles*, Auteurs et Medias (Belgium), January 2011; Columbia Public Law Research Paper, No. 11–261, January 2011.

[71] Cornish, W., et al., 'Procedures and Remedies for Enforcing IPRS: The European Commission's Proposed Directive' (2003) 25 *European Intellectual Property Review* 447.

4.   OTHER AREAS

4.1   Collective Management of Online Music[72]

The process of online rights clearance in the European Union appears complex when compared to that in the United States. With a view to reducing the disparities in licensing models, the European Commission adopted in 2005 the Recommendation on the management of online rights in musical works.[73] The Recommendation, which is not binding, is nevertheless an important policy instrument which aims to improve licensing of online services. The EU does not have a harmonized system for licensing and the growth of the cross-border Internet content industry brings about licensing problems. The Recommendation invites the establishment of a multiterritorial licensing policy by inviting the Member States to introduce systems which are best suited to the collective management of online content services. Rightholders should, under this system, have the right to choose the management society of their choice, irrespective of their residence or nationality. Rightholders should, further, have the right to choose the rights entrusted to management and the territorial scope of the mandate but should also be able to withdraw.

Prior to proposing the 2005 Recommendation, the Commission issued a detailed impact assessment on the Recommendation[74] in which it analysed the present structures for cross-border collective management of online content. It considered three options. The first was to take no action and was rejected by stakeholders. The second, favoured by commercial users, was to eliminate territorial restrictions in the existing agreements. The third option, favoured by music publishers, was to give the rightholders the option to appoint an EU-wide manager for online content ('EU-wide direct licensing'). The proposal was a hybrid of the second and third options, while introducing rules on governance, transparency and dispute settlement, and accountability of collective rights managers.

The 2005 system was criticized for avoiding true harmonization by opting for a soft-law instrument and for avoiding the introduction of a

---

[72]   For a detailed critical overview of the system in the EU see Mazziotti, G., 'New Licensing Models for Online Music Services in the European Union: From Collective to Customized Management' (2011) 34 *The Columbia Journal of Law and the Arts* 757.

[73]   Commission Recommendation of 18 October 2005 on collective cross-border management of copyright and related rights for legitimate online music services, OJ L 276/54, 21.10.2005.

[74]   Brussels, SEC(2005) 1254, 11.10.2005.

full pan-European licensing system.[75] In 2012, the Commission proposed a Directive on collective rights management.[76] Among the aims are the increased transparency and better governance of collecting societies and easier licensing of authors' rights for use on the Internet (multi-territorial and multi-repertoire licensing).

4.2 Trade Marks and Domain Names

The EU trade mark legislation approximates laws of the Member States that relate to trade marks. The legislation, which is the result of a long period of negotiation, consists of the harmonizing Trade Mark Directive[77] and the regulation creating a Community trade mark.[78]

Article 1 provides that the Directive applies to every trade mark 'in respect of goods or services which is the subject of registration or of an application in a Member State for registration as an individual trade mark, a collective mark or a guarantee or certification mark'. Article 2 provides that any sign capable of being represented graphically may be a trade mark, including words, names, designs, letters, and so on, as long as they are capable of distinguishing goods and services of one undertaking from the other. In that sense, trade marks have a similar life on the Internet.

The Directive is not a full harmonization but rather one that covers areas where disparity between Member States have in practice proved to be particularly damaging. Thus the Directive provides grounds for refusal and invalidity (Articles 3 and 4), rights conferred (Article 5), limitations of trade mark's effect (Articles 6 and 9) and exhaustion (Article 7). Furthermore, licensing (Article 8), use (Article 10), sanctions (Article 11) and revocation (Articles 12–14) are covered.

Two recent cases clarified EU trade mark protection in the Internet context. The first concerns the use of trade mark on online marketing, while the second covers its use on search engines.

---

[75] See Mazziotti, op. cit., pp. 800–808.

[76] Proposal for a Directive of the European Parliament and of the Council on collective management of copyright and related rights and multi-territorial licensing of rights in musical works for online uses in the internal market, COM(2012) 372, 11.7.2012.

[77] Directive 2008/95/EC of the European Parliament and of the Council of 22 October 2008 to approximate the laws of the Member States relating to trade marks (Codified version), OJ L 299/25, 8.11.2008.

[78] Council Regulation (EC) 207/2009, OJ L 78/1, 24.3.2009.

In *L'Oreal*[79] the online auctions marketplace eBay offered a variety of goods for sale on its website. Among these were goods which infringed the applicant's trade mark. The Court ruled that, upon proper construction of the Trade Mark Directive, the trade mark proprietor is entitled to prohibit the advertising of goods bearing its trade mark where a risk of confusion exists. The Court made a distinction between cases where the website operator plays an active role by providing assistance in the sale process and cases where it does not. In the former, the Electronic Commerce Directive (Article 14) does not insulate it from liability, whereas in the latter it does.

The *Google v Louis Vuitton* case[80] concentrated on Google's advertising practices. Google runs a search engine and operates a paid advertising service, AdWords. A search term entered into the Google search engine triggers a display of both regular search results and paid-for adverts. Louis Vuitton and others argued that search queries which contain words over which they owned trade marks display not only the legitimate sites (in the regular search window) but also AdWords-type paid sites of competitors who produced and/or sold counterfeit goods. The Court ruled that an Internet search engine which stores a keyword, which is a 'sign identical with a trademark', and displays advertisements based on that keyword, does not use the sign within the meaning of Article 5(1).

In the *Interflora* case,[81] which is a continuation of the above, Marks & Spencer used 'Interflora' and other similar trade marks in Google AdWords to attract custom for its flower delivery service. Interflora is a registered trade mark owned by Interflora Inc, a US flower delivery company. The Court held that, according to Article 5(2) of the Trade Mark Directive:

> proprietor of a trade mark with a reputation is entitled to prevent a competitor from advertising on the basis of a keyword corresponding to that trade mark, which the competitor has, without the proprietor's consent, selected in an internet referencing service, where the competitor thereby takes unfair advantage of the distinctive character or repute of the trade mark (free-riding) or

---

[79]   C-324/09, *L'Oréal SA, Lancôme parfums et beauté & Cie SNC, Laboratoire Garnier & Cie, L'Oréal (UK) Ltd v eBay International AG et al.* 12 July 2011, not yet reported.

[80]   C-236/08 and 238/08 *Google France SARL and Google Inc. v Louis Vuitton Malletier SA and Others* [2010] ECR I-02417.

[81]   C-323/09 *Interflora e.a. v Marks & Spencer.* 22 September 2011 [not yet reported].

where the advertising is detrimental to that distinctive character (dilution) or to that repute (tarnishment).

In all the mentioned cases, the Court leaves scope for further precision to the national courts, which are left with the task of working out the details.

Although domain name regulation, including disputes over domain names, is within Member States' competence, the EU regulates its own domain name. Domain name legislation is contained in the .eu Domain Name Regulation, which introduced the .eu domain name.[82]

4.3 Computer Programs

The Software Directive (Original Version)[83] allows for the protection of computer programs and accompanying design material under copyright law. The functionality and the programming language of the program is not protectable[84] and neither is the graphic user interface.[85] In *SAS*, the Advocate General suggests that performing the same function as another program or using the same programming language does not infringe copyright. Likewise, decompiling the program to achieve interoperability should be permitted. On the other hand, copying the source code should not.

Computer programs are, under Article 1, protected 'by copyright, as literary works within the meaning of the Berne Convention'. Ideas that underlie the program or its interfaces are not protected. The beneficiaries are all natural and legal persons, including groups of authors (Articles 2 and 3). Article 4 grants exclusive rights of control to the copyright owner subject to the exceptions in Article 5, which include the right to make backup copies or study the program's operation.

---

[82] Regulation (EC) 733/2002 of the European Parliament and of the Council of 22 April 2002 on the implementation of the .eu Top Level Domain, OJ L 113/1, 30.4.2002. See also Commission Regulation (EC) 874/2004 laying down public policy rules concerning the implementation and functions of the .eu Top Level Domain and the principles governing registration, OJ L 162/40, 30.4.2004.

[83] Council Directive 91/250/EEC of 14 May 1991 on the legal protection of computer programs, OJ L 122, 17.5.1991, now Directive 2009/24 on the legal protection of computer programs, OJ L 111/16, 5.5.2009 (Software Directive (Codified)).

[84] See Advocate General Bot's opinion in C-406/10 *SAS Institute*, 29 November 2011, not yet reported.

[85] C-393/09 *Bezpečnostní softwarová asociace – Svaz softwarové ochrany v Ministry of Culture of the Czech Republic* [2010] ECR I-13971.

There does not seem to be anything in the Directive which prevents it from applying purely to programs used or distributed on the Internet. Pieces of code or applications which are designed to run on the Internet itself (i.e., within a web browser) are also covered.

A question of considerable importance in computer programming is interoperability, which is the ability of one computer system to operate and exchange information with another. The leading case on interoperability in the digital context, decided in the context of competition law, is the Commission's Microsoft decision.[86] Sun Microsystems provided workgroup operating systems. In order to create operating systems that would be compatible with Microsoft Windows OS, Sun required interface information. Microsoft refused to provide this information. At the time of the case, Microsoft had dominance of the operating system market. Without making their operating systems compatible with Microsoft, the applicant could not compete. Microsoft argued that reverse engineering was the correct path for obtaining interoperability information. Sun and the others argued that reverse engineering gave few and uncertain results. This, in turn, meant that supply of the original information was necessary, which is a condition for the application of Article 102 TFEU. The Commission concluded that Microsoft's refusal amounted to abuse of its dominant position.[87]

4.4 Databases[88]

Of some interest to Internet regulation is the EU Database Directive.[89] The Directive, which defines databases as collection of 'independent works, data or other materials arranged in a systematic or methodical way and individually accessible by electronic or other means', introduces two systems of protection.

In the first category are databases which 'by reason of the selection or arrangement of their contents, constitute the author's own intellectual creation' are protected under copyright law. In order to qualify for the protection, a database needs to fulfil the usual protection criteria. No

---

[86]   Microsoft, Commission Decision COMP/C-3/37.792, 24 March 2004.

[87]   See also the Court of First Instance judgment T-201/04 *Microsoft v Commission* 2007 II-03601.

[88]   More information can be found in Herr, R., *Is the Sui Generis Right a Failed Experiment?* (DJØF, Copenhagen 2008).

[89]   Directive 96/9/EC of the European Parliament and of the Council of 11 March 1996 on the legal protection of databases, OJ L 77, 27.3.1996.

protection extends to the actual *contents* of the database, which, in any case, may be subject to a special IP protection (i.e., a photograph).

In addition to this, a *sui generis* right exists for databases in which qualitatively and/or quantitatively a 'substantial investment in either the obtaining, verification or presentation of the contents' has been made.

The Database Directive applies also in the Internet context, which has been tested in a number of cases. In the Court's view, where a database provided only a by-product of the creator's main business, it cannot be granted *sui generis* protection even when substantial effort had been put in it.[90] In *Football Dataco*,[91] following this line of cases, the Court ruled that selection or arrangement of the data must amount 'to an original expression of the creative freedom of its author, which is a matter for the national court to determine'. It is yet unclear how courts will react to the different uses to which databases can be put on the Internet and further clarification from the Court in the coming years can be expected.

4.5 Exhaustion of Rights

The principle of exhaustion of rights refers to the idea that the goods once marketed in one Member State should be freely distributable in others without intellectual property rights, such as patents, copyrights or trade marks, being in the way. The IP rights remain valid but, once the goods have lawfully been placed on the market in EU states A and B, parallel imports from and into these states cannot be prevented. Rightholders can therefore either choose not to place their goods on certain markets at all, but if they do, these will be subject to the exhaustion doctrine.[92]

The Court indirectly addressed the application of the doctrine in the *Premier League* case.[93] In that case, some UK pub owners had legally acquired Greek decoder cards with which their customers could access and watch Premier League football matches on digital television. Such cards were marketed at much higher prices in the UK. The question

---

[90] C-203/02 *British Horseracing Board v William Hill Organisation* [2004] ECR I-10415.

[91] C-604/10 *Football Dataco Ltd v Yahoo! UK Ltd*, decided 1 March 2012, not yet reported.

[92] First introduced for copyright in C-78/70 *Deutsche Grammophon* [1970] ECR 487.

[93] C-403/08 *Football Association Premier League Ltd and Others v QC Leisure and Others* and C-429/08 *Karen Murphy v Media Protection Services Ltd*, judgment of 4 October 2011, not yet reported.

posed was, essentially, whether parallel imports from another EU Member State constitute a violation of IP rights.

The Advocate General suggested in her opinion that exhaustion of rights ought to extend to services.[94] In its judgment, the Court sidestepped that particular angle of the question but answered it by analysing the free movement of services, saying that Article 56 TFEU:

> precludes legislation of a Member State which makes it unlawful to import into and sell and use in that State foreign decoding devices which give access to an encrypted satellite broadcasting service from another Member State that includes subject-matter protected by the legislation of that first State.

The grant of a limited licence, therefore, does not seem to exhaust a copyright. On the other hand, the judgment, in focusing on the services side of the question, may ultimately have far-reaching consequences for content distribution on the Internet, which also often relies on different licensing models. The message is that the ownership of intellectual property rights does not of itself suspend the free movement of services. This is a significant development, in particular in light of the Copyright Directive Article 3 right of communication to the public and its application to online works. It is likely that dissemination of most of online content falls within 'making available' under Article 3. Paragraph 3 of that Article is clear in determining that exhaustion does not apply to right of communication to the public of that article. This would mean that exhaustion cannot be applied to online distribution. The alternative route adopted in the *Premier League* case, on the other hand, leaves open the path that Article 56 provides.

4.6 Patent Regulation

Patent law is only indirectly covered in the EU, through multinational initiatives.

The European Patent Convention,[95] which is a multinational treaty out of the scope of EU law, creates a European Patent Office and provides a unified mechanism for granting European patents. Although no unitary European patent is created, the procedure for applying for patents is simplified.

---

[94]   Advocate General Opinion, paragraph 188.
[95]   Convention on the Grant of European Patents of 5 October 1973, OJ EPO 2001, (2001) Special Edition No. 4, p. 55.

Although steps towards making a unitary patent system have been taken,[96] the Court of Justice ruled[97] that a potential European and EU Patents Court (EEUPC) would be contrary to the EU Treaties. Such a system would confer on a non-EU body the ability to rule on EU law.

---

[96] More recently Council Decision 2011/167/EU of 10 March 2011 authorizing enhanced cooperation in the area of the creation of unitary patent protection, OJ L 76/52, 22.3.2011; and Proposal for a Regulation of the European Parliament and the of the Council implementing enhanced cooperation in the area of the creation of unitary patent protection, COM(2011) 215, 13.4.2011.

[97] Opinion 1/09, *The draft agreement on the European and Community Patents Court*, 8 March 2011, not yet reported.

7. Consumer protection and marketing

1. CONSUMERS AND THE INTERNET

Consumers are an important actor on the Internet. This importance is reflected in the fact that a great part of Internet activity involves consumers.[1] Hosting a website, sending an email, watching content on the Internet, ordering goods online or just visiting a web page are all inherently consumer activities. But the increase of consumer activities also increases the risk and with it the need for protection.

Internet consumer transactions need not differ significantly from regular ones except in their speed and relative ease. Hosting a web page is not significantly different from buying space in a magazine, sending an email can be equated to sending a letter, watching a television series streamed or downloaded from a web-based provider is the same as watching it on a satellite or cable channel and purchasing a video disc online is similar to ordering it on the phone from the supplier's catalogue. And yet, uncertainties prevail, as consumers seem reluctant to commit to costly purchases on the Internet.[2] Although some of the effects can be explained by a variety of psychological and economic factors, there is no doubt that the perceived or real lack of protection and lack of knowledge about the rights conferred and the applicable law play a major role. Whereas the Internet seems to have revolutionized consumer shopping habits, it would appear that consumer vulnerability has increased as demand for extra information, insurance and protection rises along with the number of fraudulent attacks.

---

[1]   Unless otherwise stated, the EU secondary legislation applies both to B2B and to B2C transactions.

[2]   See Commission Communication, A coherent framework for building trust in the Digital Single Market for e-commerce and online services, COM(2011) 942, 11.1.2012.

The European Union puts a high value on consumer protection,[3] a fact reflected both in the Treaty articles[4] and in the secondary legislation.[5] Article 169 TFEU provides that the aim is to protect 'health, safety and economic interests of consumers' and 'their right to information, education and to organise themselves'. The legal basis for consumer legislation in the EU is the Single Market (Article 114 TFEU) but Article 169 also gives the EU the necessary competence to adopt measures which 'support, supplement and monitor the policy pursued by the Member States'. Such measures, unlike laws enacted by reference to Article 114, do not pre-empt more stringent national measures.

An overview of the comprehensive EU web of consumer protection laws reveals a constant set of objectives, which revolve around transparency and certainty. In reality, consumer interests are more complex and can be tentatively divided into three groups, around which the EU legislation has been designed.[6] The first relates to fair-trading interests such as information concerning the seller and the product, payment issues and redress in case the transaction goes wrong. The second category relates to privacy: consent to gather information, access to information already gathered and security of information on hold. The third category relates to morality: issues such as pornography, hate speech and protection of minors against offensive content. There are two sources of consumer threats in all three categories. In the first case, the threat is a result of an open attempt to defraud the consumer. Recent figures confirm that fraud on the Internet is on the rise.[7] Among numerous schemes, the most popular seem to be online auctions, general merchandise fraud, the so-called Nigerian scam, electronic equipment fraud and Internet access fraud. In the second, the threat arises as a result of problematic business practices. These can be described as substandard practices relating to information provided to the consumer, conclusion

---

[3] More recently, the Commission uses the term 'consumer empowerment' to designate an environment that enables the consumers not only to have rights but also to enjoy them effectively. See Proposal for a Regulation of the European Parliament and of the Council on a consumer programme 2014–2020, Brussels, COM(2011) 707 final, 9.11.2011.

[4] Cf. Articles 39, 107 or 169 TFEU.

[5] For an overview of consumer law in the EU, see Weatherill, S., *EU Consumer Law and Policy* (Edward Elgar, Cheltenham and Northampton, MA 2005).

[6] See Dickie, J., *Producers and Consumers in EU E-Commerce Law* (Hart, London 2005), p. 11 et seq.

[7] Internet Crime Complaint Centre (IC3): *2011 Internet Crime Report*, accessed 1.8.2012 at www.ic3.gov/media/default.aspx

and performance of the contract, payment and remedies. Any EU consumer law is, therefore, an interplay of these three groups of interests as informed by the factors that threaten them.

In this chapter we will explore how the EU deals with consumer and marketing problems in the digital world. Our main focus will be on measures covering the three areas. The first relates to regular consumer transactions. Here, the new directive on consumer rights as well as its predecessors will be analysed. The second concerns protection of consumers in banking and financial transactions. The third concerns consumer protection in international litigation.

The EU regulates marketing practices extensively. In this chapter, marketing practices will be analysed only in as much as they concern consumers on the Internet.

2. CONSUMER PROTECTION DIRECTIVES

2.1 Distance Selling Contracts

The Distance Selling Directive is one of the milestones in EU consumer protection.[8] The Directive began its life in 1992 with the first proposal and culminated in 1997 with the final text. The implementation deadline was in June 2000. The Directive, therefore, began its life long before the Internet took hold in Europe and was not designed with the intricacies of the modern web in mind. Nevertheless, its technology-neutral architecture helped it withstand the test of time and made it an important instrument in consumer protection on the Internet.

In general, the Directive covers transactions that take place 'at a distance'. Article 2 provides definitions but, at the same time, sets conditions that must be fulfilled for a transaction to be treated as occurring at a distance for the purposes of the Directive. Primarily, a 'distance contract' is one concluded between a supplier and a consumer under an organized distance sale. The fact that the sale is organized means that a supplier is normally running such sales and has not approached a particular consumer on an ad hoc basis. The 'consumer', for the purposes of the Directive, is a person who is acting for purposes outside his trade. A 'supplier', on the other hand, is acting in his

---

[8] Directive 97/7/EC of the European Parliament and of the Council of 20 May 1997 on the protection of consumers in respect of distance contracts, OJ L 144, 4.6.1997, pp. 19–27. Article 31 of the new Consumer Rights Directive will, upon entry into force, repeal the Directive.

commercial or professional capacity. The parties must be, for the purposes of the contract, availing themselves of the 'means of distance communications'. Such means are defined in Annex I to the Directive, and include, among others, electronic mail or teleshopping. It must be inferred that advertising goods on the Internet also falls in this category. Finally, the distance is only relevant 'up to and including the moment at which the contract is concluded'. It is clear that the Directive applies to consumer contracts and not to contracts between business parties.

Article 3 contains a list of exceptions, contracts to which the Directive does not apply. These include contracts relating to financial services covered in a non-exhaustive list in Annex II: investment, insurance, reinsurance, banking, futures and options. The main reason for excluding those mentioned is their presence in other EU instruments. Further to that, automatic vending machines and automated commercial premises are excluded, as are public payphones, contracts relating to immovable property and auctions. The exclusion of contracts concluded through automatic commercial premises (such as ticket machines) seems understandable as such contracts do not really seem to be concluded at a distance. Websites, arguably, will not fall under such automatic premises. The exclusion of immovable property also seems understandable as such transactions are often subject to special formalities.

The exclusion of auctions, on the other hand, is a clear indication of the time in which this directive was drafted. Today, auction web pages (such as eBay) are among the most popular services on the Internet and are for direct non-auction purchases as well as auctions. At the same time, however, consumers who do use such services remain vulnerable and protection of consumers in such transactions remains inadequate. It suffices to say here that any protection will be entirely at the national level.

A further set of exceptions is located in Article 3(2), which provides that Articles 4, 5, 6 and 7(1) (see below) shall not apply to contracts for the supply of groceries intended for everyday consumption. These exceptions are somewhat puzzling, as there seems to be no particular reason why they should be there. Online food delivery is rapidly growing and more consumers are using it now than in the time when the Directive had been drafted. Also excluded are contracts by tour operators, which are to be supplied on a specific date or for a specific period.

Article 4 imposes an obligation to provide information to the consumer. Such information must be given in 'good time prior to the conclusion of any contract'. In the case of web pages, this should probably be interpreted as meaning that the information must exist at the point before the consumer clicks 'I Agree' or any such similar button. Since most websites require prior registration, this requirement will be fulfilled either if information is provided on the page before logging in, or at a later stage before the consumer commits himself. The information to be provided includes the identity of the supplier, the characteristics and price of the goods, arrangements for paying and delivery, the right of withdrawal, validity period of the offer, and so on. The said information must be provided in a clear way, so that a party to a distance commercial transaction can understand it.

The information required under Article 4 must be provided prior to the conclusion of the contract. In addition to that, however, Article 5 requires written confirmation of such information to be sent to the consumer in good time during the performance of the contract, and at the time of delivery at the latest. In particular the Article emphasizes the right of withdrawal, the address for complaints, information on after-sales services and guarantees, and the conditions for cancelling the contract, where it is of unspecified duration. No such obligation exists in respect of services provided by and paid to the operator of the distance communication. It would seem, judging from the above, that an email sent in confirmation of an order made on the Internet would satisfy the conditions of Article 5. It is also probably true that an invoice that comes with the package would be equally sufficient.

Article 6 contains the important right of withdrawal. Consumers have the right to withdraw from a contract concluded at a distance within at least seven working days, without penalty and without giving reasons for withdrawal. The supplier is in that case obliged to refund the price as soon as possible and in any case not later than 30 days afterwards and is only allowed to charge the consumer for the cost of returning the goods. The period normally begins to run from the time of delivery or from the time when the obligations in Article 5 have been fulfilled. If these obligations have not been fulfilled, the right extends to three months.[9] The right of withdrawal does not exist in respect of contracts for the provision of services if the performance has begun before the end of the seven working day period. Also, it does not exist for the supply of goods or services where the price is subject to fluctuations in the financial markets which cannot be controlled by the supplier. Finally, the right of

---

[9]   On the problems concerning the treatment of software sales under this article, see Hörnle, J., Sutter, G. and Walden, I., 'Directive 97/7/EC on the protection of consumers in respect of distance contracts' in Lodder, A. and Kaspersen, H., *eDirectives: Guide to European Union Law on E-Commerce* (Kluwer, The Hague 2002), p. 20.

withdrawal does not exist where the goods have been personalized, in the case of audio, video or software that has been unsealed and for the supply of newspapers. If the right of withdrawal is in respect of a contract financed by credit given either by the supplier or by a third party, the credit shall be cancelled.[10] However, Member States have the right to lay down detailed provisions in respect of this right.

Article 7 deals with the performance of a distance contract. The supplier's principal obligation is to execute the order within 30 days from the day following that on which the consumer forwarded his order. If the supplier is not able to fulfil this obligation as a result of unavailability, the consumer, who must promptly be informed, gets an option to refund as soon as possible and not later than 30 days afterwards. Member States are in this case given an option to set out in their law that the supplier may provide a replacement of equivalent quality and price. The consumer must be notified of this possibility prior to the conclusion of the contract.[11]

Article 8 introduces an obligation to ensure that a consumer can request cancellation of payment where fraudulent use has been made of his payment card in connection with distance contracts covered by this Directive. This provision covers the increasing occurrence of obtaining credit card details illegally, either on the Internet (for example, by using key loggers, spyware programs that memorize the sequence of key-strokes) or elsewhere, and using them to purchase goods. In such cases, consumers are entitled to a full refund of sums paid. It is worth mentioning that these rules exist under other provisions, national or EU, which deal with credit cards. In the case of debit cards, the internal banking codes usually require the same kind of refund. The practical difference between the two is therefore minimal.

Article 9 regulates inertia selling – the supply of unwanted goods or services to consumers coupled with a request for payment. This provision would not have a large impact on Internet sales if it were not for poor information provided to consumers who often believe that they are getting software or information for free or paying for one unit only whereas, in fact, they are paying a subscription on a daily, weekly or monthly basis. In a number of cases, providers of such services auto-matically subscribe consumers, upon successful download of the first unit (a ringtone, a video game, a digital magazine, a video), which is often

---

[10] Article 6(4).
[11] The usefulness of this option becomes apparent when one recollects online food supply through retailers such as Tesco or Waitrose.

advertised as being 'for free', to their often costly subscription services. In this case, the first transaction, in the absence of clearly available contractual terms stating otherwise, is not related to the subscription and the latter is provided as inertia selling.

Article 10 provides that the use by a supplier of an automated calling machine or a fax requires prior consent of the consumer. The use of other means of communication is allowed where there is no objection from the consumer. The difference between these two categories seems to be that, in respect of the first, express consent is sought in advance while the second includes a subsequent opt-out. This phenomenon has been the subject of various laws in the EU. The E-Privacy Directive contains a similar provision, the difference being that protection is extended to 'subscribers' and other non-consumer subjects.[12] The E-Commerce Directive[13] requires the consultation of opt-out registers in similar situations.

In respect of the Internet, all three provisions are inadequate to curb the spread of spam which today comprises most of the email communication on the planet. The Directive on Privacy and Electronic Communications (the E-Privacy Directive), changing the regime in the E-Commerce Directive, institutes an opt-in regime. In addition, it becomes illegal to conceal the identity of the sender and a valid return address for sending opt-out requests must be provided.[14]

2.2   Consumer Rights Directive[15]

The new Consumer Rights Directive is meant to replace the Distance Selling Directive and the even older Doorstep Selling Directive on contracts negotiated away from business premises.[16] As such, it is a codification of the basic consumer rights covered in the previously mentioned directives. At the same time, it provides 'full harmonization of some key regulatory aspects'. In respect of digital contracts, the Directive has three key regulatory directions. First, it establishes requirements for information to be provided in distance contracts (Article 6). In that

---

[12]   See Article 13, Directive 2002/58/EC; and see Chapter 8.
[13]   Article 7.
[14]   See Chapter 8.
[15]   Directive 2011/83/EC of the European Parliament and of the Council on consumer rights, amending Council Directive 93/13/EEC and Directive 1999/44/EC of the European Parliament and of the Council and repealing Council Directive 85/577/EEC and Directive 97/7/EC of the European Parliament and of the Council, OJ L 304/64, 22.11.2011.
[16]   Council Directive 85/577/EEC of 20 December, OJ L 372/31, 31.12.1985.

respect, the Directive follows similar requirements in the E-Commerce Directive. Second, the Directive establishes formal requirements for distance consumer contracts (Article 8). Third, it regulates the right of withdrawal (Articles 9–16).

Article 2 excludes a number of areas from the scope of the Directive's application, including, among others, gambling, financial services, package travel, timeshare agreements, food supplies, passenger transport, automatic vending machines and single connection Internet contracts. Article 2(5) emphasizes that the Directive does not affect national contract law. Article 2(6) confirms that *traders* (but not Member States) can go beyond minimum harmonization. In fact, Article 4 explicitly forbids Member States from introducing legislation which is more or less stringent, thus emphasizing that the Directive is a full-harmonization measure within its scope.

The Directive introduces a single set of core rules for both distance and regular contracts. Article 6 contains a comprehensive set of information to be provided to the consumer in distance contracts. The provision replicates most of the information provisions already seen in the E-Commerce and the Services Directive[17] without replacing them (Article 6(5)) but makes them clearer and more favourable for the consumer. Specific to digital contracts is the obligation to provide information on 'functionality, including applicable technical protection measures, of digital content'.[18] The trader is also under obligation to provide information on the interoperability of digital content with hardware and software.[19]

A novelty in the formal requirements section (Article 8) is the obligation to explain to the consumer that a duty to pay exists and requires the consumer to specifically acknowledge it. If buttons are used to activate payment, they need to be labelled in appropriate ways so as not to leave the consumer in doubt. This is, by analogy, extended to situations where the trader preselects the options by ticking a box on the website, or preselects the items from the fall-down menu, and so on, before the consumer has had the option to do so. Article 8(4) ensures that, where there are only limited means for displaying the required information (e.g., mobile phone screens), minimum information regarding the conditions of the transaction must still be displayed.

The right of withdrawal had been extended from 7 to 14 days (Article 9). If the trader omits the information on withdrawal, Article 10 extends

---

[17] Directive 2006/123/EC of the European Parliament and of the Council of 12 December 2006 on services in the internal market, OJ L 376, 27 December 2006.

[18] Article 6(1)(r).

[19] Article 6(1)(s).

the period from 14 days to 12 months. Annex I(B) introduces a model withdrawal form. In electronic transactions, the trader is allowed either to present the Annex I(B) form or its own, as long as appropriate information is presented and acknowledgement of receipt of the consumer's withdrawal is sent.

According to Article 16(m), the right of withdrawal does not exist in respect of the supply of digital content where no tangible medium is used and the consumer consented in advance to terms of such delivery. This is typically the case with downloading or streaming content such as books, music or videos. In the case of tangible media (CDs etc.), Article 16(i) excludes withdrawal where the seal has been removed after delivery.

The Directive introduces a comprehensive mechanism for eliminating hidden charges. Article 22 eliminates hidden transaction charges and costs in general. Consumers have to be told in advance of any such charges which are payable above the agreed remuneration and must specifically agree to them. If such consent is only inferred from default options which need to be rejected (e.g., preselected boxes or pull-down menus), the consumer will be entitled to a refund of such charges. Article 19 prohibits charging fees for using specific payment methods which go beyond the real cost. Traders are allowed to request payments for the use of, for instance, specific credit cards, but these must not exceed the real cost. Article 27 relieves the consumer from any obligation to pay for unsolicited goods, digital content or services.

2.3   Unfair Terms in E-Commerce Contracts

The Unfair Terms in Consumer Contracts Directive[20] is one of the most important consumer-protecting legal instruments in the European Union. Although drafted and enacted before the Internet age, its application to Internet cases and its importance for online transactions is well established. The aim of the Directive is simple: to minimize or eliminate unfair clauses in consumer contracts. The Directive had its origin in the Commission's policy of providing a comprehensive consumer protection system which would extend to civil contracts. Unfair terms in consumer contracts are frequent and disparities between laws of Member States aggravate the situation. The problem, as applied to the Internet, brings with it all the difficulties of instant transactions (click-wrap or browse-wrap). An average consumer does not read standard terms, is not likely to

---

[20]   Directive 93/13, OJ L 095/29, 5.4.1993.

understand them if he does and would in all likelihood not be able to spot them when he saw them.

Article 3 defines an unfair term as a contractual term which has not been individually negotiated and which, contrary to the requirement of good faith, causes a significant imbalance in the parties' rights and obligations under the contract, to the detriment of the consumer. A term not individually negotiated is one that has been drafted in advance and the consumer was not able to influence the substance. Most, if not all, contractual terms on the Internet are of this type. The Article specifically mentions preformulated standard contracts. The Article also provides that the fact that some aspects of the contract have been individually negotiated shall not preclude the rest of the contract from benefiting from the protection. The legislator targets preformulated contracts.

The unfairness of a particular term is not assessed in general but takes into account the nature of the goods or services, the circumstances and other contractual terms (Article 4). The Annex to the Directive contains a non-indicative list of terms frequently used in contracts. Some of the terms listed in the Annex are typically found on the Internet:

(a) excluding or limiting the legal liability of a seller or supplier in the event of the death or personal injury of a consumer resulting from an act or omission of that seller or supplier;

(b) excluding or limiting the legal rights of the consumer vis-à-vis the seller or supplier or another party in the event of total or partial non-performance or inadequate performance by the seller or supplier of any of the contractual obligations ... ; [...]

(d) permitting the seller or supplier to retain sums paid by the consumer where the latter decides not to conclude or perform the contract, without providing for the consumer to receive compensation of an equivalent amount from the seller or supplier where the latter is the party cancelling the contract;

(e) requiring any consumer who fails to fulfil his obligation to pay a disproportionately high sum in compensation; [...]

(g) enabling the seller or supplier to terminate a contract of indeterminate duration without reasonable notice; [...]

Article 5 requires that terms of the contract be drafted in plain language intelligible to an ordinary consumer. In cases of doubt, preference is given to terms favourable to the consumer.

The consequence of the presence of unfair terms is their nullity with the continuing existence of the remainder of the contract, if this is capable of existing without these terms. Importantly, Article 6(2) provides that the consumer will not lose the protection granted by the Directive by virtue of the choice of the law of a non-Member country as the law applicable to the contract if the latter has a close connection with the territory of the Member States. In other words, the provisions of the Directive that protect the consumer shall be treated as mandatory rules in the international sense. They are applicable irrespective of the law otherwise applicable to the contract.

It is the obligation of Member States, under Article 7, to ensure that sellers are adequately monitored for their use of unfair terms. Member States undertake to make efforts to reduce the prevalence of these terms. As an example, the second paragraph of Article 7 provides that various consumer protection bodies and similar organizations should have the right to take actions before courts or other organs to obtain decisions on whether terms of general use are unfair or not.

Article 8 provides that Member States may go above the protection provided in the Directive, as long as this is consistent with the Treaty provisions. Member States who decide to follow this path must accordingly notify the Commission (Article 8(a)).

The unfairness of a contractual term does not arise out of its length. Also, it is not the purpose of the Directive to supply for the lack of common sense. Consumers cannot rely, in legal proceedings, on their own ignorance of terms of the agreement, where they clearly had access to these. Clicking on the button 'I Agree' or 'Buy' or any similar such button constitutes a binding agreement as long as a link to 'Terms and Conditions' has been made available before such button is clicked. It is true that such terms, just like those in software agreements, are lengthy and that most consumers do not read them. The important point, however, is that the Unfair Terms Directive will provide protection against *problematic* contractual terms, whether these have been read or not, whether they have been automatically agreed or not. In fact, the very point of the Directive is to combat preformulated terms, those against which the consumer has little or no influence.

3.   BANKING AND FINANCIAL SERVICES

3.1   Distance Marketing of Consumer Financial Services Directive

The Directive[21] aims to consolidate the market for financial services, offer the widest possible choice to consumers and open up the financial

---

[21]   Directive 2002/65/EC concerning the distance marketing of consumer financial services, amending Directives 97/7/EC and 98/27/EC, OJ L 271, 9.10.2002, p. 16.

market in Member States. As such, it complements Treaty provisions and other financial instruments in this area. Distance selling of financial services is a growing area which requires additional consumer protection. It benefits both the traders, who access markets in other Member States with little or no additional cost, and the consumers who benefit from ease of access and lower prices resulting from increased competition. The Internet in particular is well suited for trading in this field as it offers easy and instantaneous comparison. An interested consumer can look up any offers for a particular financial service online and be sure that he will be able to make an informed decision in the belief that fraudulent transactions are minimized.

The Directive stands in a special relationship with a number of other instruments.[22] First, the Treaty guarantees the freedom of financial services through its Single Market provisions relating to freedom of establishment, free movement of services and free movement of capital.[23] Second, the Directive complements the Electronic Commerce Directive[24] but also limits its application to the areas not covered in the new Directive. Finally, a number of other provisions, of either Community or national provenance apply to this area.[25] In relation to them, the new Directive is a *lex specialis*. Importantly, the Directive does not apply to conflict of laws issues. Recital 8 specifically excludes the application of both the Brussels I Regulation and the Rome I Regulation on contracts.[26] This is an important feature, as both laws contain important provisions that relate to financial services.

The object of the Directive, as stated in Article 1, is the approximation of laws relating to distance selling of financial services. The Directive distinguishes between contracts that involve an initial service agreement and those that do not. The former are agreements which consist of a series of successive operations forming one whole, irrespective of whether individual operations can also be considered as contracts. These are, for example, the opening of a bank account or a credit card agreement. The opening of the account can be considered as the initial operation and each withdrawal is a successive one. In such cases, the provisions of the Directive will only apply to the initial agreement and not to the successive ones.

---

[22] The 97/7/EC Directive on distance selling specifically excludes financial services.
[23] Articles 49, 56 and 63 TFEU.
[24] See Chapter 2.
[25] See Articles 17–19 and Chapter 9.
[26] See Chapter 3.

The first obligation, set out in Article 3, is the duty to provide information prior to the conclusion of the contract. Before the consumer is bound, he must receive information regarding the supplier of the service, the financial service itself, the contract and any redress he may be entitled to. In terms of the supplier, such information includes all the usual details which may be expected in such situations, such as the identity, addresses of representatives and any relevant authorization details. The data regarding the financial service include particularly the price to be paid, costs, taxes, any limitation periods and arrangements for payment and performance. Of particular importance for the consumer will be the right of withdrawal, the duration of the contract and any right to terminate it. The consumer must also be informed of any provision relating to the competent court and the applicable law. The Directive has a favourable view of out-of-court settlement and provides that the consumer shall be informed if any such redress exists.

The Directive does not derogate from information requirements contained in other Community instruments and Member States have the right to introduce more stringent criteria as long as they are properly communicated to the Community.[27] In addition, the communication requirements of Article 3 and 4(1) shall also be forwarded in paper form before the consumer is bound and also immediately after the conclusion of the contract if this has not been done in a form where they are immediately visible (i.e., telephone of VoIP).[28] The consumer may request the terms and conditions in paper form at any time during the duration of the contract and may also change the means of communication, if appropriate.

Article 6 introduces the right of withdrawal. This right can be exercised within 14 days without any obligation to give reasons and without penalty. Life insurance and pensions contracts covered in the Life Assurance Directive[29] have the deadline extended to 30 days. The right does not exist for financial services normally subject to market fluctuations such as trade in foreign exchange, securities and other financial instruments listed in paragraph 2(a), short-term travel insurance or contracts where performance has already taken place. Importantly, Member States may exclude property credits, credits secured by a mortgage and declarations using the services of an official.[30]

---

[27]　Article 4.

[28]　Article 5.

[29]　Directive 2002/83/EC of the European Parliament and of the Council of 5 November 2002 concerning life assurance, OJ L 345, 19.12.2002.

[30]　Article 6(3).

Unsolicited services are covered in Article 9 of the Directive. The supply of financial services without prior request is prohibited when this request includes payment, prior or deferred. Specifically, the Directive provides that not replying shall not constitute consent and exonerates the consumers from any liability that arises from it. Likewise, Article 10 prohibits unsolicited communications by automated calling systems or fax unless prior consent has been obtained from the consumer. Unfortunately, the same standard has not been used for unsolicited email (spam). Article 10(2) gives the option to Member States to choose between two regimes: opt-in (a) or opt-out (b). Under the first, spam can only be sent if the consumer has expressed consent in advance. Under the second, the consumer only has the right to object once he starts receiving it.

The final provisions of the Directive provide extra protection to consumers. Article 11 obliges Member States to introduce adequate sanctions for violations of the provisions of the Directive. Article 12 provides that the Directive has a mandatory nature, from which consumers cannot derogate. Comprehensive obligations lie on Member States in respect of redress.[31] Member States have to: (a) ensure adequate and effective compliance; (b) allow consumer organizations, public bodies and professional organizations access to courts to ensure that national implementing measures are applied; and (c) force the operators and suppliers to stop practices which are incompatible with the Directive. Out-of-court dispute resolution is promoted in Article 14.

The Directive has been subsequently amended and needs to be read in conjunction with the Payment Services Directive (PSD) – see below.

3.2 Fraudulent Use of Payment Cards

In the early days, financial transactions that took place on the Internet, including payment by credit cards and money transfers, were limited and so was fraud. With the growth of electronic commerce, consumer fraud increased. A financial transaction on the Internet can typically take two forms. First, it can be a traditional contract followed by the issuing of an invoice, the payment by cash, cheque, money order or bank transfer. These transactions differ little from orders on the phone or by fax. Second, it can be an instant contract where payment is effected by credit or debit card or the use of one of the proxy services, such as PayPal or Western Union. This brings the added security of a trusted and reputable intermediary but

---

[31]   Article 13.

also adds another step in the transaction chain and therefore increases the risk. Proxy accounts require usernames and passwords, increasing the length of chain and exposing the customer to scams and 'phishing' attacks. The contract can also involve a payment by credit or debit card. The fact that details from these cards are transferred over the Internet and then stored at the other end increases the risk of interception. For that reason, most reputable web pages encrypt this information while it is in transit and keep it secure on local servers or delete it.

Fraudulent use of payment instruments is covered in the Distance Selling Directive, the Distance Marketing of Consumer Financial Services and the Payment Services Directive, among others.

Article 8 of both the Distance Selling Directive and the Distance Marketing of Consumer Financial Services Directive contained a provision obliging Member States to introduce legislation allowing the consumer 'to request cancellation of a payment where fraudulent use has been made of his payment card in connection with distance contracts covered by this Directive' and allowing the consumer 'to be recredited with the sums paid or have them returned'. The provision is less clear and less useful than would otherwise be desirable.

Under most national laws, fraudulent use of credit cards is subject to compensation from the moment the consumer had notified the card issuer. Similar arrangements usually exist for debit cards as a result of an agreement between the banks. In this case, it would have to be assumed that the right to compensation also exists from the moment the notification was received by the issuer. It is not clear what happens with transactions which occur between the moment of loss and the moment of notification, but these would in any case be subject to national law. In addition, the Article does not cover the issue of responsibility for fraudulent use. The loss and subsequent abuse of banking/credit card details may result either exclusively from hacking or other illegal activity on the side of the perpetrator or from the combination of these and negligence on the part of the user (who may not have bothered to use passwords, kept the PIN code together with a credit card, etc.). National laws legally limit the right to be recredited to cases where the consumer has not acted negligently.

The Commission's Recommendation on Electronic Payments from 1997,[32] drafted as a non-binding but nevertheless informative document,

---

[32] Recommendation 97/489/EC of 30 July 1997 concerning transactions by electronic payment instruments, OJ L 208/52, 2.8.1997., since integrated into the Payment Services Directive (see below).

covers some of the mentioned problems. The general regime of application of the Recommendation included electronic cash withdrawals and transfers of funds, but not electronic money instruments, unless they were used to load or unload value onto an account.[33] Electronic money instruments were defined as reloadable payment instruments such as stored-value cards or computer memory.[34] Like other similar EU laws, the issuer had to communicate to the consumer all the terms and conditions, charges, and so on, *prior* to the delivery of the money instrument.[35] Likewise, subsequent to a transaction, the issuer had to provide information that would enable the identification of individual transactions, the amounts, any charges or exchange rates.[36]

The user's obligations include the duty to be as diligent as possible about account information, including the duty not to disclose access information or to notify of any theft, loss or unauthorized access. Article 6 of the Recommendation provides that, up to the time of notification, the holder bears the consequence of the loss or theft of the electronic payment instrument up to a certain limit (the then ECU 150), unless he has acted negligently, in contravention of his obligations or fraudulently, in which case the limit does not apply. The holder stops being liable from the moment he has notified the issuer. Importantly, however, paragraph 3 of Article 6 provides that 'the holder is not liable if the payment instrument has been used, without physical presentation or electronic identification (of the instrument itself). The use of a confidential code or any other similar proof of identity is not, by itself, sufficient to entail the holder's liability'.

The Recommendation exonerates the holder from any liability in the event of his payment data being presented electronically without the actual card. This is the case where credit card numbers and other associated information (start date, end date, name on card, security code) have been stolen, obtained fraudulently or generated. Moreover, the presentation of any extra security information (such as a password or security code) does not make the holder liable. This high standard of consumer protection effectively prevents the banks from claiming, without proving the contrary, that fraudsters have the data because the holder had been negligent.

The issuer will be liable for any defective execution of the user's transactions even if the defect is not directly attributable to the issuer.

---

[33] Article 1.
[34] Article 2.
[35] Article 3.
[36] Article 4.

Likewise, the issuer is liable for transactions not authorized by the holder or errors attributable to the issuer in administering the account.[37] This provision firmly puts the onus of liability on the issuer, which is in harmony with a number of national laws

In reality, it will be difficult to apply even this regime, which is favourable to diligent consumers. For instance, will the user who does not have anti-spyware software installed or has not updated it be potentially liable for any financial loss resulting from an attack and the electronic theft of financial information? If Articles 6 and 7 are applied strictly, the answer would almost certainly be yes. In reality, the range and sophistication of attacks would make a very large number of consumer claims unenforceable. Also, when will the victims of phishing attacks, which involve fake emails purporting to be from banks but demanding access codes, passwords, and so on, actually be liable if they fall for such attacks? These and similar questions cannot be reliably answered at the time. The banks in many countries have shown remarkable flexibility towards consumers and have compensated the victims in all cases where they have been reasonably careful. All of this, however, is a result of private regulation rather than direct EU intervention.

A study on the implementation of the Recommendation has been carried out, resulting in a report published in 2001.[38] The study, based on the analysis of legislation in then 15 Member States as well as on anonymous questionnaires, found a general lack of transparency from issuers to holders. There was a significant non-compliance in respect of a number of issues, in particular notification of loss or theft and the subsequent liability. Worryingly, in a number of states the burden of proof was placed on holders and the means of dispute settling inadequate. Finally, Denmark was in 2001 the only country to specifically adopt the Recommendation. Most other states complied differently with various parts of the document, either as part of other laws or through voluntary codes.

The present regime is a big and significant step towards Internet security. The Distance Marketing of Consumer Financial Services Directive, although a necessary and welcome instrument, has its limitations.

---

[37]　Article 8.
[38]　Herveg, J., et al., 'Study on the implementation of Recommendation 97/489/EC concerning transactions carried out by electronic payment instruments and in particular the relationship between holder and issuer', Call for tender XV/99/01/C, Facultés universitaires Notre-Dame de la Paix and Queen Mary and Westfield College, Final report of 17 April 2001.

Rather than talk about 'electronic payment instruments', as the Recommendation does, it limits itself to payments in general or credit cards. PayPal transactions, an increasing phenomenon, are not covered by Article 8.

3.3 Payment Services Directive[39]

The Payment Services Directive (PSD) can be described as an attempt to achieve a single European payments market.[40] Judging the European payments to be fragmented, inefficient and non-competitive, the Commission reviewed the then legislative framework[41] and proposed a new one. The Directive sought to increase competition and market transparency while standardizing providers' rights and obligations.

The subject matter is payments institutions except central banks and public authorities when they act in a public capacity (Article 1). The Directive applies to 'payment services provided within the Community' (Article 2) but does not apply to a number of specifically listed categories (Article 3). The Directive does not replace the Electronic Money Directive, which regulates who can issue electronic money and under what conditions.[42] Payment institutions are, therefore, not allowed to issue electronic money but can handle payments where electronic money is used.[43]

Title 2 of the Directive sets out the rules for payment institutions, title 3 information requirements and transparency conditions and title 4 rights and obligations in relation to the provision and use of payment services. Titles 5 and 6 contain transitory and final provisions.

Title 3 introduces stringent information and transparency requirements. Recital 22 reinforces the already-established consumer protection installed with the precontractual information requirements of the Unfair Commercial Practices Directive (see below), the Electronic Commerce Directive (see Chapter 2) and the Distance Marketing of Consumer Financial Services Directive but clarifies the relationship between these and the PSD.

The Directive introduces measures for minimizing the fraudulent use of payment instruments. The user of the payment instrument is obliged to notify the issuer of any unauthorized or incorrectly executed payment

---

[39] Directive 2007/64/EC, OJ L 319, 5.12.2007.
[40] See Recitals 1–3.
[41] See Recitals 3–5.
[42] See Chapter 2.
[43] See Recital 9.

transactions within 13 months of the debit date.[44] If the user denies having made a particular payment, the burden of proof will be on the payment service provider.[45] In such cases, the fact that there is a record of a particular transaction will not of itself constitute proof that the payment was authorized nor that the user had acted fraudulently or in negligence.[46] Article 60 obliges the payment providers to compensate the users who have notified in accord with Article 58.

Exceptions to the regime are introduced in Article 61, which says that the user will be liable up to the amount of €150 in cases of lost or stolen payment instruments or in cases where the user had failed to keep the personalized security features safe. This provision puts a top limit on the user's liability in cases of negligence. Nevertheless, the user who acted fraudulently or failed to follow the terms of use or to notify of loss, theft or misappropriation with intent or gross negligence will be liable in full. This means that a user who loses a credit card or fails to keep the pin code secret can avail itself of the upper limit of €150 whereas the one who, for example, writes it down or gives it to another cannot. Member States may reduce liability in cases where the user acted neither fraudulently nor with intent ignored terms of use or the obligation to inform. This will be done by taking the nature of the personalized security features and the circumstances of loss into consideration. The notification has, in any case, the effect of exonerating a bona fide user. The provider has an obligation to enable the user to notify properly at all times. This must be taken to mean a 24/7 hotline available at normal telecoms prices.

This leaves a number of cases in a grey area. Should a user who guards his banking details but fails to update its Internet protection (such as anti-virus and similar measures) be able to avail himself of the protection? There is no clear answer to this question, and it seems that some disparity will remain between Member States who attempt to deal with these issues.

4. MARKETING REGULATION

The Internet revolves around advertising, it requires new models of getting product information to consumers at the lowest possible cost and the consumers' ability to adequately (in the advertiser's view) respond to

---

[44] Article 58.
[45] Article 59(1).
[46] Article 59(2).

the products. Advertising on the Internet is a new field for both consumers and corporations. The advertisers, on one hand, are finding consumers inundated with competitive products, often ready to change products and suppliers and ready to use the Internet to explore the alternatives. Consumers, on the other hand, find a bewildering array of products and services advertised on almost every site accessed. In such a climate, choices become difficult and resorting to reputable websites, such as Google or Yahoo, becomes tremendously important.

From the consumer's perspective, Internet advertising suffers from two problems. The first is: how will a consumer be able to choose between a fraudulent advert and a genuine one? A number of adverts promote fake goods or are operated by scammers who do not intend to fulfil their contractual obligations. They sell products that do not exist or their purpose is to extract money without providing adequate goods or services in exchange. Spam attacks in which consumers are offered the opportunity to buy cheap stocks at unrealistically low prices or phishing attacks where they are coerced into parting with their personal details, which would then be used for criminal purposes, are examples of these. Such advertising is subject to civil and criminal laws at both national and European level.

The second problem is: if the advert is genuine, how can a bona fide consumer ensure that the goods or services fit the description and the perceived purpose and that the transaction is described in sufficient detail? This problem relates to both the lack of information about a feature or a transaction (i.e., dimensions not stated clearly, hidden charges not declared) and the incorrect information (e.g., pictures do not correspond to the goods delivered).

4.1 Misleading and Comparative Advertising

A considerable achievement in answering both of the above questions and furthering consumer protection in the EU is the Misleading and Comparative Advertising Directive.[47] The aim of the Directive is to protect consumers from misleading advertising and its consequences and to lay down the conditions for comparative advertising. The Directive defines advertising in Article 2 widely, as representation in any form in connection with the trade that aims to promote goods or services. In such terms, it is not limited only to registered corporations but applies also to

---

[47] Directive 2006/114 of the European Parliament and of the Council on misleading and comparative advertising, OJ L 376/21, 27.12.2006.

individuals (selling on eBay, for instance, falls within the scope of the Directive).[48] Secondly, misleading advertising 'deceives or is likely to deceive' and because of its deceptive nature either affects consumers' economic behaviour or injures a competitor. This includes not only selling goods or services that do not exist, that is, false advertising, but also any other deception in relation to the representation of products. Comparative advertising is simply advertising which identifies the competitor or their goods or services.

Article 3 provides that, in determining whether there is misleading advertising, account must be taken of all the circumstances of the case, including characteristics and price of the goods and services and the attributes of the advertiser. Comparative advertising, that which identifies the competitor, is allowed under the conditions set out in Article 3(a). These conditions prevent the comparative advertiser from creating confusion, discrediting or misleading or, in the case of a trade mark with a reputation, from taking unfair advantage from such a trade mark. Article 4 of the Directive allows comparative advertising if eight conditions are met.

Article 5 obliges Member States to provide adequate sanctions against misleading advertising and to combat comparative advertising. This includes the possibility for organizations such as consumer associations to bring legal action. Voluntary control by self-regulatory bodies is allowed and encouraged (Article 6).

As the measure is a minimum-harmonization measure, more stringent ones can be adopted at national level by virtue of Article 8. Since the entry into force of the Unfair Commercial Practices Directive (below) the Directive's scope has changed. It now covers business-to-business misleading advertising and comparative advertising which may harm a competitor but where there is no direct consumer detriment.[49]

4.2   Unfair Commercial Practices Directive[50]

The Unfair Commercial Practices Directive (UCP) was drafted in 2005 as major reform legislation aiming to improve consumers' rights and

---

[48]   Article 2.

[49]   See Article 14 of the UCP Directive.

[50]   Directive 2005/29/EC of the European Parliament and of the Council of 11 May 2005 concerning unfair business-to-consumer commercial practices in the internal market and amending Council Directive 84/450/EEC, Directives 97/7/ EC, 98/27/EC and 2002/65/EC of the European Parliament and of the Council

positively influence cross-border trade. The Directive is based on two ambitious tasks. The first is to harmonize unfair trade terms across the EU by preventing Member States from distorting the free movement of goods or services for reasons falling within the scope of the Directive.[51] The second is to introduce a general obligation on traders to treat consumers fairly. The Directive is a full harmonization measure, precluding Member States from acting within its scope.[52] The Directive does not affect contract law nor rules determining the jurisdiction of the courts.[53] The consumer protection provisions deriving from either contract law or private international law are therefore left in place.

The Directive applies to unfair business-to-consumer commercial practices.[54] These are defined very widely as those being contrary to the 'requirement of professional diligence' and 'materially distorting the economic behaviour' of the consumer.[55] The Directive covers misleading and aggressive advertising practices (Article 5) with misleading practices being divided into actions and omissions.[56] The Directive operates with the notion of an average consumer which is to be understood in light of the Court's interpretation as an 'average consumer who is reasonably well informed and reasonably observant'.[57]

The Directive introduces objective criteria for determining whether a practice is misleading. It says that it will be so if it is untruthful or deceives or is likely to deceive an 'average consumer' (Article 6.1). In Section 1, the Directive particularly lists misleading acts (Article 6) or misleading omissions (Article 7) and aggressive commercial practices (Article 8) or harassment, coercion or undue influence (Article 9) as examples of unfair commercial practices.

---

and Regulation (EC) 2006/2004 of the European Parliament and of the Council, OJ L 149/22, 11.6.2005.

[51] Article 4.

[52] C-540/08, C-304/08, C-261/07 and C-299/07 *Mediaprint; Zentrale zur Bekämpfung unlauteren Wettbewerbs eV; Galatea BVBA v Sanoma Magazines Belgium NV*, 9 November 2010, not yet reported.

[53] Article 3(2) and 3(7).

[54] Article 3.

[55] Article 5.

[56] On scope, the Court's tasks in interpreting and the behavioural economics aspects, see Trzaskowski, J., 'Behavioural Economics, Neuroscience, and the Unfair Commercial Practices Directive' (2011) 34 *Journal of Consumer Policy* 377–92.

[57] See C-210/96 *Gut Springenheide GmbH and Rudolf Tusky v Oberkreisdirektor des Kreises Steinfurt – Amt für Lebensmittelüberwachung* [1998] ECR I-04657.

Whereas the practices in Articles 6–9 are assessed judicially on a case-by-case basis, Annex I contains a list of practices which are regarded as being inherently unfair. No analysis is necessary for these as they are unfair in all circumstances. The list contains 31 items of which many will be easily recognized in the digital world. For example, the Annex speaks of codes of conduct abuse (item 1), cases where traders falsely claim that their products have endorsements from public or private bodies (item 4) or paying for editorial content in the media without making this known to consumers.

The Directive has no special provisions for advertising on the Internet and such provisions do not seem to be necessary. The Directive's general scope should adequately cover most unfair practices on the Internet. Nevertheless, a number of questions are specific to the Internet and need to be answered. First, traders can operate partially or wholly through Internet sites. Such traders are caught in the scope of the Directive. If a trader is 'hidden', that is, uses the Internet to hide its real identity by, for instance, leaving favourable comments on websites, it will also fall within the scope of the Directive.[58] Second, social media, user-generated sites, blogs and comparison or reviewing sites fall under the scope of the Directive in all cases where they are not independent but operated by, paid for or used by the traders to promote their goods or services.[59]

5.   CONSUMER PROTECTION IN PRIVATE INTERNATIONAL LAW

Consumer protection in EU private international law predates the emergence of the Internet by more than 20 years. It dates back to the 1968 Brussels Convention on Jurisdiction and Foreign Judgments, which contained special rules on jurisdiction over consumer contracts. The effort to protect consumers was continued in the 1980 Rome Convention on the Law Applicable to Contractual Obligations, which, in Article 5, addressed the issue of 'certain consumer contracts'. In addition to that, a number of Directives mentioned in this chapter have a private international law dimension. This is usually limited to a declaration that consumers shall not lose, by virtue of the operation of choice-of-law rules, a right granted by a particular directive[60] or that a directive does

---

[58]   See Annex I, no. 22.

[59]   See *Carrefour c/Galaec (la coopérative groupement d'achat des centres Leclerc)*, 29 mars 2007, Tribunal de commerce de Paris.

[60]   Article 6 of the Unfair Terms in Consumer Contracts Directive

not establish additional rules on private international law.[61] In either case the accent is on protection – a consumer must not be deprived of security that an instrument gives them by virtue of a conflict with private international law.[62]

Consumers are vulnerable to litigation. They do not normally have the financial and other means to fight legal battles, either as plaintiffs or as defendants. This often leads them either to seeking alternative means of dispute resolution[63] or simply deciding to cut their losses.[64] The consumers who nevertheless seek to assert their rights through the courts in cross-border disputes face two problems. The first concerns the courts which have jurisdiction to decide the case, whereas the second is about the law applicable to it.

5.1 Jurisdiction Rules

Regulation 44/2001[65] harmonizes rules on jurisdiction in civil and commercial contracts and rules on recognition and enforcement of judgments. Section 4 (Articles 15–17) are dedicated exclusively to consumer contracts.

Jurisdiction in consumer contracts is regulated in Articles 15, 16 and 17 of the Regulation. Their purpose is to enable consumers, who are defined in Article 15 as individuals concluding contracts outside their 'trade or profession', to avail themselves of the potentially more favourable jurisdiction regime in the place of their domicile. These rules apply to instalment credit contracts, loans repayable by instalments and all other contracts where commercial or professional activity has been pursued in the Member State of the consumer's domicile or 'by any means' directed towards that state.

---

[61]   As is the case with Article 1(4) of the E-Commerce Directive.

[62]   In reality, however, this relationship is more complex, as was demonstrated in the case of Articles 1(4) and 3 of the E-Commerce Directive.

[63]   Exclusive arbitration clauses in consumer contracts have, in spite of criticism, been upheld in the US Supreme Court. See, for instance, *CompuCredit Corp. v Greenwood*, No. 10–948, 10 January 2012.

[64]   See Hill, J., *Cross-Border Consumer Contracts* (OUP, Oxford 2008), Chapter 2.

[65]   Council Regulation (EC) 44/2001 of 22 December 2000 on jurisdiction and the recognition and enforcement of judgments in civil and commercial matters, OJ L 12, 16.1.2001.

Article 15(1)(c), which brings a slight change from the Brussels Convention text,[66] caused some controversy in the drafting stages as it was claimed by e-commerce businesses that the 'introduction' of the 'destination principle' would expose them to litigation in all Member States.[67] To the opponent of this provision, it seemed that a mere availability of content on the Internet allows the consumer to invoke the jurisdiction Article 15(1)(c). The Article activates special consumer jurisdiction where:

> the contract has been concluded with a person who pursues commercial or professional activities in the Member State of the consumer's domicile or, by any means, directs such activities to that Member State or to several States including that Member State, and the contract falls within the scope of such activities.

In reality, the mere accessibility of a website is not, in itself, enough to trigger protective jurisdiction:

> The mere fact that an Internet site is accessible is not sufficient for Article 15 to be applicable, although a factor will be that this Internet site solicits the conclusion of distance contracts and that the contract has actually been concluded at a distance, by whatever means. In this respect, the language or currency which a website uses does not constitute a relevant factor.[68]

Further clarification is provided in the Commission's proposal:

> The concept of activities pursued in or directed towards a Member State is designed to make clear that point (3) applies to consumer contracts concluded via an interactive website accessible in the State of the consumer's domicile. The fact that a consumer simply had knowledge of a service or possibility of buying goods via a passive website accessible in his country of domicile will not trigger the protective jurisdiction. The contract is thereby treated in the

---

[66] Article 13(1)(3). The original Convention activated consumer protection in all cases where the contract was concluded pursuant to specific invitation or advertising and the consumer took the necessary steps for concluding the contract in that state. No policy change was intended by this rephrasing, see Nielsen, P.A., 'Comment on Article 15', in Magnus, U. and Mankowski, P. (eds), *European Commentaries on Private International Law: Brussels I Regulation* (Sellier, European Law Publishers, Munich 2007), p. 315.

[67] See in more detail, Øren, J., 'International Jurisdiction over Consumer Contracts in e-Europe' (2003) 52 *International and Comparative Law Quarterly* 665.

[68] Statement on Articles 15 and 73, accessed 1.8.2012 at http://ec.europa.eu/civiljustice/homepage/homepage_oo_on_declaration.pdf.

same way as a contract concluded by telephone, fax and the like, and activates the grounds of jurisdiction provided for by Article 16.[69]

Two things must be clear from this. First, from the litigation management perspective, a consumer *defendant* would, in any case, have to be sued in that consumer's domicile because that is where his assets are most likely to be found. Second, the consumer as *plaintiff* will not be able to sue in the state of his domicile simply because he has been able to access a web page there. On the contrary, more substantial contacts, akin to American 'active web sites' would be required. In that respect, it can be expected that European courts will develop their own versions of the Zippo Test.[70]

In the *Hotel Alpenhoff* case,[71] which involved an Austrian consumer and a German website, the Court decided that the application of Article 15(1)(c) depends on whether 'it is apparent from those websites and the trader's overall activity that the trader was envisaging doing business with consumers domiciled in one or more Member States, including the Member State of that consumer's domicile, in the sense that it was minded to conclude a contract with them'. If so, the website was directing activities and will be subject to Section 4 jurisdiction. Importantly, the Court provides a non-exhaustive list of factors which should be taken into consideration when deciding whether directing took place:

> the international nature of the activity, mention of itineraries from other Member States for going to the place where the trader is established, use of a language or a currency other than the language or currency generally used in the Member State in which the trader is established with the possibility of making and confirming the reservation in that other language, mention of telephone numbers with an international code, outlay of expenditure on an internet referencing service in order to facilitate access to the trader's site or that of its intermediary by consumers domiciled in other Member States, use of a top-level domain name other than that of the Member State in which the trader is established, and mention of an international clientele composed of customers domiciled in various Member States.

In any case, it will be for the national courts to develop their own approaches which, ultimately, may lead to divergence.

Article 15(2) allows a non-EU website, which otherwise has a 'branch, agency or other establishment' in the EU, to be subject to Section 4,

---

[69] European Commission, Proposal, COM(1999) 348, 14.7.1999.

[70] See Chapter 3.

[71] *Peter Pammer v Reederei* Karl Schlüter GmbH & Co. KG (C-585/08) and C-144/09 *Hotel Alpenhof GESMBH v Oliver Heller* ECR [2010] 0000.

provided that the dispute arises out of the operations of that branch. An American site with a branch in Ireland will therefore be subject to the consumer jurisdiction regime of Section 4 if a consumer contract arises out of a dealing of that branch with the consumer. It will be less clear whether consumers can sue in the state where they are domiciled if their dealings are exclusively with a generic website (e.g., the Facebook company is based in Palo Alto, California but has offices in various EU countries) if they cannot prove that they were dealing directly with the branch, agency or establishment.

Article 16 contains the protective regime that is the centre of Section 4 of the Regulation. Article 16(1) provides that a plaintiff consumer may *bring proceedings* either in the state where the defendant is domiciled or in the state where the consumer is domiciled. The discretion, in this case, is the consumer's. Article 16(2), on the other hand, says that proceedings may be brought *against* a defendant consumer only in the state where the consumer is domiciled.

Jurisdiction clauses in consumer contracts are subject to the special regime of Section 4. A choice-of-forum clause that violates the consumer protection provisions will normally be invalid. Article 17 provides that the mandatory protective provisions of Section 4 of the Regulation may only be departed from after the dispute has arisen, or if they allow plaintiff consumers extra forums or if both parties are domiciled or habitually resident in the same Member State at the time of conclusion and if the agreement confers jurisdiction on that state.

A choice-of-court agreement which satisfies the conditions of Article 23 remains valid if it does not contradict the provisions of Article 17. The majority of contracts concluded on the Internet which contain a clause to the effect that 'parties submit to the exclusive jurisdiction' of a state other than the state of the consumer's domicile will simply have the effect of allowing the consumer to sue in that state but cannot have the effect of preventing the consumer from taking action in the state provided for in Articles 15 and 16.

The Consumer Injunctions Directive codified EU law concerning injunctions which may be applied for and used in protecting consumers' interests.[72] The Directive harmonizes national law relating to injunctions aimed at protecting consumers' collective interests arising out of the Directives specifically listed in the Annex. The obligation lies on Member States to designate bodies (Article 2) which can respond to actions brought by qualified applicants (Article 3). The overall aim is to

---

[72]   Directive 2009/22/EC, OJ L 110/30, 1.5.2009.

improve the efficiency of consumer protection in the Directives listed in the Annex.

5.2 Choice-of-Law Rules

The Rome I Regulation[73] harmonizes national rules on law applicable to contracts. Article 6 of that regulation introduces a special regime for consumers. Article 6(1) provides that the law of the country where the consumer has his habitual residence shall govern consumer contracts. This will be the case only if one of the two conditions are fulfilled: either the professional had pursued his activities in the country where the consumer is habitually resident (the 'seller moves' situation) or the seller had 'by any means' directed his activities to that country 'or to several countries including that country'. The first situation includes a seller who physically operates on the territory of another country.

The second involves a seller who advertises his services and actively seeks custom, including the situation where the Internet is used for that purpose. Recital 24 expressly admits that it applies to Internet contracts, drawing an analogy with the Brussels I Regulation. Although the choice of language or the currency will not, on their own, constitute relevant factors, they help determine the seller's intentions. Determining factors may include information displayed in different languages, different currencies, local contact numbers or any attempt to target local customers.[74]

The parties may choose the law applicable to the contract in accordance with the regular rules on choice of law (Article 3).[75] Their choice may not have the effect of depriving the consumer of the protection of mandatory rules (which are defined as provisions that cannot be derogated from by agreement) of the law which would have been applicable, that is, the law of the consumer's habitual residence. This should be taken to mean that the parties are freely allowed to choose the law of a country other than the consumer's habitual residence, but that the consumer would always be allowed to invoke its mandatory rules.

---

[73] Regulation (EC) 593/2008 of the European Parliament and of the Council of 17 June 2008 on the law applicable to contractual obligations (Rome I), OJ L 177/6, 4.7.2008.

[74] Cf. Chapter 3.

[75] Article 6(2).

Special protective measures do not apply to contracts for the supply of services where these services are supplied in a country other than that of the consumer's habitual residence.[76]

Mandatory rules other than those referred to in Article 6(2) may be applicable and some of them will derive directly from Community law. Article 25 of the Consumer Rights Directive, for instance, says that provisions of that Directive are mandatory and cannot be waived.

5.3   Alternative Dispute Resolution

In spite of the existence of a consumer-favourable litigation regime, the low value of most disputes coupled with the discouraging nature of an adversarial resolution mechanism creates an intimidating climate. This can be resolved with more diversification in the alternative dispute resolution field and the creation of industry-driven mechanisms. The EU, aware of the problem, took modest steps towards these ends with recommendations on out-of-court settlement of consumer disputes[77] as well as with later measures generally aimed at ADR.[78] In 2011, two specific proposals for ADR in consumer disputes were tabled.

A directive on consumer ADR was proposed[79] with the aim of improving 'procedures for the out-of-court resolution of contractual disputes arising from the sale of goods or provision of services' in alternative dispute resolution. The directive is primarily concerned with the issues of access and principles that govern ADR (Chapter II) and information and cooperation (Chapter 3). Whereas the former improves general accessibility and makes sure ADR is transparent, impartial and fair, the latter improves communication between the parties.

---

[76]   Article 6(4)(a).

[77]   Commission Recommendation 98/257/EC of 30 March 1998 on the principles applicable to the bodies responsible for out-of-court settlement of consumer disputes, OJ L 115, 17.4.1998; Commission Recommendation of 4 April 2001 on the principles for out-of-court bodies involved in the consensual resolution of consumer disputes not covered by Recommendation 98/257/EC, OJ L 109, 19.4.2001.

[78]   See also the Mediation Directive 2008/52/EC of the European Parliament and of the Council of 21 May 2008 on certain aspects of mediation in civil and commercial matters, OJ L 136, 24.5.2008.

[79]   Proposal for a Directive of the European Parliament and of the Council on alternative dispute resolution for consumer disputes and amending Regulation (EC) 2006/2004 and Directive 2009/22/EC (Directive on consumer ADR), COM(2001) 793, 29.11.2011.

In 2011, the Commission also proposed a Regulation on online dispute resolution for consumer disputes (Regulation on consumer ODR).[80] The regulation is aimed at the 'out-of-court resolution of contractual disputes arising from the cross-border online sale of goods or provision of services'. Its main purpose is simply to ensure that ADR mechanisms exist for the resolution of all consumer disputes. Article 5 creates the European online dispute resolution platform in the form of a website accessible locally throughout the EU. The platform's main function is to facilitate ADR rather than act as a tribunal itself. In that sense, it brings the parties together, offers a list of competent ADR bodies and acts as a point of information for all sides.

---

[80] Brussels, COM(2011) 794 final, 29.11.2011.

8.   Data protection and privacy

1. INTRODUCTION

1.1   Private Life in the Digital World

Privacy, as a modern European understands it, is the ability to withhold information about oneself or, put differently, the ability to have a secluded sphere of life and to select which parts of one's life will be public. Historically, a 'private' person was one that did not participate in the public life.[1] The term was often taken as a pejorative, as an indication of the person's unwillingness to participate or lack of capacity to. Privacy as a *desire* to keep one's life from public view only became a value and was legally protected recently.[2]

Until late into the twentieth century the ability to guard one's life from the view of others was rudimentary and enjoyed by the few. This was not because the potential to violate it was absent, but rather because it was omnipresent. In addition, one's life took place in public, on streets, squares and markets, and people were expected to participate in it even before most were accorded the right to vote. An average nineteenth-century European or American would be familiar with the need and importance of confidentiality, understood as a right to protect information one guards in secrecy, but would have difficulties with the notion that *non-confidential* information may also be private. Modern privacy law is still locked into this paradigm of privacy as secrecy.[3]

In the modern age, as life retreated from squares into offices, houses and institutions, privacy became a protected value, and with it came the potential and desire to invade it. Once, the governments were the most likely to profit from such invasions. As late as the beginning of the

---

[1]   *Privatus*, in Latin, denoted an individual deprived of public or military office.

[2]   Warren and Brandeis are credited with 'inventing' privacy law in Warren, S. and Brandeis, L., 'The Right to Privacy' (1890) 4 *Harvard Law Review* 5.

[3]   See also, Richards, N. and Solove, D., 'Privacy's Other Path: Recovering the Law of Confidentiality' (2007) 96 *Georgetown Law Journal* 124; and Solove, D., *The Digital Person* (New York University Press, New York 2004), p. 8.

twentieth century, only a handful of states were democracies and most of them did not accord women the right to vote. The interest was, therefore, to control all elements perceived as being a threat to stability of the regime. Keeping records and spying, an activity as old as political life itself, obtained new dimensions as wealth and with it political freedom spread. But, as threats increased, so did legal responses to them and the first statutes and court cases came into being.

A significant portion of modern life no longer takes place in the public eye. Although homes and family lives, telephone conversations and correspondence may be protected, public participation in the digital world has made everybody exposed to new privacy threats. First, technology has enabled public dossiers to be assembled and be accessible more easily than ever while the law has made information gathering mandatory in many more situations than had previously been the case. Additionally, the information may be easily collated, creating more meaningful links between previously disjointed pieces of information. Second, businesses can assemble large quantities of information about their users with relative ease. The information thus gathered can then be used to target marketing or, being itself a commodity, can be traded. Third, the dynamism of modern digital life requires participation on a level which forces us to voluntarily relinquish information about our activities, the places we visit, the books we read or the people we befriend.

In our times, the desire to invade privacy comes no longer only from governments but also, and possibly primarily, from corporations and our fellow citizens. Governments expend the power of collecting data or accessing data that others have collected, often with little regard to the actual power to process the information and render it useful. The corporations, in a constant bid to gain an edge over the competition, strive to learn consumers' habits and use them to improve their marketing techniques. At the same time, other individuals stand to gain from having an insight into our lives. Their reasons range from illegal ones, such as identity theft, to illegitimate ones, such as gaining advantage by learning what our superiors think of us, to relatively harmless ones driven by curiosity about others' television or reading habits.

In the digital age, the potential to gather data is vast, the means to violate accessible and cheap and the potential damage high and un-predictable. The reason for legislative intervention seems, therefore, to be obvious. On the other hand, lack of privacy has other unforeseen and deeper circumstances. It reduces the willingness to engage in activities

that 'promote democratic self-rule'.[4] 'A realm of autonomous, un-
monitored choice ... promotes a vital diversity of speech and behaviour'[5]
and is essential for developing and maintaining a democratic society.

The availability of data, in itself, is not a novelty. Neither is the ability
to access it quickly, which has existed for several decades. Automatically
processed data has been the subject of regulation for some time now and
long before the advance of the Internet in the 1990s. What makes
databases in the digital age sensitive, however, is their ability to be
quickly and accurately brought into relation with other databases. This
ability has been created by the emergence of cheap raw processing
power. Searching for a name, a telephone address or an email on the
Internet will often result in data being presented which contains other
information of which the search term is just a part. Such information may
contain property or tax records, political interests or medical history.

Privacy needs to be in balance with other constitutionally protected
values such as the right to free speech, the right of the public to know or
the right to security. It is normally assumed by Internet scholars that the
advent of the digital age presents particular problems for privacy, but
the relationship between technology and privacy is complex.[6] While
the debate continues, it seems increasingly clear that some features of the
Internet do pose a particular threat to privacy. Among those is the
decreasing cost of storage capacity and the availability of networked
systems as well as the availability to collate information.[7]

In the United States, the right to privacy in common law came to be
discussed only towards the end of the nineteenth century.[8] The American
Constitution does not protect privacy directly but infers it from other
constitutional provisions or other laws. Initially, the right to privacy was
cast as 'the right to be let alone' but, as Solove puts it, has in the
twentieth century also been conceptualized as 'limited access to the self',

---

    4   Schwartz, P., 'Privacy and Democracy in Cyberspace' (1999) 52 *Vanderbilt
Law Review* 1609.
    5   Cohen, J., 'Examined Lives: Information Privacy and the Subject as
Object' (2000) 52 *Stanford Law Review* 1373.
    6   See Posner, R., 'Orwell versus Huxley: Economics, Technology, Privacy
and Satire' in Gleason, A., et al., (eds), *On Nineteen Eighty-Four: Orwell and
Our Future* (Princeton University Press, Princeton 2005), p. 183.
    7   Cf. Bellia, P., Berman, P., Frischmann, B. and Post, D., *Cyberlaw –
Problems of Policy and Jurisprudence in the Information Age* (4th ed., West, St.
Paul 2011), pp. 625–7.
    8   On 'second generation of information privacy principles', see Kirby, M.,
'Privacy in Cyberspace' (1998) 21 *University of New South Wales Law Journal*
323.

secrecy, control over personal information, personhood or intimacy.[9] An important element of privacy, which protects against government surveillance, came through the Fourth Amendment. In *Katz v United States* the Supreme Court ruled that privacy cannot be invaded where reasonable expectations of privacy exist unless there is prior judicial authorization.[10] *Katz* was extended to electronic communications in the Electronic Communication Privacy Act 1986.[11] The act prohibits or limits the interception of electronic communications, the access to stored data and access to dialling and signalling information. The contribution of the American debate is in singling out those concepts and definitions of privacy which can be of particular importance for the Internet.

1.2 EU and Privacy

The European Union places a high value on privacy. Member States' constitutions directly grant protection while several EU constitutional documents do the same at EU level. The European Convention on Human Rights[12] protects privacy through Article 8:

1. Everyone has the right to respect for his private and family life, his home and his correspondence.
2. There shall be no interference by a public authority with the exercise of this right except such as is in accordance with the law and is necessary in a democratic society in the interests of national security, public safety or the economic well-being of the country, for the prevention of disorder or crime, for the protection of health or morals, or for the protection of the rights and freedoms of others.

The Article is the subject of a number of decisions of the European Court of Human Rights, which reflects its complex nature and which largely mirror the difficulties encountered in American courts of defining privacy. This chapter looks into some of the important EU legal instruments that apply to Internet privacy but does not reflect upon deeper underlying issues not specific to the European Union.[13]

---

[9] On the definition, see Solove, D., 'Conceptualizing Privacy' (2002) 90 *California Law Review* 1087.

[10] Supreme Court, 1967, 389 US 347.

[11] 18 USC §§2510–22.

[12] Which, in turn, was inspired by the United Nations Declaration of Human Rights of 1948.

[13] For an overview of data protection laws from the UK's perspective, see Carey, P., *Data Protection: A Practical Guide to UK and EU Law* (OUP, Oxford 2004).

The EU constitutional law also regulates privacy. The Charter of Fundamental Rights of the European Union provides in Article 8:

1. Everyone has the right to the protection of personal data concerning him or her.
2. Such data must be processed fairly for specified purposes and on the basis of the consent of the person concerned or some other legitimate basis laid down by law. Everyone has the right of access to data which has been collected concerning him or her, and the right to have it rectified.
3. Compliance with these rules shall be subject to control by an independent authority.

Finally, the Treaties also protect privacy.[14] Article 16 TFEU specifically provides a legal basis for action:

1. Everyone has the right to the protection of personal data concerning them.
2. The European Parliament and the Council, acting in accordance with the ordinary legislative procedure, shall lay down the rules relating to the protection of individuals with regard to the processing of personal data by Union institutions, bodies, offices and agencies, and by the Member States when carrying out activities which fall within the scope of Union law, and the rules relating to the free movement of such data. Compliance with these rules shall be subject to the control of independent authorities.

The rules adopted on the basis of this Article shall be without prejudice to the specific rules laid down in Article 39 of the Treaty on European Union.

The fundamentals of EU data protection were built in the 1995 Data Protection Directive.[15] In 2002, the E-Privacy Directive[16] addressed some

---

[14] Article 39 TEU, Article 16 TFEU.

[15] Directive 95/46 of the European Parliament and the Council of 24 October 1995 on the protection of individuals with regard to the processing of personal data and on the free movement of such data, OJ L 281, 23.11.1995. For more details, see Kaspersen, H., 'Data Protection and E-Commerce', in Lodder, A. and Kaspersen, H., *eDirectives: Guide to European Union Law on E-Commerce* (Kluwer, The Hague 2002), p. 119; Carey, P., *Data Protection: A Practical Guide to UK and EU Law* (OUP, Oxford 2004); Kuner, C., *European Data Privacy Law and Online Business* (OUP, Oxford 2003); Article-by-article comment in Büllesbach, A., et al., (eds), *Concise European IT Law* (Kluwer, The Hague 2006).

[16] Directive 2002/58/EC of 12 July 2002 of the European Parliament and of the Council concerning the processing of personal data and the protection of privacy in the electronic communications sector, OJ L 201, 31.7.2002. Amended in Directive 2009/136/EC, OJ L 337/11, 18.11.2009.

of the challenges of the digital world while leaving the main Directive in place. Acutely aware of the technological challenges of modern life, the Commission reassessed the regime in the 2010 Communication on data protection,[17] proposing a new General Data Protection Regulation[18] and a new Police and Criminal Justice Data Protection Directive[19] in 2011.

2. DATA PROTECTION DIRECTIVE

2.1 Introduction

The current directive on data protection was not the first European instrument to cover the issue of data protection. It was preceded by the convention on the protection of automatically processed personal data drafted by the Council of Europe in 1981.[20] The convention, which came into force in 1985, was a source of law in many European states and the Commission's original plan was for all Member States to ratify it. In the EU, however, not all Member States did. Further to that, there was some dissatisfaction with the rules it provided, which were viewed as antiquated and unsuitable for a digital world. Therefore, the Community began work on its own instrument in the early 1990s, culminating in the adoption in 1995 of the final text.

The European regime is made up of elements of data protection found in Member States, notably French and German, adopting the best solutions, some of which accord a high level of protection to privacy. As recognized in Recital 8, disparities in levels of protection between Member States may obstruct the flow of data. However, the Directive is

---

[17] Communication from the Commission to the European Parliament, the Council, the Economic and Social Committee and the Committee of the Regions, A comprehensive approach on personal data protection in the European Union, COM(2010) 609 final, Brussels, 4.11.2010.

[18] Proposal for a Regulation of the European Parliament and of the Council on the protection of individuals with regard to the processing of personal data and on the free movement of such data (General Data Protection Regulation), COM(2012) 11 final, 25.1.2011.

[19] Proposal for a Directive of the European Parliament and of the Council on the protection of individuals with regard to the processing of personal data by competent authorities for the purposes of prevention, investigation, detection or prosecution of criminal offences or the execution of criminal penalties, and the free movement of such data, COM(2012) 10, 25.1.2012.

[20] Convention for the Protection of Individuals with regard to Automatic Processing of Personal Data, ET NR 108, or 'Convention 108'.

used as a framework instrument for national legislators, giving them enough flexibility, as evidenced in Article 5, but instituting a high level of protection which other instruments may complement (as is the case with the E-Privacy Directive).

The Directive aims at a high level of protection. This is based on the idea that an Internal Market requires not only conditions for a free flow of data but also a high level of protection of fundamental rights, including the right to privacy. The information economy brings with itself an increasing flow of data between Member States and with it the increased risk of privacy violation. The Directive aims at full harmonization, precluding Member States' action in the area falling within its scope.[21]

The Directive has dual aims, as evidenced in Article 1. The first aim is to enable the free flow of data, and in this respect the Member States take the obligation of preventing any obstacles that may arise to this. The second obligation is to protect 'fundamental rights and freedoms of natural persons' with the particular aim of protecting the right to privacy.

The scope of the Directive is defined in Article 2(a) – it applies to 'any information relating to an identified or identifiable natural person'. The directive applies to personal data of natural, not legal, persons. Such information is personal if 'it enables the direct or indirect identification of the person concerned'. This definition creates a sufficiently wide scope for the directive. The exclusion of corporate data means the exclusion of trade secrets law from the scope of the Directive.

The processing of personal data is defined as any operation performed on data, but the Directive only applies to personal data processed 'wholly or partially by automatic means'.[22] Also, it applies to processing other than by automatic means where personal data form part of a filing system.[23] It specifically does not apply to police and judicial co-operation,[24] and also specifically not to security or defence. If processing of data is carried out for journalistic, artistic or literary purposes solely, Member States are allowed to introduce various exceptions 'to reconcile the right to privacy with the rules governing freedom of expression'.[25]

---

[21] C-101/01 *Bodil Lindqvist* [2003] ECR I-1297, §96–7.

[22] See Article 3. Manual processing is covered only in so far as it forms part of a filing system.

[23] This means, under Article 2(c), a structured set of personal data accessible according to specific criteria.

[24] Which used to be the Second and Third Pillar structure of EU law, now eliminated under the Lisbon Treaty.

[25] See Article 9.

Finally, activities of natural persons in a private or household context are also excluded.

The main addressees of the obligations in the Directive are 'controllers' – persons, natural or legal, who 'determine[s] the purposes and means of processing of data'. This is a wide definition but, in practice, applies to *any* body, corporate or not, in the position to manipulate personal data. The concept is different from 'operator', which is simply a person who manipulates the data on behalf of the controller. A national gas company, an airline and a university are, according to this, all controllers of data.

Article 4 regulates the territorial application of EU data protection law. If the controller is established in an EU Member State, the controller will be subject to the law of that state. Where the controller is established in several Member States, the laws of each of them have to be complied with. The controller will also be subject to the laws of the Member States in which the controller is not established but in which the equipment for processing personal data (except for transitory purposes) is situated.

The chosen territorial regime is awkward.[26] It leads to situations where EU law applies to controllers who have no connection with the EU other than the fact that they use or rent the equipment physically located in the EU. It also leads to situations where EU law does *not* apply to controllers outside the EU who deal exclusively or largely with EU customers and have no processing equipment located in the EU.

2.2 Data Controllers – Quality and Legitimacy in Collection and Processing

A number of principles were developed that bind the controllers in their processing of data. The Directive distinguishes between collection and processing. The first principle contained in Article 6 is that data should be *processed* 'fairly and lawfully'.[27] The second principle is that data

---

[26] See Moerel, L., 'The Long Arm of EU Data Protection Law: Does the Data Protection Directive apply to Processing of Personal Data of EU Citizens by Websites Worldwide?' (2011) 1 *International Data Privacy Law* 28.

[27] In practice, this coincides with the conditions set out in Article 7 of the Directive (legitimacy). For example, an illegally collected list of email addresses will not meet these conditions, as the data subject has not given his consent. The data controller must provide certain information to the data subject when it collects data for the first time. Most important here is the data subject's consent, which may be obtained by a number of methods. The most famous are the opt-in

shall be *collected* for 'specified, explicit and legitimate purposes'. Moreover, legitimately collected data may be subject to illegitimate processing. For instance, information on online purchasing habits collected with the aid of cookies may be used to push advertising. Therefore, Article 6(1)(b) leaves it to Member States to provide adequate safeguards for further processing of such data. This may be for historical, statistical or scientific purposes. The third principle is that personal data must be adequate, relevant and not excessive for the purpose for which they are collected. They must be accurate, and if not, shall be erased or corrected.

Article 7 sets out the criteria which make the processing of data legitimate. Personal data, according to that Article, may only be processed if either of six conditions is fulfilled. The first is that the data subject has given his consent. This can be given in the simplest of forms and is, in case of the World Wide Web, normally accomplished with the aid of a simple click on the button that signifies the acceptance, usually located at the end of the conditions. The second option is if the processing is necessary for the performance of a contract to which the data subject is party. An e-commerce sale agreement, for instance, will have a shipping and billing address and credit card details and may have a number of other situation-specific items, some of which may be sensitive (such as data on medicines taken). Other options are if the processing is necessary for compliance with a legal obligation to which the controller is subject or if the processing is necessary for the protection of vital interests of the data subject. Processing may also be necessary for the performance of a task carried out in the public interest or in the exercise of official authority. In this case the authority may either be in the hands of the controller or a third party to whom data is disclosed (such as the police or judicial authorities). Finally, processing may be necessary in pursuing legitimate interests, as long as these are not overridden by the fundamental rights and freedoms of the data subject. The last criterion seems to be too vague.

Certain categories of data are treated with extra care and their processing is prohibited, save in special circumstances. These are data relating to racial and ethnic origin, political, religious, philosophical beliefs, trade union memberships and those concerning health and sex life. The processing of these shall exceptionally be allowed where

---

or the opt-out clauses. In the opt-in, the user specifically adds his name to the register. In the opt-out, the user is automatically added, with the possibility to remove his name if he wishes so. Either method may be legitimate.

explicit consent has been given,[28] where employment law so requires or where vital interests of the data subject are concerned. Non-profit bodies and foundations with political, philosophical or trade union aims may process data if it relates to its members. Finally, processing may be carried out for data manifestly made public or necessary for processing of a legal claim. Specific derogation is inserted for preventive medicine and the medical profession, under the obligation of secrecy. Data concerning criminal convictions, other offences and judgments are subject to specific protection.

Processing of personal data is subject to a specific derogation in relation to journalistic, literary or artistic purposes where freedom of expression comes into conflict with the right to privacy. In such a case, derogations may be made in relation to special categories of data (Article 8), Chapter IV (transfer to third countries) and Chapter VI (Supervisory Authority and Working Party).

2.3 Data Subjects – Rights of Information, Access and Objection

The data subject has the right[29] to be adequately informed of the gathering and processing of data, including what is being collected, by whom and who has access to it. Furthermore, the subject has the right to access the data, correct it, object to its processing or object to its use for commercial purposes.

Articles 10 and 11 give the data subject the right to be informed of who the controller is and why data is being collected. The subject of this obligation is the controller. In cases where information is collected directly from the data subject, that subject has the right to know who the controllers and recipients are, the purposes for which data is collected, whether replies to questions are mandatory or voluntary and the consequences of not replying, that a right of access exists, and that data can be rectified.[30]

Where data has not been obtained from the data subject, the information is subject to the conditions set out in Article 11, negligibly different from Article 10. This relates to any case where the data subject has no control over whether they give information, such as in public places, but also cases where information is simply compiled without their knowledge. In such cases, the controller is under obligation to disclose the data to the data subject at the moment when they gather the

---

[28] National laws may provide that the data subject cannot give consent.
[29] Articles 10–15 of the Directive.
[30] Article 10.

information or, at the latest, when this information is being disclosed to third parties. The conditions include: (a) the identity of the controller; (b) the purpose of the processing; (c) other information, such as categories of data, recipients, the existence of right to access and the right to rectify.

The potential to obtain data on the Internet is considerable. The obvious means of such enterprise are not necessarily illegal. Cookies have been around for a considerable time and are a valuable source of information for those who place them. The Internet, however, exposes us to various hacking and piracy attacks where information is gathered illegally.

An important right of data subjects is the right to access data.[31] This is exercised by the subject against the controller. The latter shall, without constraint, at reasonable intervals, without delay or expense: inform the data subject whether data relating to him are held or processed; why they are processed; what categories of data they include; and who they are disclosed to. If this is performed automatically, the information shall also include the logic behind the automation. This is particularly emphasized in relation to automated decisions brought under Article 15. The data subject has the right to obtain from the controller the blocking, erasure or rectification of data that does not comply with the provisions of the Directive and the right to inform third parties that this action has been performed.

Article 14 covers the data subject's right to object. This shall, at least, consist in the right to object to data gathered in the public or legitimate interest as referred to in Article 7. A separate right to object exists in cases where data is processed for direct marketing or is disclosed to third parties for the first time or used on their behalf. Member States have a specific obligation to make the data subjects aware of the possibility to object to data gathering for commercial purposes.

Both Articles 11 and 14 are of considerable importance in practice as the incentive to obtain commercially valuable information at low cost has dramatically increased in recent years. Particularly valuable and marketable information includes names and credit records, valid email addresses and shopping habits. These are traded both legally and illegally for large sums of money. Electronic commerce on the Internet depends on the speed of transactions. Such speed often results in us overlooking the small print, which may include a consent form for the information to be shared with or passed on. Such passing of commercial information to

---

[31]   Article 12.

third parties is a sensitive issue normally covered in national legislation. In a number of test cases in the United Kingdom,[32] certain corporations engaged in advertising practices on their own or on behalf of other corporations. They included distribution of leaflets of third parties (*Midlands Electricity*, *Thames Water*) or passing on their own customers' details to third parties (*British Gas*) or an electoral register being sold for commercial purposes (*Robertson*). The common thread in all cases was the fact that data subjects whose information was held and subsequently passed on did not give consent. In some cases (*British Gas*), the data subject had the opportunity to remove his name from the register that the Tribunal ruled to be unfair.

Automated decisions are a reality of the society in which we live. They may relate to any issue, starting from banking and credit rating to various administrative decisions. Because of their importance, Article 15 specifically regulates them. Data subjects, according to this Article, have the right not to be subject to such decisions where the decision has legal effects or affects them in other ways. The exception is when the decision is authorized by another law or is taken in the course of entering into or performance of a contract.

The sanctions for violation of the provisions of the Directive are left to Member States but an obligation is imposed to ensure that those suffering damage as a result of unlawful processing are entitled to compensation.[33]

Controllers are allowed to outsource data processing to third parties under controlled conditions. The first safeguard is contained in Article 17(2), which provides that data controllers must, where processing is carried out on their behalf, choose a processor providing sufficient guarantees in respect of safety. It would seem that the data controller bears the main responsibility in terms of the Directive and that a contractual obligation exists between it and the processor. The Commission published in 2001 a set of model contract clauses for the transfer of data to processors located outside the European Economic Area (EEA).[34]

---

[32] *British Gas Trading Limited v Data Protection Registrar* [1998] TLR 393, Data Protection Tribunal; *Midlands Electricity Plc v Data Protection Registrar* [1999] TLR 217 Data Protection Tribunal; *Decision by The Data Protection Commissioner re Thames Water Utilities Limited* (unreported); *Brian Reid Robertson v Wakefield Metropolitan Council, Secretary of State for the Home Department* [2001] EWHC Admin 915.

[33] Articles 23 and 24.

[34] See Commission Decision of 27 December 2004 amending Decision 2001/497/EC as regards the introduction of an alternative set of standard

The clauses do not change the nature of the relationship between the controller and the processor but make it clearer.

In *Bodil Lindqvist*,[35] the Court had an opportunity to clarify some important Directive concepts in light of the Internet. The case concerned a private individual who, in the course of her engagement with the local church, had a web page set up. The web page contained private information about some of the parishioners. The Court first ruled that the act of naming persons on the Internet or referring to them by other means constitutes processing of personal data in light of Article 3(1) without any of the exceptions of Article 3(2) applying. The question concerning Article 25 was whether posting of data accessible to the public on a webpage means the transfer of data to a third country. The Court answered that it does not.

2.4   Prohibition of Data Export and the EU/US Safe Harbour Agreements

An essential feature of the data protection regime in the EU is a general prohibition of transfer of data outside the EU except when certain conditions are met. The reason for the prohibition is the fear of losing data protection standards in countries with a lower threshold of protection. Since data is regularly transferred on the Internet, this restriction is of particular importance.

The potential for infringement of the provision on the Internet is considerable. Computer networks of corporations present in more than one country typically make some or all of that information available in all of their branches. The practice of 'list trading' is also present on the Internet. The practice of outsourcing – transferring some of the work to another corporation – is dependent on modern infrastructure, including the Internet.

Transfer of data to third countries is regulated in Chapter IV. The main provision, Article 25, is that data transfers can be undertaken only to countries which ensure an adequate level of protection (adequacy criterion). Paragraph 2 lists the criteria to be taken into consideration, which include situation in both countries, the rule of law, professional and security measures, and so on. Data may be transferred to third countries in derogation of Article 25 in a number of situations listed in Article 26 and which include, among others, the user's consent, performance of a contract, public interest, and so on. The third possibility for transfers to

---

contractual clauses for the transfer of personal data to third countries, OJ L 385/74, 29.12.2004.
35   See C-101/01 *Bodil Lindqvist* [2003] ECR I-1297.

third states arises in Article 26(2), which allows transfers in cases where the controller 'adduces adequate safeguards with respect to the protection of the privacy and fundamental rights and freedoms of individuals and as regards the exercise of the corresponding rights' from, among others, contractual clauses. This, then, needs to be notified to the Commission and other Member States.

Article 25 of Data Protection Directive provides a basis:

> transfer to a third country of personal data which are undergoing processing or are intended for processing after transfer may take place only if, without prejudice to compliance with the national provisions adopted pursuant to the other provisions of this directive, the third country in question ensures an adequate level of protection.

The adequate level of protection is defined in Article 25(2), which does not provide a precise method for assessing this adequacy but provides, instead, the elements which shall be taken into consideration. Power is given in Article 25(6) to the Commission to create white lists of countries that are considered to fulfil the adequacy criteria in Article 25(2). The EU has set up, under powers given in Article 29, a Data Protection Working Party. The Working Party's role is advisory. It gives counsel to Member States, promotes Data Protection Directive and advises the Commission.

Exemptions may be granted for the export of data to third countries under the conditions set out in Article 26. Article 26(1) first introduces some general rules for exempting the export of information. The conditions that need to be satisfied are strict: the data subject must have given his consent or the transfer must be necessary, either for the performance of the contract or with a view to entering into a contract, or necessary for entering into a contract between the data controller and a third party but at the request of the data subject. Another ground is if the transfer is necessary for reasons of public interest or for one of the other reasons concerning the interests of the data subject (in legal proceedings, for instance).

Further to this, a specific exemption method for model contracts exists in Article 26(2) of the Directive. The idea is that a transfer may be authorized in the case where a potential controller issues guarantees in respect of the protection of privacy and fundamental rights. In particular, the Article provides, these may result from contractual clauses. The European Commission has issued a set of standard contractual clauses in

2010.[36] The clauses are designed in such a way as to guarantee the rights of data subjects and minimize the potential for exposure of information. Transfers of data to processors in third states, as opposed to controllers, are subject to lower standards.

A very important exemption, negotiated outside the scope of Article 26, relates to the transfer of data to the United States. The US and EU data protection regimes are different. In order to bridge the differences and minimize damage to trade, the EU and the US negotiated a set of principles that enable the US companies to comply with the requirements of the Data Protection Directive in a streamlined manner. The principles are based on Article 25(1) and 25(2). The significance of the exemption must be seen in light of the volume of data crossing the Atlantic in either direction but also in terms of political events.

The Safe Harbour principles were first agreed in 2000.[37] They are designed to permit the transfer of data to carriers in the United States on the condition that certain standards are respected and that guarantees are given by bodies of the US government which serve as overseers. In order to obtain a Safe Harbour status, an organization can either enter a self-regulatory program or design one itself. The self-certification is renewable annually at the Department of Commerce. In addition, the Federal Trade Commission or the Department of Transportation act as overseers.

The Safe Harbour regime imposes upon controllers the obligation to inform individuals that their data are held and what the purposes of the collection are. Data subjects are allowed to opt out of uses that fall out of the scope for which they were originally gathered. The opt-in system is accepted for sensitive information. The data subject must have access to information held about him and the right to amend it. Additional requirements relate to such issues as forwarding of information to third parties or enforcement.

The Safe Harbour regime is enforced both by corporations themselves and by the government. There are, on the other hand, both positive and

---

[36]   Commission Decision of 5 February 2010 on standard contractual clauses for the transfer of personal data to processors established in third countries, under Directive 95/46/EC, OJ L 39/5, 12.2.2010.

[37]   Commission Decision of 26 July 2000 pursuant to Directive 95/46/EC of the European Parliament and of the Council on the adequacy of the protection provided by the safe harbour privacy principles and related frequently asked questions issued by the US Department of Commerce (notified under document number C(2000) 2441), OJ L 215, 25.8.2000.

negative sides to using model clauses and the Safe Harbour regime.[38] The former provides a typical contractual regime, with all its benefits and failings while the latter benefits from government monitoring.

The situation for transfer of passenger data had to be negotiated separately. After the September 11 attacks, the US passed legislation requiring that airlines flying into the US provide specific information concerning passengers at reservation and check-in time. There were a number of items required, among these names, addresses, dates of birth, nationalities and credit card numbers, referred to as passenger name records (PNR). This information may include private and sensitive data. The US authorities typically demand that PNR be transferred prior to flights taking off for the United States. Non-complying airlines face penalties. Since such data transfers would contravene the Data Protection Directive, a separate agreement was concluded in May 2004.[39] The Parliament objected to the Agreement, claiming that adequate levels of protection were not provided. On 30 May, the Court of Justice concluded that the transfer of passenger records was a matter of public security and, therefore, outside the scope of the Data Protection Directive. The Court also ruled that the Agreement was illegal, having found that it was based on the wrong legal grounds.[40] In July 2007, the EU and the US had concluded a new agreement (the '2007 Agreement').[41] The new agreement sets out requirements concerning the purpose, technology, amount, type, retention, level of protection, access, redress and review. The present regime dates to 2011 and was finally adopted in the Council in 2012.[42]

3. PROPOSAL FOR REFORM

The desire to reform the EU data protection framework arises from the challenges posed by modern technology. The changes such as the global

---

[38] For more, see Carey, P., *Data Protection*, op. cit., footnote 13.

[39] The agreement presently in force is the 2011 Agreement between the United States of America and the European Union on the use and transfer of Passenger Name Records to the United States Department of Homeland Security, 2011/0382 (NLE), 8.12.2011.

[40] Joined cases C-317/04 and C-318–04 *European Parliament v Council of the European Union and Commission of the European Communities* [2006] ECR I-4721.

[41] The 2007 Passenger Name Records (PNR) Agreement, Council Decision 2007/551/CFSP/JHA of 23 July 2007, OJ L 204/16, 4.8.2007.

[42] See footnote 39.

rise of mobile technologies and user-generated content lead to increased productivity but pose threats to privacy. The new proposals aim to strengthen the rights of data subjects while enhancing the internal market dimension and improving enforcement.[43] The proposal consists in the General Data Protection Directive and the Police and Criminal Justice Data Protection Directive.

3.1   General Data Protection Regulation

The General Data Protection instrument is based on the new Article 16 TFEU and is issued in the form of a regulation to minimize the disparities between the Member States. The new instrument relies on the Data Protection Directive, retaining its key ideas but also adding new concepts and making a number of provisions more precise.

Territorial scope of the Regulation differs to that of the Directive. Article 3 provides that the Regulation applies to situations involving controllers in the EU but also to processing of data subjects resident in the Union by a controller not established in the Union where the processing either relates to goods or services offered in the Union or to the monitoring of the EU consumers' behaviour. Arguably, this connecting factor is both more flexible and more useful than that in Directive Article 4 which ties the applicability with the physical presence of the processing equipment in the EU.

Article 4 modifies a number of definitions and adds new ones for, among others, 'personal data breach', 'generic data', 'biometric data', 'data concerning health' and a 'child'. The principles relating to data processing have been clarified in Article 5 with the new principles of transparency, data minimization and controller liability added.

The criteria of lawfulness of processing have been improved. Article 6(f) now prohibits processing in the legitimate interests of the controller where the fundamental rights of the subject require data protection. This is particularly true of a data subject who is a child.

Although consent is only one of the bases on which data can lawfully be gathered, its practical importance forced the drafters to introduce a new Article 7, which regulates conditions under which this consent can be given. Importantly, the burden of proving that consent had been given lies on the controller. Where consent is given in the context of a written

---

[43]   Reading, V., 'The Upcoming Data Protection Reform for the European Union' (2011) 1 *International Data Privacy Law* 3.

declaration on another matter, the consent must be singled out. Data subjects have the right to withdraw their consent at any time.

A new provision (Article 8) now protects personal data of children. Data concerning children below the age of 13 years old can only be processed with the parents' consent.

Controllers' policies on data protection must be both transparent and easily intelligible (Article 11). The language must not be technical but 'clear and plain'. The controllers are obliged to install procedures and mechanisms (Article 12) for exercising data subjects' rights, which include provision of information, rights of access, ratification, erasure and portability.

Rectification and erasure are now placed in a special section, Section 3, which regulates the right to rectification (elements of Article 12(b) in the old Directive, now Article 16), right to be forgotten and right to erasure (elements of Article 12(b) in the old Directive, now Article 17) and right to data portability (Article 18). The latter, which is a new right, consists of the right to obtain a copy of the data from the controller for further use by the data subject.

The right to object is made more precise in the new Article 19 (previously Article 14). Of particular interest is the right to object to processing for direct marketing purposes, which shall be free of charge and offered clearly and explicitly and distinguishable from other information. The provision concerning profiling (ex-Article 15) is elaborated in the new Article 20.

The controller's obligations of accountability are spelled out in Article 22. A special obligation is inserted in Article 23 which obliges the controller to obtain state-of-the-art technology for processing data and to ensure that, by default, only the minimum of data necessary is processed.

The security of processing is regulated in Section 2, which is a set of more elaborate instructions than that contained in the old legislation.[44]

Finally, the provisions for transferring data to third countries have been significantly improved. Transfer may be undertaken pursuant to Article 41 when a third country meets the adequacy criteria. The proposed Regulation clarifies the principles controlling the Commission's decision and introduces a new geographical and sectoral application (i.e., transfer to federal and regional units). Transfer can also be effectuated through appropriate safeguards (Article 42) in cases where no adequacy decision had been taken or by way of binding corporate rules (Articles 43 and 58).

---

[44] Ex-Articles 17(1) Data Protection Directive and 4(3) E-Privacy Directive.

3.2   Criminal Justice Data Protection Directive

The EU instrument for personal data protection in criminal matters is Framework Decision 2008/977/JHA.[45] This measure is a minimum-harmonization measure which applies to the cross-border exchange of personal data. This instrument has limited scope as it applies only to cross-border data processing and not to processing which takes place only at national level nor to processing by police and judicial authorities.

The new Directive protects individuals in situations where 'competent authorities' process their personal data 'for the purposes of the prevention, investigation, detection or prosecution of criminal offences or the execution of criminal penalties' only.[46] The purpose of the Directive is to ensure that fundamental rights are respected in such situations and that exchange of data by these authorities is not restricted or prohibited for reasons concerning data protection rules. The Directive does not apply to issues falling outside the scope of EU law.

The Directive subjects data to the principles of Article 4 and requires Member States to distinguish between personal data of different data subjects (Article 5). These persons are suspects, those convicted of criminal offences, victims and third parties. These categories are granted certain rights (Chapter III), whereas duties of controllers and processors are covered in a separate section (Chapter IV). Data can, under Chapter V, be transferred to third countries under the principles and mechanism similar to those in the General Data Protection Regulation.

4. DATA RETENTION DIRECTIVE

The Data Retention Directive was adopted in early 2006[47] with the specific aim of aiding the fight against terrorism and related crime.[48] The Directive mandates the retention of data relating to phone calls and emails for a period of between six months and six years. The data thus

---

[45]   Council Framework Decision 2008/977/JHA of 27 November 2008 on the protection of personal data processed in the framework of police and judicial cooperation in criminal matters, OJ L 350, 30.12.2008.

[46]   Article 1.

[47]   Directive 2006/24/EC of the European Parliament and of the Council of 15 March 2006 on the retention of data generated or processed in communication with the provision of publicly available electronic communications services or of public communication networks and amending Directive 2002/58/EC, OJ L 105/54, 13.4.2006.

[48]   See Recital 10.

gathered is then available to national security authorities. The directive does not allow retention for any other purpose than those designated nor does it make it available to others than the designated authorities.

The Directive is a special law in relation to the Data Protection Directive and is related to the E-Privacy Directive and the Framework Directive.[49] The Directive specifically derogates from the E-Privacy Directive according to which data is only retained as long as justified. Article 1 provides that the Directive only applies in respect of communication services and data generated or processed by them. As confirmed in Recital 13, the generated data only refers to communication or the communication service and not to actual content of information communicated. Paragraph 2 of Article 1 confirms that data gathered does not relate to actual content. What is, therefore, retained is not copies of data itself but information *about* the data. The data relates to identification of the subscriber or registered user. The Directive applies to traffic and location data for both legal persons and individuals.

The categories of data to be retained are defined in Article 5. In general, the data relates to several categories of situations: data necessary to identify the source, the destination, date, time and duration, type of communication and equipment used (whether fixed or mobile). For the Internet and email, the data retained to identify the source is the user ID, the telephone number and the name and address of a subscriber to whom these have been allocated. Subparagraph 2 specifically prohibits retention of data relating to the content of communication. The period of retention is between six months and two years.[50]

The obligation imposed on the Member States by virtue of Article 3 is the retention of data specified in Article 5, when this data is generated or processed by public networks. This obligation is in specific derogation of the E-Privacy Directive.[51] The gathering of data does not relate to private networks or to private computers not connected to public networks. This includes the so-called Intranets, which are networks within an organization only available to their own members.

The right of access to data retained in accordance with the provisions of Articles 3 and 5 shall only be granted to national authorities and even then only in accordance with national law. Each Member State has a right to define the conditions under which this data can be accessed. This right

---

[49]   Directive 2002/21/EC of the European Parliament and of the Council of 7 March 2002 on a common regulatory framework for electronic communications networks and services, OJ L 108/33, 24.4.2002.

[50]   Article 6.

[51]   Specifically Articles 5, 6 and 9 of that Directive.

is specifically subject to the European Convention of Human Rights as interpreted by the European Court of Human Rights, to international and to EU law, a choice which may lead to disparities between Member States.

Member States are under an obligation to provide supervisory authorities, which may be the same as those required under the Data Protection Directive. These authorities have the task to ensure that the data complies with the requirements of Article 7 (which relates to, among other things, quality, integrity and access).

Three important points can be made about the Directive in its present form. First, the Directive is more restrictive than necessary. The European Parliament's Civil Liberties, Justice and Home Affairs Committee (LIBE) recommended that data be retained for up to 12 months only, and be obtainable exclusively upon presentation of a judicial warrant and even then only for crimes that would qualify for an European Arrest Warrant. In this proposal, there would also be compensation for the subjects of the obligation.[52]

The second point is that the Directive is a direct derogation of the important principles relating to security and integrity of information found in the E-Privacy Directive and the Data Protection Directive. The three instruments contain three separate lists of situations under which data may be retained. The derogation in Article 6 of the E-Privacy Directive says that traffic data must be erased or made anonymous if no longer needed and Article 9 states that location data must be made anonymous before processing. Data retention is allowed only in exceptional cases (Article 15) for safeguarding national security, defence, public security and prevention, investigation, detection and prosecution of criminal offences or unauthorized use of communications systems. The Data Protection Directive, on the other hand, talks of economic or fiscal interest and regulated professions. These divergent approaches create uncertainty.

The final point is that actual surveillance and extraction of meaningful information, even if the Directive's otherwise questionable legitimacy is accepted, is an expensive and difficult exercise that depends on human resources and adequate technology. Automated data monitoring can help the extraction of such information but meaningful decisions depend on human analysis, which is labour-intensive.

---

[52]   See European Parliament, Report on the proposal for a directive of the European Parliament and of the Council on the retention of data processed in connection with the provision of public electronic communication services and amending Directive 2002/58/EC, A6 0365/2005, 28.11.2005.

Finally, the Directive left the rules regarding the access to data or its use by public authorities to national lawmakers. In its judgment of 2 March 2010, the German Supreme Court ruled the German implementation of the Directive to be unconstitutional in its present form.[53]

5. E-PRIVACY DIRECTIVE – SPECIFIC PROBLEMS OF DATA PROTECTION AND PRIVACY ON THE INTERNET

The Electronic Privacy Directive has been drafted specifically to address the requirements of the new digital technologies, ease the advance of electronic communications services and create favourable market conditions for the digital economy. The development of new technologies should, according to Community drafters, coexist with the fundamental rights of which the most notable is privacy. The Directive complements the Data Protection Directive[54] and applies to all matters which are not specifically covered by that Directive. In particular, the subject of the Directive is the 'right to privacy in the electronic communication sector' and free movement of data, communication equipment and services.

Article 1 delimits the Directive's scope of application. The Directive does not apply to areas falling out of the scope of EU law. Likewise, it does not apply to issues concerning public security and defence, state security and criminal law. As a result, interception of communications of individuals or legal persons is allowed in the cases where state security demands it. At present, such interception is partially covered by the new EU Data Retention Directive.

In spite of its declared compatibility with the Data Protection Directive, the two instruments operate with somewhat different scope. Contrary to the Data Protection Directive, which specifically addresses only individuals, Article 1(2) makes it clear that the E-Privacy Directive also protects legal persons' interests. The inclusion of legal persons is an interesting addition. There is no doubt that unsolicited communication, spyware, viruses, and so on, affects corporations and individuals alike. In fact, the cost of such communications to businesses is considerable. On the other hand, the declared aim of the Directive is 'processing of personal data and the protection of privacy', a title distinctly targeting

---

[53] *Vorratsdatenspeicherung* [Data retention], judgment of 2 March 2010, 1 BvR256/08, 1 *BvR* 263/08, 1 *BvR* 586/08.

[54] See Article 1.

individuals. Recital 12 of the Directive does talk of the 'legitimate interests of legal persons'. These are not defined, but the Recital clarifies that Member States shall not have an *obligation* to apply the Data Protection Directive to those. It would seem that the Directive does not aim here to fight the more general data protection problems affecting legal persons but rather to protect them in their role as clients of various Internet Service Providers. In other words, the E-Privacy Directive protects ISPs' customers irrespective of the nature of their legal personality.

Article 2 of the E-Privacy Directive adopts the definitions of the Data Protection and the Framework Directive[55] and only introduces definitions that do not feature in these two. Thus, a 'user' is any person who accesses an electronic communications service, and not only a subscriber, 'communication' is any information exchanged electronically and 'electronic mail' is any text, image or audio which can be stored at the destination until requested. This liberal approach is welcome, as Internet traffic today does not follow the subscriber–provider model of the 1990s. The majority of people in the developed countries access the Internet both at home and at work and can access it in any number of wireless spots and often on their mobile devices. Had the Directive adopted the subscription model, their protection would have been significantly limited.

The services concerned are described somewhat awkwardly as 'processing of personal data in connection with the provision of publicly available electronic communication services in public communication networks'. The definition includes 'data collection and identification devices'. In reality, the aim of such a definition is to include as broad a spectrum of information society service providers as possible as long as personal data is being transferred on their networks and as long as those networks are public. Therefore, anyone who is publicly providing services – not necessarily for remuneration and not necessarily as an ISP – is to be included.

The first general obligation in the Directive is a mandatory obligation to provide security of processing (Article 4). The Directive recognizes that ISS providers are often not related to network service providers and demands that the two cooperate on providing security. Two factors determine the quality and degree of protection. The first is risk/threat

---

[55]   Directive 2002/21/EC of the European Parliament and of the Council of 7 March 2002 on a common regulatory framework for electronic communications networks and services (Framework Directive), OJ L 108, 24.4.2002, as amended by Directive 2009/140/EC, OJ L 337, 18.12.2009.

presented, which is to be understood as real or threatened danger. The second is state of the art of technical solutions needed and their cost. The duty imposed is to ensure, at least, that only authorized persons can access data and that data cannot be destroyed by accident. Paragraph 2 introduces a general obligation to inform subscribers of the risk of breach and any measures which may be taken. Paragraphs 3–5, added in the 2009 revision, deal with notification procedures in cases of breach.

The second general obligation (Article 5) is to maintain the confidentiality of information. The addressees are Member States, who are required to prohibit listening, tapping, storage or other kinds of interception or surveillance of communication and 'related traffic', unless the users have given their consent or the conditions of Article 15(1)[56] have been fulfilled. The confidentiality of communication is not violated by simple caching nor for purposes of providing a proof of the transaction. In reality, it is difficult to keep track of the exact purpose for which the information is stored.

The Directive obliges the providers of services to erase or anonymize the *traffic* data processed when no longer needed, unless conditions from Article 15 have been fulfilled.[57] Retention is allowed for billing purposes but only while the statute of limitation allows the payment to be lawfully pursued. Data may be retained for marketing and value-added services upon the user's prior consent (which may later be withdrawn). Article 6(5) expresses concern that data handling might be outsourced to organizations with low standards outside the EU and restricts the categories of actors who can handle data.

Where data relating to *location* of user or other traffic can be processed, Article 9 provides that this will only be permitted if such data is anonymized, where users have given consent or for provision of value-added services. Like in the previous case, users must be informed beforehand of the character of information collected and have the option to opt out.

5.1 Cookies

A particular problem concerning the lawfulness of gathered information arises in relation to 'cookies'. Cookies are small pieces of computer code, often no longer than a line, left by a website on the visitor's

---

[56] Derogations from the E-Privacy Directive under the conditions set out in the Data Protection Directive.
[57] Article 6.

computer. Cookies have three primary uses: session management, personalization and tracking. They help the website memorize the user's
identity and 'steer' his browsing, they 'tailor' the web page to the needs
of individual users and they gather information about the users' habits.
From the viewpoint of those who post the code, cookies are a source of
information both of immediate commercial value and a valuable and
tradable resource. From the consumers' viewpoint, cookies avoid the
need for constant authentication by memorizing the users' preferences.

Cookies do not carry viruses or malware but the risk to privacy they
pose arises from their data collecting capacity and the potential to pass
this data on to unauthorized persons. Whether cookies are a threat to
privacy depends on the amount of privacy-sensitive information they hold
and on whether the collector shares the information obtained with others
on the Internet. The information held will mostly consist of programming
code not comprehensible to an average user. This code may contain
sensitive information, such as username and/or password, the collection
of which is controlled by the web operator.

Cookies may be left by the issuer himself or they may be left on behalf
of third parties (tracking cookies). In this case, third parties are advertisers who track information about users, such as shopping habits and
preferences. What information the cookies store depends on the issuer
and user preferences. Some record only the identity of the user's
computer but others may contain more sensitive information. The users
are able to technically set the browser to accept all, none or only some
cookies. Cookies are considered an easy and convenient way for obtaining information about users but may be difficult to manage. First, an
average Internet user is not very likely to track the individual cookies
stored on the computer. Cookies are easily accessible in most browsers'
preferences but need to be looked at and analysed on a case-by-case
basis. Second, cookies, even if analysed, do not easily reveal what
information is being sent back to the service provider.

Where identity information is contained in a cookie, the issuer must
comply with data protection legislation contained in the E-Privacy
Directive. The Data Protection Directive does not contain special provisions applicable to cookies.

The early drafts of the Directive on Privacy and Electronic Communications proposed a ban on the use of cookies without consent. This was a
result of the Parliament's fear that customer data is being collected
without their knowledge and consent. The threat to consumer privacy was
perceived as something that would ultimately undermine consumers'
confidence in electronic commerce and seriously damage the prospect of
it being at the forefront of development in the EU. The proposed

measure, however, would have failed, as most sites today depend on cookies without which basic functionality would have been lost. The later drafts and the final version of the Directive introduced a more flexible opt-out regime: they allow the use of cookies but oblige the issuer to give the final user the opportunity to refuse the storage.[58]

In reality, modern browsers allow different privacy settings and permit the consumers to determine which cookies would be stored, for how long and when. Most consumers would, arguably, use these facilities rather than depend on reading certificates on individual websites. But it is also true that a majority of consumers have poor understanding of the basic technicalities of browser operation.

The 2009 revision of the Directive adds changes to Article 5(3), which affects information collected from users' computers, including cookies:

> Member States shall ensure that the storing of information, or the gaining of access to information already stored, in the terminal equipment of a subscriber or user is only allowed on condition that the subscriber or user concerned has given his or her consent, having been provided with clear and comprehensive information, in accordance with Directive 95/46/EC, inter alia, about the purposes of the processing.

The addition effectively requires the operators to obtain permission (opt-in approach) in all cases where information is collected in addition to explaining clearly the purposes and operation of the collection. The solution attracted strong criticism for being practically unworkable or very difficult to achieve. The Preamble (item 66) states that 'where it is technically possible and effective, ... the user's consent to processing may be expressed by using the appropriate settings of a browser or other application'. Although this almost certainly means that browsers *deliberately* set to accept cookies would satisfy the requirements of Article 5(3), problems remain with this solution. First, it leaves important questions to the Recital rather than the main text of the Directive. Second, technology, which is capable of reacting more quickly and being more flexible to problems than law, is and will remain a better way of protection against privacy invasion than any regulatory effort in the near future.

The Article is written in a technology-neutral manner, deliberately not naming any specific technological means which may be used to store data. This leaves the Article open to future technological developments.

---

[58]   Cf. Edwards, L., 'Articles 6–7, ECD: Privacy and Electronics Communications Directive 2002' in Edwards, L. (ed.), *The New Legal Framework for E-Commerce in Europe* (Hart, London 2005), p. 31, at 57.

Recital 25 of the Directive helps clarify some of the ambiguities of Article 5(3). Among other things, it provides that 'information and the right to refuse may be offered once' but may cover 'any future use'. Practically, this means that the option to opt-in should pop up the first time a web page is visited but need not reappear again. However, by default, this information does not appear and even if it did most users would probably disable the feature. The general policy of Recital 25 is that cookies should be allowed provided that: (a) users are given clear information according to the Data Protection Directive; and (b) given the opportunity to reject cookies. The Recital emphasizes the importance of this in cases where third parties may have access to cookies, such as computers in public places (libraries, universities, etc.).

Since Article 5(3) is technologically neutral, it covers any other files similar in form and function to cookies. Other files left on the client's computer, with or without their knowledge, can, for example, be the 'keys' that certain credit institutions place on hard drives to enable the users to access internet banking facilities. Viruses, Trojans, spyware and other similar software left without the user's consent also fall within the principle of lawfulness.

5.2 Spam

The instrument that initially dealt with the protection of personal data in the telecommunications sector was Directive 97/66/EC (Telecommunications Privacy Directive).[59] It covered such issues as itemized billing or unsolicited calls. The proposal to amend Directive 97/66/EC, ultimately resulting in the E-Privacy Directive, was motivated by the desire to bring it in line with the recent developments in the digital world.

Article 13(1) of the E-Privacy Directive introduces the opt-in regime for email for marketing purposes:[60]

> The use of ... electronic mail for the purposes of direct marketing may be allowed only in respect of subscribers or users who have given their prior consent.

---

[59]   Directive 97/66/EC of the European Parliament and of the Council of 15 December 1997 concerning the processing of personal data and the protection of privacy in the telecommunications sector, OJ L 24/1, 15.12.1997.

[60]   The sending of unsolicited text messages, either in the form of SMS messages, push mail messages or any similar format designed for consumer portable devices (mobile phones, PDAs) also falls under the prohibition of Article 13.

Emails for purposes of direct marketing can be sent only with prior agreement of the recipient. A natural or legal person who initially collected the data has the right to use it for their own commercial purposes, provided the customers have the right to reject such communications, either where it was collected either initially or subsequently.[61]

Member States have the obligation to ensure that unsolicited communication, other than those mentioned in Article 13(1), is prohibited. There are two exceptions in Article 13(3), either of which the Member States can implement into their legislation at their discretion. The first is situations 'where the consent of the subscribers' had been obtained. The consent required is not 'prior consent'. The second is 'in respect of subscribers who do not wish to receive these communications'. It is unclear in what form this lack of desire is to be expressed and at what point in time. The confusing formulations should be interpreted to mean that the Member States are allowed to choose between the opt-in and the opt-out regime. Articles 13(1) and 13(3) apply only to natural persons.

Article 13(2), which applies to both natural and legal persons, allows controllers who have obtained data in the context of a sale of a product or service to use them to market their own products as long as the customers can object to this, included in each email they are sent from the controller. Article 13(5) essentially prohibits communications to which the subscriber cannot respond or which conceals the necessary information.

Article 13(6) allows ISSs, as persons having a 'legitimate interest in the cessation or prohibition of such infringements', to bring legal proceedings in respect of the infringements. This measure is intended to enable ISSs, who have the financial and the legal power, to pursue violations which individual users otherwise would not be interested in.

A particularly sensitive problem is the use of location data – data that can help establish the exact location of the user's mobile device and target marketing to that location (e.g., sending book adverts when the consumer is in a bookstore). Article 9 of the Directive covers such eventuality. The Article allows the processing of location data only when processing can be done anonymously or where the user has given consent in advance. Users must be informed, prior to giving their consent, of all the details concerning the processing. The user, in such circumstances, must retain the possibility to opt-out.

---

[61]   Article 13(2).

The 2009 reform introduced an enforcement mechanism which obliges Member States to introduce civil and criminal sanctions.[62] The Member States retain, in addition to this, the power to order the cessation of any violation

6. CONCLUSION

There is no doubt that scope exists for improving the Data Protection Directive, notably in relation to new developments in information technology, new threats to privacy and enforcement issues.[63] In the short to medium term, the Commission's aim to concentrate on better enforcement seems both necessary and reasonable.[64]

The new regime, consisting of a general regulation and a special criminal directive, goes far in the direction of addressing new technologies and providing better enforcement mechanisms while protecting citizens. At the same time, the reformed E-Privacy Directive successfully supplements the Data Protection Directive while bringing the innovation necessary to cover digital technologies.

At present, it seems clear that the EU has gone further in protecting privacy than the United States.[65] Although this may be seen as a welcome development, the difficulties seen in the transfer of data arrangements demonstrate the complexity of the issue.

---

[62]   Article 15a(1).

[63]   European Data Protection Supervisor's opinion on Data Protection Directive implementation, 25 July 2007, OJ C 255/1, 27.10.2007.

[64]   So much was recognized in the Commission's Communication on implementation of data protection, Brussels, COM(2007) 87 final, 7.3.2007.

[65]   Specifically, cf. Samuelson, P., 'Privacy as Intellectual Property' (2000) 52 *Stanford Law Review* 1125.

9. Digital identity and electronic payments

1. IDENTITY AND CYBERSECURITY

Strictly, identity is 'the quality or condition of being the same in substance'. In other words, it is the 'condition or fact that a person or thing is itself and not something else'.[1] Digital identity is the quality of sameness as mediated by the Internet. It is the ability of an individual (or legal person) to prove that they are who they claim to be. The importance of the quality of identity arises from the desire to treat the Internet as a secure domain. Identity, in other words, is an element of cybersecurity[2] which, in turn, can be defined as the safety of the Internet as a platform for those who use it.

In everyday life, identity is proved by various means. A good but not always conclusive proof can be in the form of a formalized document such as a passport or a national identity card or a more complex one such as a face-to-face interview often conducted by immigration or passport authorities. Sometimes, presenting similar documents, such as birth certificates, driving licences or utility bills can have the same purpose as can presenting witnesses. What is common with these forms of identification is that an individual presenting the document is usually also present. This is never the case on the Internet. Increasingly, proof of identity on the Internet is becoming important for activities ranging from electronic government (e-voting and similar) to commercial transactions. The strictness of the proof of identity is proportional to the sensitivity and importance of the transaction. An e-vote in national elections, for instance, requires conclusive evidence that the individual voting is indeed the individual on the electoral register. A purchase of alcoholic beverages, pornography or certain kinds of medicines may only require proof

---

[1] Oxford English Dictionary Online (2007), accessed 1.8.2012 at www.oed. com.

[2] Rundle, M.C. and Laurie, B., 'Identity Management as a Cybersecurity Case Study', Berkman Center Research Publication No. 2006–01, September 2005, accessed 1.8.2012 at http://ssrn.com/abstract=881107.

that the individual in question is over 18 years old, without also proving the address or any other information.

The difficulties of proving identity on the web arise from two separate issues. The first is the result of technical limitations of the medium and the inability of a single platform to gain ground. The methods of proving identity are many.[3] They range from different authentication options operated by businesses or governments (such as combinations of login screens on banking websites) or mediated by third parties (the likes of NET Passport, PayPal and similar) to those that also require additional hardware (fingerprint or smart-card readers and eye-scanners attached to clients' computers). What is clear today, after almost two decades of Internet use, is that there is no common platform. The existence of such a platform would require that needs are similar where they are not and that basic international standards can be adopted where they cannot.

The second difficulty is the value placed on privacy by individuals and companies. At present, proving identity would require a database of records that could be consulted. Such a database would have to be managed either by an international body, or by a private corporation or by individual states. The first model is impossible to achieve in reality. The second is possible but sensitive for a number of reasons ranging from security to antitrust. The third model is more easily achievable but suffers from problems of international recognition to which non-electronic documents are also subject. In reality, although individual platforms such as national (electronic identity schemes) or corporate (PayPal) may work, there is no one efficient way of proving electronic identity today.

Authentication on the Internet can have two distinct aspects. The first concerns authentication of a person or a corporation on the Internet. This aspect relates to situations where an individual or a corporation acting on the Internet needs to prove to the other side that they are who they claim to be. One important aspect of the question has been covered in the EU in the Electronic Signatures Directive. The second aspect concerns authenticating one's payments in commercial transactions on the Internet. This is partially covered in the EU Electronic Money Directive.

---

[3] Rundle, M.C. and Trevithick, P., 'Interoperability in the New Digital Identity Infrastructure', Berkman Center Research Publication No. 2006–01, 13 February 2007, accessed 1.8.2012 at http://ssrn.com/abstract=962701.

2. ELECTRONIC SIGNATURES

2.1 Introduction

The purpose of electronic signatures is the same as written signatures: they indicate the originator of the document, confirming that the person who claims to have created it indeed did so. The terms 'digital signature' and 'electronic signature' are often taken as being synonyms but, in reality, they may designate different systems. A digital or electronic signature is a digital rendering of an ordinary signature (i.e., a photographic copy) or simply data in electronic form (words typed in the document). A special kind of electronic signature is achieved where a public or private authentication body confirms the identity of the individual using the signature, making such a signature qualified.

There are several approaches to the regulation of digital signatures. The first sets down requirements for the use of a particular technology. Electronic signatures are not recognized as such unless they are rendered in that technology.[4] Under the second approach, electronic signatures are valid in principle, with certain exceptions. Here, electronic signatures may have different impacts based on the strength of the technology used but the choice is left to individual authorities. This approach, which places no restriction on future development of the technology, has been adopted in the United States. Finally, the Electronic Signatures Directive combines the two approaches in that it recognizes electronic signatures in principle, but posts guidelines as to what constitutes a reliable technology.[5]

The United Nations proposed the UNCITRAL Model Law on Electronic Signatures in 2001.[6] The Model Law met with success and was adopted relatively widely, being seen as a step forward in facilitating electronic commerce between Member States, where divergent rules and lack of accreditation of certification service providers threatened to create barriers to the use of electronic contracts in business.

Article 7 of the 1996 UNCITRAL Model Law on Electronic Commerce follows a simple approach to electronic signatures:

---

[4] See German law: Informations-und Kommunikationsdienste-Gesetz [Information and Communication Services Act], BT-Drs. 13/7934, 11 June 1997.

[5] See Article 2 and the Annexes of the E-Signatures Directive.

[6] This is complementary with the 1996 UNCITRAL Model Law on Electronic Commerce.

(1) Where the law requires a signature of a person, that requirement is met in relation to a data message if:

(a) A method is used to identify that person and to indicate that person's approval of the information contained in the data message; and

(b) That method is as reliable as was appropriate for the purpose for which the data message was generated or communicated, in the light of all the circumstances, including any relevant agreement.

Directive 1999/93/EC (Electronic Signatures Directive)[7] was first proposed in May 1998, subsequently amended in 1999 by the European Parliament, approved in 2000, and was due to be implemented by July 2001. The Directive was designed to use 'public key cryptography' technology. The sender of the message encrypts it using a 'private key' – an electronic code which is kept secret by the sender and is used to authenticate him. The sender also provides a 'public key' – a piece of information available to the recipient, which he, the recipient, will use to test whether the sender is in the possession of the private key. The keys are, simply, two pairs of numbers. They are not government-issued and can be faked or manipulated.

Directive 1999/93/EC on the community framework for electronic signatures is narrower than the 1996 UNCITRAL Model Law in that it only affects a certain class of electronic signatures. On the other hand, unlike the 2001 Model Law, it has the potential to apply outside the scope of commercial activities. For example, Recital 19 of the Directive quotes 'public procurement, taxation, social security, health, and justice system' as some areas where electronic signatures might be used in communication between citizens and government and/or economic entities.

2.2 The Operation of Directive 1999/93/EC

An electronic signature is defined as 'data in electronic form which are attached to or logically associated with other electronic data and which serve as a method of authentication'[8] This definition, which is the same as in the 2001 Model Law is intended to convey the link between data

---

[7] OJ L 13/12, 19.1.2000. See also Communication from the Commission to the Council, the European Parliament, the European Economic and Social Committee and the Committee of the Regions, Action Plan on e-signatures and e-identification to facilitate the provision of cross-border public services in the Single Market. COM(2008) 798, 28.11.2008.

[8] Article 2(1) of the Directive.

and the signature used to authenticate it. A signatory is defined in the 2001 Model Law as a 'person that holds signature creation data and acts either on its own behalf or on behalf of the person it represents'. A certificate in the Directive is 'an electronic attestation which links signature-verification data to a person and confirms the identity of that person'. The certification service provider is a person in charge of issuing the certificate.

Article 2(1) does not set requirements for an electronic signature other than that it has to be electronic and attached to other electronic data as the means of authentication. Any signature, therefore, can be recognized as such and will be so, under Article 5(2), which provides that Member States shall ensure that an electronic signature is not denied legal effectiveness and admissibility as evidence in legal proceedings solely on the ground that it is in electronic form, not based on a qualified certificate or not created by a secure device. The sender's name, added at the end of an email can, under these circumstances, be admitted in court as evidence.

The Directive makes a difference between ordinary and 'advanced electronic signatures'.[9] The latter have to meet more stringent criteria and are admissible as evidence and, for all purposes, must be taken to play the same role that ordinary hand-written signatures play in administrative and legal proceedings. In order for a signature to be treated as 'advanced' it must be:

- uniquely linked to the signatory;
- capable of identifying the signatory;
- created using means that the signatory can maintain under his sole control; and
- linked to the data to which it relates in such a manner that any subsequent change of the data is detectable.

On the other hand, Recital 21 says that 'national law governs the legal spheres in which electronic documents and electronic signatures may be used'. The Directive is 'without prejudice to the power of a national court to make a ruling regarding conformity with the requirements of this Directive and does not affect national rules regarding the unfettered judicial recital of evidence'. In other words, national courts will have open hands in deciding whether to admit evidence based on electronic certificates.

---

[9]   See Article 2(2).

It seems from Recital 20 that the aim was to equate 'advanced' certificates with hand-written signatures. However, the Recital says that 'advanced electronic signatures which are based on a qualified certificate and which are created by a secure-signature-creation device can be regarded as legally equivalent to hand-written signatures only if the requirements for hand-written signatures are fulfilled'. Member States are required to make electronic signatures equal with hand-written ones. They are, on the other hand, still allowed to deny them validity on substantive terms, such as because they object to the quality of the technology used in the particular case.

An important principle of the 2001 Model Law was technological neutrality, which enables any electronic signature technology to satisfy the technological requirements in Article 6(1). Article 5(2) of the Directive is meant to serve the same purpose. That Article, however, seems to be based on public key cryptography technology and does not spell out the equality of all electronic signing technologies, casting the success of that approach into question.

Article 6 of the 2001 Model Law provides:

1. Where the law requires a signature of a person, that requirement is met in relation to a data message if an electronic signature is used that is as reliable as was appropriate for the purpose for which the data message was generated or communicated, in the light of all the circumstances, including any relevant agreement.
2. Paragraph 1 applies whether the requirement referred to therein is in the form of an obligation or whether the law simply provides consequences for the absence of a signature.

Article 5(1) of the Electronic Signatures Directive provides:

Member States shall ensure that advanced electronic signatures which are based on a qualified certificate and which are created by a secure-signature-creation device ... satisfy the legal requirements of a signature in relation to data in electronic form in the same manner as a hand-written signature satisfies those requirements in relation to paper-based data.

Annex I of the Directive gives criteria for determining a qualified *certificate*. The *certification service provider*, on the other hand, must meet the criteria in Annex II of the Directive. A *device* that creates electronic signatures, 'Secure-Signature-Creation Device', must satisfy the requirements in Annex III. Finally, Annex IV sets out recommendations for *verification* through 'Secure Signature Verification'

The requirement, in Article 5(1), that electronic signatures be accepted as evidence is unnecessary.[10] Firstly, Member States already all recognize them as such. Secondly, the Directive recitals point to the national courts as final arbitrators of the admissibility of electronic signatures.

It will be noted that the requirement that an electronic signature has to fulfil in order to get the status similar to that of a written signature, is as set out in Article 6 of the 2001 Model Law. Arguably, this is a flexible solution that expands the number of signatures that can potentially be accorded this status. The Directive, on the other hand, introduces in Article 5(1) some technical requirements that need to be fulfilled initially. First, the signature must be an 'advanced electronic signature'. To be recognized as such, it must meet four criteria: it must be uniquely linked to the signatory; it must be capable of identifying the signatory; it must be created using means that the signatory can control; and it must be linked to the related data, making subsequent changes of data detectable.[11] Second, it needs to be based on a qualified certificate and, third, it has to be created using a secure-signature-creation device. This is a relatively high threshold. In the 2001 Model Law, Article 6(3), an electronic signature will be considered to be reliable where (a) the signature creation data is linked to the signatory only, (b) the signature creation data were, at the time of signing, under the control of the signatory only, and (c) any alteration to the electronic signature is detectable.

On the other hand, Article 5(2) provides that an electronic signature that otherwise does not satisfy the conditions in the first paragraph shall nevertheless be accorded 'legal effectiveness and admissibility as evidence in legal proceedings'. This can also be seen as an interesting derogation from the requirements of Article 5(1) and a silent admission of the difficulty of their satisfaction.

In reality, 'advanced electronic signatures' are not widely accepted and their increased use in the future will depend on market forces. On the other hand, public key infrastructure (PKI), which is meant to make digital signatures widely available and used in daily transactions, suffers from problems relating to the certification authority's liability, operating

---

[10] See also Dumortier, J., 'Directive 1999/93/EC on a Community Framework for Electronic Signatures' in Lodder, A. and Kaspersen, H., *eDirectives: Guide to European Union Law on E-Commerce* (Kluwer Law International, The Hague/London/New York 2002), p. 56.

[11] See Griffiths, D.H. and Harrison, J., 'European Union' in Campbell, D., *E-Commerce and the Law of Digital Signatures* (Oceana Publications, Inc., Dobbs Ferry, NY 2005), p. 743.

standards and security. The technology, although largely in place, is simply too risky both in terms of security and in terms of its openness to litigation.

There is no provision in the Directive that regulates the conduct of *signatories*. This is an omission, as Article 8 of the 2001 Model Law has detailed provisions in this area. It provides, among other things, that signatories shall exercise reasonable care and notify any person who may rely on the signature that data might have been compromised.

The story is entirely different with the conduct of *certification service providers* (CSPs). These are liable for acts and omissions that result from the services they provide. There is a difference in the approach between the 2001 Model Law and the Directive. The former sets out, in Article 9(1), a number of requirements that providers have to fulfil and then provides that they shall bear the consequences for failing to do so. The latter provides that a certification service provider is liable for damage caused by inaccuracies and omissions at the time of issuing and failure to register revocation. This is a somewhat more rigid approach than that found in the 2001 Model Law, although the standard is, in both cases, that of negligence.[12]

Article 10 of the 2001 Model Law sets out a number of requirements that help determine whether the certification service provider's systems, procedures and human resources are trustworthy. No direct equivalent exists in the Directive, although Annex II covers most of Article 10, with the exception of the requirements of an independent audit and of accreditation.

The conduct of the relying parties is left for regulation by the Member States in both the 2001 Model Law and the Directive.

A certificate issued by one Member State shall be fully recognized by another, as if it was issued in that other Member State. For certificates *issued* in third states, Article 7 of the Directive provides that these shall be recognized if (a) the certification service provider fulfils the requirements laid down in the Directive and is accredited under a voluntary scheme, or (b) is issued by a certification service provider established within the Community or (c) either the certificate or the provider is recognized in a bilateral or multilateral agreement.

---

[12]   See Article 9 in the United Nations, UNCITRAL Model Law on Electronic Signatures with Guide to Enactment 2001 (United Nations, New York 2002).

Article 8 of the 1996 Model Law provides that, where the law requires information to be presented or retained in its original form, that requirement can be met by a data message if there exists reliable assurance as to the integrity of the information from the time when it was first generated in its initial form and where the information is capable of being presented. There is no equivalent provision in the E-Commerce Directive.

Data messages can, according to Article 9 of the 1996 Model Law, be admitted as evidence. There is no similar provision in the E-Commerce Directive. The only way to challenge this is through Article 9 of the Directive, on grounds of creating an obstacle for electronic contracting.[13]

2.3 Liability of Certification Issuing Authorities

Article 6 of the Directive introduces a minimum standard of liability for certification service providers. These provisions apply where the certificate has been issued as a qualified certificate according to the Directive. This is understandable, as the criteria introduced by the Directive guarantee the security of the certificate. The certificate has to have been issued to the public, a remark based on Recital 16 which makes a distinction between open and closed systems. The former are systems open to the public, the latter are systems based on 'voluntary agreements' based on private law. A certificate 'guaranteed' to the public is equated to a certificate issued to the public.

The liability is for damage caused to any entity or legal or natural person who relies on the certificate. Reliance can take place on three distinct elements. First, it can be as regards the accuracy of the information and the details contained in the qualified certificate. Second, it can relate to the fact that the identified signatory held the data corresponding to the data in the certificate. Finally, for the fact that data used to create and verify the signature can be used in a complementary manner, where they were issued by the same certification service provider. In all cases, the relevant time is the time of issuance of the certificate.

Liability is based on negligence and the certification service provider must prove that it has not acted negligently. The certification service provider will also be liable for failing to register revocation of the certificate.[14]

---

[13] See Griffiths, D.H. and Harrison, J., op. cit., p. 750.
[14] Article 6(2).

The certification service provider is entitled to register limitations on the use of the certificate, provided they are recognizable to third parties.[15] The issuer will not be liable for damage arising out of use that exceeds this limitation. In addition to this, a limitation may be imposed by the provider on the value of the transaction to which the certificate applies.[16] This limit also needs to be recognizable to third parties. In any case, the Unfair Terms in Consumer Contracts Directive will apply.[17]

Some doubt is caused by the wording of the Directive in relation to the claimant. The claimant is labelled as the 'relying party'. This is, naturally, a person who receives the signature and acts in reliance on it. Can the signatory be the relying party? It would not appear so, judging from Recital 16 that clearly excludes closed systems. Here, the law applicable to the transaction would be the law that governs the contract between the signatory and the certification service provider.[18] On the other hand, there is no reason why the provisions of the Directive would not also apply to this relationship, as there is nothing that explicitly excludes its application. In any case, national law is allowed to go above the 'minimum harmonization' standards imposed in the Directive.

3. ELECTRONIC PAYMENT

3.1 Difficulties of Paying Online

One traditional means of payment online is the use of debit, charge and credit cards. The use of such cards is regulated by various financial and consumer laws, all of which apply also to electronic transactions.[19] The use of such cards on the Internet differs little from their use on the telephone, where the transaction is recorded as being conducted with an absent cardholder. Electronic money performs a similar function to a credit card or real money, with the difference that monetary value is stored on the card itself. The information can normally be read either by specific instruments or by ordinary computers fitted with appropriate readers. For these to be useful in an internet transaction, a computer would have to be fitted with the appropriate reader. At the beginning of

---

[15]   Article 6(3).
[16]   Article 6(4).
[17]   Directive 93/13/EEC of 5 April 1993, OJ L95/29, 21.4.1993.
[18]   In this sense, see Dumortier, J., op. cit., p. 59.
[19]   For issues concerning consumer protection in financial transactions, see Chapter 7.

this century this was still a rarity. Today, however, there are a number of devices, notably fingerprint readers or smart-card readers that are typically found on laptops and, increasingly, on desktop machines. In such a climate, it is easy to envisage a situation where electronic money software is used to store the money and one of the readers is used to authenticate the user. In reality, however, this procedure is still not used widely, and is nowhere near as popular as PayPal or the use of payment cards.

Electronic money is not restricted to Internet use. On the contrary, it is particularly useful in situations where electronic readers may be widely available, such as in supermarkets, at gas stations, hotels, and so on. The role that electronic money plays on the Internet is directly related to the difficulties, real and perceived, of online payment. Recent surveys show that a large proportion of consumers still feel uncomfortable with making payments online. Some of that fear can be attributed to decreasing safety online, but others are a result of inability or inaccessibility of adequate payment means.

3.2 The Electronic Money Directive 2009[20]

The first Electronic Money Directive[21] was drafted at the time when it was widely believed that electronic means of payment would catch up faster than they did. In reality, the majority of consumer transactions on the Internet still use credit cards or electronic payment services such as PayPal. It was felt that the Consolidated Banking directive,[22] which already allowed electronic money, did not provide an adequate basis for this task.[23] Whereas Recital 4 of the old Directive made clear that the

---

[20] Directive 2009/110/EC of the European Parliament and of the Council of 16 September 2009 on the taking up, pursuit and prudential supervision of the business of electronic money institutions amending Directives 2005/60/EC and 2006/48/EC and repealing Directive 2000/46/EC, OJ L 267, 10.10.2009.

[21] Directive 2000/46/EC of the European Parliament and of the Council of 18 September 2000 on the taking up, pursuit of and prudential supervision of the business of electronic money institutions, OJ L 275, 27.10.2000.

[22] Directive 2000/12/EC of the European Parliament and of the Council of 20 March relating to the taking up and pursuit of the business of credit institutions, OJ L 126, 26.5.2000, p. 1, amended in Directive 2000/28/EC, OJ L 275/37, 27.10.2000, see especially point 5 in Annex I.

[23] The problem was that electronic money does not normally constitute deposit-taking activity as deposited funds would be immediately exchanged for surrogate money.

approach adopted was minimum harmonization, with the mutual recognition and general good system found in banking and other similar directives kept in place, the new Directive, in Article 12, confirms that the approach now taken is full harmonization.

Article 2.2 defines electronic money as:

> electronically, including magnetically, stored monetary value as represented by a claim on the issuer which is issued on receipt of funds for the purpose of making payment transactions [as defined in the PSD Directive] and which is accepted by a natural or legal person other than the electronic money issuer;

Recital 7 confirms that this means 'pre-paid stored value in exchange for funds, which can be used for payment purposes because it is accepted by third persons as a payment'.

The aim, as evident from that Recital, was to establish a technology-neutral framework that could be used for future products as they were developed. At present, electronic devices can be understood to be software systems, smart cards or account-based programs.[24]

In the first situation, proprietary software is used to store electronic money on the user's hard drive. Such information would normally be encrypted or secured in other ways to ensure that only the user can access it. It is worth remembering that, at the time of drafting, there were actually no successful electronic money products of this sort. The second method involves the use of smart cards which are similar in appearance to credit cards. These seem to have been taken up in limited contexts, although some shops have introduced them, and experiments have been conducted using mobile phones as smart cards.

The final method relies on user authentication and is not tied to a specific machine. The user has a registered account with some value stored on it, but authenticates by entering a combination of a password, username and other similar information. By far the most successful system so far is PayPal which has attracted millions of users. The system is simple. The buyer opens a PayPal account and registers and authorizes for use a credit or a debit card. The seller does the same. At the time of transaction, the buyer logs into his PayPal account and authorizes the amount of sale. The seller logs into his and collects the money. It is also possible to preload a certain sum of money or use a credit or debit card.

---

[24]   See Guadamuz, A. and Usher, J., 'The EC Electronic Money Directive 2000; Electronic Money: The European Regulatory Approach' in Edwards, L. (ed.), *The New Legal Framework for E-Commerce in Europe* (Hart, Oxford and Portland 2005), p. 173, at 176.

The advantage of the system is its simplicity. It avoids the complexity and cost of accepting credit and debit cards and gives the option to register different cards with only one account/password combination.

The mentioned issue illustrates the difficulties faced by the drafters in the Commission. On one hand, the Directive proclaims to be technology neutral. On the other, it clearly leans towards smart-card systems. The Directive has the potential to be applied to other new technologies but not without difficulty. Redrafting may appear to be the best solution.

The Directive applies to electronic money institutions, which means, according to Article 2, a legal person which has been granted authorization under Title II to issue electronic money. These requirements, which are in line with the PSD Directive, relate to prudential supervision and have been made substantially easier to fulfil since the 2001 version of the Directive. The Directive explicitly does not apply to monetary value stored on devices or cards which can only be used on the issuer's premises.[25] In addition, and according to Article 1(5), the Directive does not apply to:

> payment transactions executed by means of any telecommunication, digital or IT device, where the goods or services purchased are delivered to and are to be used through a telecommunication, digital or IT device, provided that the telecommunication, digital or IT operator does not act only as an intermediary between the payment service user and the supplier of the goods and services.

In other words, the Directive does not apply to digital purchases of goods which are used digitally but applies to purchases where the IT equipment is only used as an intermediary, that is, payment is effectuated online but goods are physically delivered.

In order for the payment method to be recognized as electronic money, Article 2 provides that it has to be (a) stored electronically or magnetically, (b) represented as a claim on the issuers issued on the receipt of funds, (c) for the purpose of making payments as defined in the PSD Directive, and (d) accepted by natural and legal persons other than the issuer. This last point disqualifies various store reward cards (such as those used in supermarkets or chemists) or cards used for paying within corporations (e.g., for meals). Importantly, this would also exclude some digital cash systems used for payment on the Internet in case they only operate with a closed number of participating institutions and are therefore more like proprietary cash. Such transactions would still be governed by regular credit laws.

---

[25] Article 1(4).

There are some reasons to believe that PayPal does not fall under the provisions of the E-Money Directive.[26] Primarily, the company does not store money in an electronic device but rather uses the already existing bank accounts to mediate between the seller and the buyer. More importantly, an account-based organization appears to fall both under the provisions of a traditional credit-taking institution and the provision of the E-Money Directive. In other words, they appear to be taking deposits within the meaning of the Consolidated Banking Directive. On the other hand, such deposits are not used for investments or for operational costs, taking them out of the scope of provisions applicable to credit institutions.[27] Also, PayPal styles itself as an 'e-money payment service' and is recognized as such in the United Kingdom. The issue remains unresolved but the majority of Member States' legal systems are likely inclined towards recognition of PayPal as electronic money.

Only the credit institutions as defined in Article 1.1 may issue electronic money. Such institutions wishing to conduct activities other than issuing electronic money must fall under one or more of the provisions of Article 6. Otherwise, for areas out of the scope of this directive, other EU and national banking provisions shall apply to the business of credit institutions.[28]

The Directive introduces a number of specific rules designed to facilitate electronic money transactions. Article 11 provides that electronic money must be redeemable at par value during the period of validity. The initial capital, originally set at not less than €1 million and with own funds amounting to 2 per cent or more of the previous six months' proceedings, has now been lowered to €350,000.[29] The safeguarding requirements of the institutions are regulated in Article 7 and serve the purpose of minimizing the risk. Article 9 allows the Member States to waive some of the requirements in a number of exceptional situations.

---

[26]   For a more detailed discussion, see Guadamuz, A. and Usher, J., op. cit., pp. 196–200; and Guadamuz, A., 'PayPal: Legal Implications of a C2C Electronic Payment System' (2004) 20 *Computer Law and Security Report* 1.

[27]   In the United States, the service is explicitly not a bank, as it lacks the all-important charter.

[28]   Article 2.

[29]   Article 4.

10. Cybercrime

1. CYBERCRIME IN THE EU

Criminal activity on the web takes many forms. Identities are stolen, computer systems broken into, software illicitly traded, child pornography peddled, money laundered. Share scams, botnets and keyloggers for hire, hacking, phishing, credit card fraud, espionage and political crime have marked the beginning of this century. The perpetrators are numerous and spread widely over the globe. The cost of this activity is measured in hundreds of billions of dollars[1] and the figures are likely to rise as the numbers of Internet users increase, particularly in the developing world.

This chapter is an outline of some of the issues that have provoked reaction at a European level. The most important one is the Cybercrime Treaty (see below), which is a Council of Europe coordinated initiative open to signature by other states.

1.1 Legal Basis

The European Union has limited capacity to legislate in the area of criminal law, which has always been regarded as a symbol of state sovereignty.[2] Although the European Union is primarily a trade organization, it has partial competence to regulate criminal law. This is because crime is an obstacle to trade between Member States but also because better cooperation in criminal matters is necessary for a more stable economic and social development.

---

[1] Symantec, 'Internet Security Threat Report Vol. 17' (Symantec Corporation, Mountain View 2011), accessed 1.8.2012 at www.symantec.com/threatreport.

[2] C-176/03 *Commission v Council* [2005] ECR I-7879, where the Court said 'neither criminal law nor the rules of criminal procedure fall within the Community's competence'. On the global approach to regulating cybercrime, see Gercke, M., 'The Slow Wake of a Global Approach against Cybercrime' (2006) 7 *Computer Law Review International* 140.

Both the Maastricht (1993) and the Amsterdam (1999) Treaties introduced changes which affected criminal law to some extent, notably in the field of 'justice and home affairs', but the actual competence to create criminal law was lacking. Approximation of rules in criminal matters was allowed under Article 29 of the Nice Treaty (TEU 2001).

Article 83(1) TFEU allows the EU to adopt *directives* containing minimum rules defining criminal offences and sanctions. This can only be done for particularly serious crimes with a cross-border dimension, which include:

> terrorism, trafficking in human beings and sexual exploitation of women and children, illicit drug trafficking, illicit arms trafficking, money laundering, corruption, counterfeiting of means of payment, computer crime and organised crime.

The Council may decide that other crimes be added to the list. Another possibility exists in Article 83(2) in respect of crimes that are normally not 'particularly serious':

> If the approximation of criminal laws and regulations of the Member States proves essential to ensure the effective implementation of a Union policy in an area which has been subject to harmonisation measures, directives may establish minimum rules with regard to the definition of criminal offences and sanctions in the area concerned. Such directives shall be adopted by the same ordinary or special legislative procedure as was followed for the adoption of the harmonisation measures in question, without prejudice to Article 76.

Article 84 further allows promotion and support of actions in Member States, without harmonization measures. Eurojust, the EU agency for cooperation in criminal matters established in 1999, is entrusted with various coordination tasks.

In recent times, however, a number of developments forced a gradual rethinking of this approach. In *Pupino*,[3] the Court ruled that framework decisions made in the area of criminal law have an effect in national legal systems. In *Commission v Council*,[4] it said that the lack of Community competence in this area does not 'prevent the Community legislature ... from taking measures which relate to the criminal law of Member States'. This will be true when taking action is necessary for the effectiveness of Community law. This means that national criminal law

---

[3] C-105/03 *Criminal Proceedings against Pupino* [2005] ECR I-5285.
[4] C 176/03, see footnote 1.

may be used to further a Community policy, but a more direct action to harmonize national law under Article 83 may still be allowed.[5]

Compared to its other IT-related interests, the European Union showed an interest in the area of cybercrime relatively late with two 2001 communications.[6] The communications were primarily intended to raise awareness of computer security issues. Three categories of more recent instruments followed. The first is the noted Council of Europe Convention on Cybercrime (the Cybercrime Treaty) signed in Budapest in 2001.[7] The second can be grouped under a general title of 'Computer Misuse' and cover a variety of issues of interference with computer systems. This category relates to unsolicited email messages or spam too. The final category includes measures for the protection of certain vulnerable groups on the Internet, including women and children.

In a recent Proposal,[8] the Commission considered several policy options in the area of cybercrime. Two of the options considered were the 'introduction of comprehensive EU legislation against cybercrime' (policy option 4) and an 'update of the Council of Europe Convention on Cybercrime' (option 5). The Commission was aware of the difficulties which either of these would bring and opted for a more targeted approach instead. Interestingly, referring to option 4, it said that comprehensive law, in its view, would encompass attacks against information systems, financial cybercrime, illegal Internet content, transfer of electronic evidence and jurisdiction rules.

2. CYBERCRIME TREATY

The Convention on Cybercrime was signed under the patronage of the Council of Europe. Although not an EU instrument, the Convention

---

[5]   Cf. Crosby, S., 'European Criminal Law: Some Introductory Reflections' (2006) 1 *Journal of European Criminal Law* 7. A similar provision existed in Article III-271 of the 2004 Constitutional Treaty (Treaty establishing a Constitution for Europe).

[6]   Communication, Creating a Safer Information Society by Improving the Security of Information Infrastructures and Combating Computer-related Crime, COM(2000) 890, 26.1.2001; and Communication from the Commission, Network and Information Security: A European Policy Approach, Com (2001) 208, 6.6.2001.

[7]   Convention on Cybercrime, CETS No: 185.

[8]   Proposal for a Directive on attacks against information systems, see section 3 below.

effectively represents the Community's interests in its field of application.[9] The timing of the Convention coincides with the increased
importance of electronic commerce, intellectual property and deeper
penetration of fast Internet access and mobile telephony. The perceived
borderless nature of the covered offences has prompted an effort on a
European level.

The Convention effectively creates an obligation for Member States to
introduce the provisions of Chapter II into their substantive law and to
enable cooperation in the matters within its subject area.

The Convention has a threefold purpose. Firstly, it defines substantive
criminal law (Chapter II, Section 1). This is a harmonizing effort aimed
at creating a common base of offences. Secondly, it harmonizes measures
of investigation and criminal proceedings (Chapter II, Section 2). Thirdly,
it opens up avenues for international cooperation (Chapter III). These
will be analysed in turn.

2.1 The Offences

The Convention has a relatively wide scope. The offences are grouped
into four categories. The first are breaches of confidentiality, integrity and
availability of computer data and systems. These are well-known
offences of interference with computer systems that predate the Internet
age. The second category includes computer-related offences, such as
forgery or fraud. The third category includes offences related to content,
primarily child pornography. The final category comprises infringements
of copyright and related rights. A Protocol to the Convention, signed in
Strasbourg in 2003, adds to these the dissemination, threat or insult by
racist and xenophobic material through computer systems and the denial,
minimization or approval of genocide.

The first category of offences, those against the integrity of computer
systems, covers illegal access.[10] The offence consists of breaking into a
system, in whole or in part, without proper permission. Parties may
require that the offence is committed by infringing security measures or
with the intent of obtaining data or with dishonest intent, or in relation to
a computer system that is connected to another system. The Article
essentially covers hacking into a computer system. The offence is
relatively easily committed on the Internet, which allows several types of

---

[9] See Commission Staff Working Paper, Brussels, SEC(2001) 315,
19.2.2001, expressing a desire for a disassociation clause to be inserted, to claim
precedence of EU law over the Convention in matters covered in both.

[10] Article 2 of the Convention.

connections, from a simple unencrypted connection to a connection with several levels of security. The offence consists of unauthorized access, intention being an optional element. Given the possibility of accidental access this may be too harsh, but is in practice of limited importance, as most computer systems holding data of any value would have such security measures that intent would be a necessary part of the offence anyway.[11]

Article 3 of the Convention introduces the offence of illegal interception. The offence consists of intercepting without right, by technical means, non-public transmission of computer data to, from or within a computer system, including electromagnetic emissions. Dishonest intent, once again, may be added by parties, as may be a connection to another computer system. The offence can also be committed with electronic equipment, provided that the perpetrator's was sufficiently sophisticated. In the age of the Internet, the most common form would be unauthorized use of wireless or LAN facilities but more sophisticated methods may involve reading and extracting data from physical wires or a transmitted non-encrypted signal. This provision has a limited impact on financial fraud targeting individual consumers (such as identity theft or phishing), as fraud is typically committed not by intercepting data but by stealing it in physical form (e.g., paper records) or by illegally obtaining digital data (e.g., by purchasing it). As such, these offences are more effectively covered in other provisions of the Convention or EU law.

Article 4 targets a similar offence of data interference. This involves intentional damaging, deletion, deterioration, alteration or suppression of computer data without right. A party may require that the conduct results in serious harm. The offence involves hacking attacks, the purpose of which is not to obtain access to a system (although most of them inevitably do) or to intercept data but to *alter* it. A typical Internet example involves hacking into websites to alter their content for the perpetrator's purpose. The presence of the second paragraph that mentions serious harm serves as recognition that most of the attacks of this type are more akin to vandalism than to criminal behaviour.

Article 5 introduces the offence of system interference, which involves intentional hindering, without right, of functioning of a computer system by the inputting, transmitting, damaging, deleting, deteriorating, altering or suppressing of computer data. This Article largely covers the same subject as Article 4. It would seem that the legislator's intent was to

---

[11]   The presence of a login screen, at least, would leave the potential offender in no doubt.

distinguish the situation where the purpose of data interference is to *hinder* the functioning of a computer system from the situation that involves only *interference* which does not affect the system. If so, this was unnecessary, as the purpose of the legislation must be to prevent any unauthorized interference, whatever the effect on the system. If interference results in subsequent damage to the system itself, that may be taken as an aggravating factor.

Article 6 deals with intentional and unauthorized misuse of devices that can help commit offences mentioned in the previous articles. The offence can consist in the production, sale, procurement for use, import, distribution or other making available of a device (including a computer program) designed or adapted for the purpose of committing offences in Articles 2–5. Also included are computer passwords, access codes or similar data through which computer systems can be accessed. The possession of the item with the purpose of committing the offences is also criminalized, but a party may put a quantitative limit on items before criminal liability arises. No offence is committed where devices are used for testing of computer systems' protection.[12] Parties may put reservation on this article, with the exception of provision (a.ii) relating to passwords or access codes.

The Article is underlined by a commendable motive of stopping piracy on a large scale. Devices, software or access codes for breaking into commercial systems are widely available on the Internet, often free of charge. The Article is unambiguous about its target, which is explained in paragraph (a.i) as comprising devices 'designated or adapted primarily for the purpose of committing any of the offences'. This leaves a considerable margin of discretion to national lawmakers and to national judges. A strict interpretation may lead to illegality of a number of devices that have mixed uses.

Articles 7 and 8 introduce the 'computer-related offences'. Article 7 deals with computer-related forgery, criminalizing intentional and unauthorized input, alteration, deletion or suppression of computer data, resulting in inauthentic data. The essential element of the offence is the intent that data be considered or acted upon for legal purposes as if they were authentic. An intent to defraud or similar dishonest intent may be additionally required by the party.

This article covers forgery applied to computers. In reality, an electronic forgery is not more difficult to commit than an ordinary one. First, electronic documents are usually not images (either in JPG or PDF or

___

[12]   See Article 6(2).

any other such form) of paper documents, but discreet database entries that can be transmitted electronically or exported or converted to other formats. The ability to forge an entry in such a database would depend on the forger's ability to enter into the system, an offence also subject to Article 2. A skilled forger would simply illegally enter the system and change the values in the database.

Article 8 criminalizes computer-related fraud. The offence is committed intentionally and without authorization and involves input, alteration, deletion or suppression of data or interference with the functioning of a computer system, in both cases with the fraudulent intent of obtaining an economic benefit for oneself or another. The offence consists, in other words, of some or all of the elements of the previous offences, with the addition of economic motivation. There seems to be some repetition in this, as most of the offences in Articles 2–7 are normally committed for obtaining economic benefit.

Article 9, the only content-specific offence, criminalizes child pornography offences. The offence consists of the intentional and unauthorized production, offering, making, distributing, transmitting, procuring or possessing of child pornography. The aggravated nature of the offence is reflected in the criminalization of mere possession, on a computer or on another medium. Child pornography is described as material that visually depicts a minor engaged in sexually explicit conduct or a person appearing to be a minor engaged in sexually explicit conduct or realistic images representing a minor engaged in sexually explicit conduct. A minor is defined as a person less than 18 years of age, although the parties may require a lower age, but not less than 16 years. Parties are free to put a reservation on procuring and possessing as offences and on the definition of 'child pornography' so that it only includes visual depictions of minors engaged in sexually explicit conduct, and not pretend or 'artistic' images.

Article 10 criminalizes certain behaviour relating to infringements of copyright and related rights.[13] The first paragraph of the Article invokes the obligations that parties have undertaken under the Bern Convention,[14] the TRIPS Agreement and the WIPO Copyright Treaty 1996, with the exception of any moral rights. The offences must have been committed wilfully, on a commercial scale and by means of a computer system.

---

[13] On the problem of criminal sanctions for copyright violation, see Chapter 6.

[14] Paris Act of 24 July 1971, revising the Bern Convention for the Protection of Literary and Artistic Works.

The second paragraph invokes the Rome Convention,[15] the TRIPS Agreement and the WIPO Performances and Phonograms Treaty 1996, with the exception of moral rights, where committed wilfully and on a commercial scale and by means of a computer system. If other effective remedies exist, the parties may reserve the right to impose criminal liability and that party's international obligations remain intact.

Aiding and abetting in committing any of the offences under Articles 2–10 as well as attempting is, under Article 11, also an offence when committed intentionally. An attempt to commit is an offence in the case of Articles 3, 4, 5, 7, 8 and 9.1.a and c of the Convention.

Corporate liability is established under Article 12. Legal persons are liable for offences committed for their own benefit by a natural person, who acted independently or as part of an organ of a legal person. In the latter case, which is included to ensure that directors', managers' or other employees' actions can make their corporations criminally liable, such organ must have a power of representation, or an authority to take decisions on behalf of the legal person or an authority to exercise control within the legal person. Paragraph 2 of Article 12 emphasizes that liability exists in cases where the lack of control or supervision over the natural person has led to the offence. The liability of the corporation in all these cases can be criminal, civil or administrative and is without prejudice to the liability of the natural person.

The sanctions for offences in Articles 2–11 shall be effective, proportionate and dissuasive and shall include deprivation of liberty. In case of Article 12 – corporations – such sanctions may or may not be criminal but can in any case be monetary.

2.2 Procedural Measures

Procedural provisions of the Convention establish powers and procedure for criminal investigations relating to the crimes committed under the provision of the previous section. Significantly, under Article 14, these powers and procedures apply not only to criminal offences established in Articles 2–11, but also to other criminal offences committed by means of a computer system[16] and to the collection of evidence in an electronic form.[17] In other words, the Convention's procedural provisions aim to

---

[15] 1961 International Convention for the Protection of Performers, Producers of Phonograms and Broadcasting Organizations.

[16] Article 14(2)b.

[17] Article 14(2)c.

apply not only to the Convention itself, but to harmonize parties' procedural law applicable to computer misuse.

Article 15 introduces important safeguards for the application of procedures in Section 2. The powers and procedures of that section shall be used primarily under the safeguards of domestic law of the party. Such protection includes human rights and liberties as required under the 1950 European Convention on Human Rights, the 1966 UN Convention on Civil and Political Rights, and other international instruments. The safeguards shall include judicial and other independent supervision grounds justifying application and other limitations of scope and duration.

The provisions on the scope and the safeguards, contained in Articles 14 and 15, apply to most of Section 2. In fact, most of the Articles specifically say so. The exceptions are Articles 20 and 21. Parties are allowed to place a reservation on the application of Article 20 (real-time collection of traffic data) so that it will apply only to some offences, provided that such range is not narrower than that of Article 21 (interception of data).[18] The reservation is understandable, considering the political sensitivity of governmentally sponsored monitoring. A party may also reserve the right not to apply the procedural measures in Articles 20 and 21 to communications within a closed computer system (such as that operated by the military).

Article 16 allows parties to retain computer data, including traffic data, stored by a computer system, especially where that data is vulnerable to loss. Parties are required to pass laws in cases where they make orders to persons to preserve data. In such cases, the maximum duration of data maintenance is 90 days, but is renewable if the parties so wish. Custodians of data may be required to keep such gathering of data confidential. The powers under Article 16 do not depend on the number of service providers involved.[19] Such disclosure of data must involve a sufficient amount to enable identification of service providers.

Article 18 establishes a 'production order'. This order empowers the parties' authorities to request a person to submit computer data, either stored in the computer system itself or in a data storage medium. More significantly, the service provider offering its services in the territory of the state *must* submit subscriber information relating to such services. The importance of the latter provision is reflected in the recent case law in the United States, where the Recording Industry Association of

---

[18] Article 14(3)a.
[19] Article 17(1)a.

America has successfully requested information held by ISPs to facilitate actions against individual file-sharers in copyright infringement cases. The obligation applies not only to ISPs established on the territory of a party but also to any ISP that offers its services in that territory, which significantly enlarges the scope of the provision.

The information that may be requested is referred to as 'subscriber information' and includes: the type of service used, the technical provisions and the period (e.g., ADSL connection); the subscriber's identity and address, contact details and billing and payment information; and any other information relating to computer equipment. Such powers are extensive and may force the ISPs to provide more information than is in reality necessary. The order is subject to Articles 14 and 15 and can only be applied to the stipulated criminal offences and under the safeguards. Nevertheless, the scope of such offences is as wide as is the order itself. It remains to be seen whether the sweeping powers so provided would actually have an impact on combating crime on the web.

Article 19 introduces the measure of search and seizure of computer data. Either a computer system or a data storage medium may be searched, provided that these are located on the party's territory. This last requirement may turn out to be more elusive than the legislator intended. Is the storage medium located in a contracting party where the business headquarters are in the United States and only a backup server is physically located in the party? The power under paragraph 1 extends to other computer systems accessible through the primary computer system, provided that both are in the same territory.

The computer data accessed under Articles 19(1) and (2) may be seized or secured, copied, rendered inaccessible, removed or its integrity maintained in other ways.[20] Orders may be made to competent persons to make information available to protect data, the search or seizure of which is required.[21]

Jurisdiction is regulated in Article 22. It provides that jurisdiction of national courts over offences in Articles 2–11 shall exist where these are committed on their territory, on board a ship flying their flag, on board an aircraft registered under their flag or by one of their nationals, provided that the offence is punishable where it was committed or if the offence is committed outside the jurisdiction of any state. The penultimate provision is problematic. For, if the offence committed by a national of state A in state B is punishable in state B, then surely it is for

---

[20]   Article 19(3).
[21]   Article 19(4).

state B to pursue the matter. If it does not want to or cannot, why would state A show an interest in it, only on the basis of the nationality of the perpetrator? This was recognized and a reservation was allowed to all of the mentioned provisions save for the first one (offence committed on the territory).

A confusing provision on extradition is added in paragraph 3. The paragraph requires the party to establish jurisdiction over the offences referred to in Article 24 (namely Articles 2–11) in cases where the perpetrator is present on its territory but cannot be extradited due to nationality. Apart from being a duplication of paragraph 6 of Article 24, the provision does not make much sense. A party is, according to this, either forced to prosecute or to extradite. If it cannot extradite, because, for example, its constitution prohibits it from doing so, it must prosecute even where it normally would not.

2.3 Data Retention

All EU Member States and all members of the Council of Europe have data protection laws in place.[22] The standard of these laws differs, being stricter in some states while more lax in others. EU data protection laws introduce minimum harmonization in this area. But the operation of these laws is not smooth. The problem of data retention arises out of at least three sources. The first can tentatively be called political – Internet users, whether private or corporate, are wary of any attempts to monitor their activity on the Internet. They are protected with constitutional guarantees of privacy and they see the data retention efforts as an infringement on it. Second, the political appetite in the Member States for demanding data retention grows, as they face increasing security problems. Finally, even if one agrees with the statement that data retention is necessary and useful in combating crime (which is at this stage still uncertain), one is faced with the problem of the quality of large amounts of data that cannot be analysed without using significant human and financial resources.[23]

Data retention is covered in two separate Articles in Section 2 of the Cybercrime Convention. Article 20 sanctions real-time collection of traffic data. The Article empowers the parties' authorities to collect or technologically record traffic data in real time, on its territory and

---

[22] On the data protection regime in the EU in connection with the Internet, see Chapter 8.

[23] On problems of surveillance in general, see Singh, S., et al., 'Technology Surveillance', in Campbell, D., *Legal Issues in the Global Information Society* (Oceana TM/OUP USA, New York 2005), p. 87.

transmitted by means of a computer system. It also authorizes parties to compel a service provider to do the same or to cooperate and assist the authorities in collecting data. Provision exists in the second paragraph of the Article, where a party cannot, due to its domestic legal system, comply with the first paragraph, to adopt other measures it can to ensure real-time collection through technological means. The service providers are, under paragraph 3, obliged to keep confidential the fact that any collection is taking place.

Article 21 applies to the interception of content data. Structurally, it is the same as Article 20. It applies only to a range of serious offences to be determined by domestic law. It enables national authorities to collect or record through technological means, content data in real time, on its territory and transmitted by means of a computer system. It may also compel the service provider to collect or record data or to cooperate and assist in its collection.

In 2006, the Commission adopted the Data Retention Directive.[24] The Directive harmonizes Member States' laws concerning the obligations of public providers of electronic communication services in respect of the retention of data and is inextricably linked with the Data Protection Directive.[25] Article 13 of the Directive deals with remedies, liabilities and penalties. It provides that Member States must take measures to implement Chapter III of the Data Protection Directive and provide sanctions in respect of data processed under that Directive. In particular the Directive criminalizes the intentional access to or transfer of data retained in accordance with the Directive that is not permitted under national law adopted pursuant to the Directive. Such transfer is punishable by penalties, including administrative or criminal, that are 'effective, proportionate and dissuasive'.

2.4 International Cooperation

International cooperation is established in Article 23 of the Cybercrime Treaty, which simply says that the parties should cooperate in criminal matters applicable to the Internet in all possible ways.

---

[24] Directive 2006/24/EC of the European Parliament and of the Council of 15 March 2006 on the retention of data generated or processed in communication with the provision of publicly available electronic communications services or of public communication networks and amending Directive 2002/58/EC, OJ L 105/54, 13.4.2006.

[25] For more details on its operation, see Chapter 8.

Importantly, Article 24 introduces the possibility of extradition of offenders. Such extradition is possible in respect of offences set out in Articles 2–11, provided that they are punishable by the laws of both parties and would result in deprivation of liberty for a maximum period of at least a year or more. Where a different minimum penalty applies, the minimum shall be taken as a basis. The Convention shall serve as a legal basis for extradition even where a treaty normally does not exist between the parties.[26]

Article 25 speaks of mutual assistance in matters which the Treaty covers. One form of such assistance is the spontaneous provision of information.[27] Another form is the requests for assistance either where agreements exist or where they are absent.[28]

2.5 Analysis

The Cybercrime Treaty, in spite of the positive elements that it brings by encouraging a global fight against digital crime, can be criticized on several grounds. Some of the activities it criminalized continue to be condemned by civil liberties groups. It places a massive surveillance apparatus in force, criminalizes a host of activities that were hitherto not deemed to be harmful and imposes rigid standards on a still-developing medium.

As an example, the Treaty makes it a crime to create, download or post on a website any computer program that is 'designed or adapted' primarily to gain access to a computer system without permission. Also banned is software designed to interfere with the 'functioning of a computer system' by deleting or altering data.[29] A number of computer programs that fit the latter description also have a harmless use that is limited by criminalizing their creation or adaptation.

Second, it allows governments to order the encryption keys to be revealed.[30] In some states, such the US, the constitutional provisions on self-incrimination may prevent the correct implementation of this provision. It also allows authorities to order the passphrase for an encryption key to be revealed.

Also worrying is the requirement imposed on Internet Service Providers in Articles 16, 17, 20 and 21 to collect information about their

---

[26] Article 24(3).
[27] Article 26.
[28] Article 27.
[29] Article 6 of the Treaty.
[30] Article 18.

users, a rule that would potentially limit anonymous use and that may be in conflict with Article 15 of the E-Commerce Directive as well as with the Court's case law on this matter.

Finally, the requirements imposed in Chapter III would force governments to help enforce the criminal laws of other Member States, even if those were vastly different or, in their view, unjustified. In cases concerning speech that is protected in state A but illegal in state B, this leads to a serious curtailment of acquired Internet rights. Doubts remain about whether this mode of enforcement is a good use of limited financial and human resources.

3. ATTACKS AGAINST INFORMATION SYSTEMS – THE EU FRAMEWORK DECISION

The Decision, adopted in 2005, is intended to address certain forms of criminal activity against information systems.[31] The specific aim of the Framework Decision is harmonization of the criminal law relating to information systems in the EU. This is part of a more general objective of achieving an area of freedom, security and justice that has been highlighted in the Tampere European Council in 1999 and in the Lisbon European Council of 2000. The lack of harmonized law was perceived as an obstacle to achieving a proper Community cooperation in criminal matters. The Framework Decision on Attacks Against Information Systems[32] is intended to be consistent with the Convention. The purpose of the Framework Decision, however, is not to duplicate the work done under the Convention but to combat crime against computer infrastructure.

'Information systems' are defined as any device which perform automatic processing of computer data, and the computer data stored, processed, recovered or transmitted by them for the purposes of their operation, use, protection and maintenance. The Decision makes three categories of crime against information systems punishable.

The first (Article 2) consists of illegal access to information systems. This comprises a variety of attacks colloquially referred to as hacking.

---

[31]   The Framework Decision was adopted under the Third Pillar. It is binding on the Member States as to the result to be achieved but leaves the choice of form and methods to the national authorities.

[32]   Council Framework Decision 2005/222/JHA of 24 February 2005 on attacks against information systems, Brussels, OJ L 69, 16.3.2005. The legal basis was found in Arts 29, 30(a), 31 and 34(2)(b) of TEU.

The offence consists of accessing intentionally and without right the whole or any part of an information system. The offence must not be minor. Member States may decide that conduct will only be incriminated where a security measure is breached. The convenience of this measure consists in its flexibility. It comprises not only cases where a person has logged into a computer system with real or false credentials and without authorization, but also all attacks having a further aim which necessarily consists of illegally accessing the system. For instance, in order to send thousands of unsolicited email messages, a perpetrator may use its own resources. More likely, however, an unguarded or poorly secured system will be found which will then be used as a base for launching the attacks. An even more efficient effort would consist of planting a bot, a small piece of computer code that would then hijack the victim's computer and, in turn, start sending email messages on behalf of the perpetrator.

The second offence[33] consists of illegal system interference. It consists of the intentional serious hindering or interruption of the functioning of an information system by inputting, transmitting, damaging, deleting, deteriorating, altering, suppressing or rendering inaccessible computer data. As in the previous Article, minor offences are excluded. This offence is more flexible than the previous one, as it does not require unauthorized access to the system. This is important as persons otherwise authorized to use the system but misusing it on a particular occasion often commit this crime. The most notorious form of system interference is the denial-of-service attack. To put it simply, that is an attempt to make computer resources unavailable to users. It is usually performed by forcing the victim computer to waste all its resources on the attacker, thus making it unable to respond to users' requests.

Other forms that fall under this provision are various kinds of virus attacks. A computer virus in a general sense is any piece of computer code that can copy itself without the user's knowledge. This need not be malicious but nearly always takes valuable computer resources. A virus often installs malicious code which in turn may have various purposes, ranging from simply damaging the user's computer to extracting valuable data (bank and credit card accounts, email addresses, etc.).

Finally, Article 4 of the Framework Decision criminalizes illegal data interference. The offence consists of intentional deletion, damaging, deterioration, alteration, suppression or rendering inaccessible of computer data on an information system. The difference between this offence and the previous one would appear to be in the purpose. Article 3 covers

---

[33] Article 3.

offences intended against computer systems affected through tampering with data. Article 4, on the other hand, targets attacks against data.

Much that was said for the previous Articles can be repeated here. In fact, it would appear that most cyber-related criminal activities fall under several or even all of the Articles mentioned in the framework decision. This is not surprising, as much of cybercrime today requires access to or interference with the system and access to data. The two are rarely separable.

Instigating, aiding and abetting is punishable as the criminal offence itself as are attempted offences, although Member States have the capacity to opt out of this. Member States are obliged, under Article 6, to introduce 'effective, proportional and dissuasive penalties'. In particular, the offences in Articles 3 and 4 must be punishable by criminal penalties of a maximum of at least between 1 and 3 years of imprisonment. This is a sensible policy intended to send a clear message about the seriousness with which cybercrime is viewed in the EU. A special case is created for the offences referred to in Articles 2(2), 3 and 4. These should be punishable by criminal penalties of a maximum of at least between 2 and 5 years of imprisonment when committed within the framework of a criminal organization.[34] The same measures may be taken in respect of Article 2(1) when the offence has caused serious damage or has affected essential interests.

An important measure is Article 8, which allows legal persons to be prosecuted for crimes in Articles 2–5, where they are committed for their benefit by any person who acts either individually or as part of an organ. In either case, the person must have a leading position within the organization. This may be based on a power of representation, authority to take decisions on behalf of the legal person or an authority to exercise control. Liability is also ensured in cases of lack of supervision or control that lead to the committing of the offence. Finally, liability of a legal person itself does not exclude liability of a natural person as a perpetrator, instigator or accessory in the commission.

The penalties for legal persons[35] include criminal or non-criminal fines and other penalties, for example: exclusion from entitlement of public benefit or aid, disqualification from practice, judicial supervision or judicial winding-up.

Jurisdiction for offences committed by Internet use is a contentious issue in civil law. In criminal law, jurisdiction for prosecuting crimes exists, under Article 10: (a) where the offence has been committed

---

[34]   The definition of a criminal organization is provided in Joint Action 98/733/JHA, OJ L 351/1, 29.12.1998

[35]   Article 9.

wholly or partially on the territory of a Member State; or (b) by one of its nationals; or (c) for the benefit of a legal person with a head office in the territory of that Member State.[36] In relation to offences committed on the territory of a Member State, it is enough that the perpetrator is physically located there, irrespective of the actual location of the computer system against which the activity is directed. Likewise, this includes cases where the information system is on its territory but the perpetrator is not.[37]

It should also be clear that a single offence can affect several Member States. For instance, interference with a computer system in country A where data is also affected in countries B and C. On the Internet, this is particularly true of websites/services which typically have a presence in more than one Member State. Likewise, there may be several perpetrators independently targeting the same Internet service, in which case there will be several offences for each event.[38]

Article 10(4) of the Framework Decision provides for cases where more than one state is interested in prosecution. It says that, where an offence falls within the jurisdiction of more than one Member State and when any of the States concerned can validly prosecute on the basis of the same facts, the Member States concerned shall cooperate in order to decide which of them will prosecute the offenders with the aim, if possible, of centralizing proceedings in a single Member State. Member States may avail themselves of any mechanism or body in the European Union that would facilitate these aims. A sequence is suggested (not imposed) that the Member States may follow in deciding which of them will prosecute the perpetrator. The first in line, according to the sequence, is the Member State where the offence is committed. The second is the State of which the perpetrator is a national. The final one is the State in which the perpetrator has been found. The last category, in our opinion, provides too tenuous a link and is not very likely to be employed.

Extradition, although not explicitly regulated in the Framework Decision, is mentioned in Article 10(3), which provides that those Member States that do not extradite their nationals must take measures to establish their jurisdiction over offences in Articles 2–5 in all cases when they are committed by their nationals outside their territory. This refers to cases where the perpetrator has committed an offence in state A and then returned to a non-extraditing state B, of which he is a national.

---

[36] Member States are, in Article 10(5), allowed to opt out of items (b) and (c).

[37] Article 10(2).

[38] Typical examples are concerted attacks, such as denial of service, by hacker groups.

The Framework Decision aims in Article 11 to kick-start the 'existing network of operational points of contact'. A General Secretariat and the Council are established as the main bodies for exchanging information regarding information systems crime.

There are some obvious problems with the Framework Decision. The first concerns Article 3 and illegal system interference. The Article does not differentiate between serious crimes, such as persistent denial-of-service attacks arranged by organized crime with the aim of, for example, extorting money, and attacks arranged by individuals for political purposes. The first is normally malign and violent, the second often peaceful and short-lived. Political campaigning on the Internet is as old as the network itself. It is undeniable that a number of attacks by various political groups can be disruptive, even damaging. It is also undeniable that some of them are harmful and expensive to rectify. On the other hand, it is not clear why these protests would not benefit from constitutional protection of free speech when their 'real-world' counterparts do.

Another apparent problem is broadness of definition in Article 2. Unauthorized access is normally regarded as hacking which, in turn, has a relatively precise definition. It involves unauthorized access to a protected system which, in turn, is defined by standards of a reasonably skilled hacker. The Framework Directive, however, talks of 'illegal access'. This includes unauthorized access to what is otherwise an open system. The exclusion of minor offences does not help here in the absence of a proper definition. Neither does paragraph 2, a measure that is nearer reality but which is optional.

There are also differences between the Cybercrime Treaty and the Framework Decision. Article 2 of the Cybercrime Treaty, at the parties' option, criminalizes access by infringing security measures only when this is done with the intention of obtaining data or in the case of a networked computer system. No such requirement exists in the Framework Decision. The latter seems a more sensible solution at first, as the intention of obtaining data may indeed not form part of a serious offence or the offence may not be directed towards a network. On the other hand, the difference may be important for situations involving free speech.

Furthermore, the Cybercrime Treaty includes categories that the Framework Decision does not. One of these is the category of 'interception of communication' under Article 3.[39]

---

[39] For further on the differences, see Flanagan, A., 'The Law and Computer Crime: Reading the Script of Reform' (2005) 13 *International Journal of Law and Information Technology* 98.

Although recognized as an instrument promoting cooperation between Member States on serious issues of cybercrime, doubt remained about the Decision's effectiveness. In a proposal for revision of the Framework Decision,[40] the Commission revisited some of the unanswered questions. The desire was primarily to address the new forms of attacks against information systems, such as large-scale attacks.

The proposed Directive retains the provisions of the Decision and adds new substantive elements:

- Article 7 penalizes production, sale and procurement of devices used for committing criminal offences. This specifically covers not only technical devices but also computer programs and passwords.
- Article 10 now covers aggravating circumstances which may be in the scale of the attack (botnets are specifically quoted) or when the attacks are committed through false identities.
- Article 6 introduces illegal interception of non-public transmissions.
- Article 14 improves European criminal justice cooperation.
- Article 15 harmonizes rules on handling statistical data.

4. SPAM AND ADVERTISING

4.1 Political, Individual and Commercial Problems

Spam is one of the costliest problems on the Internet today. For consumers, it represents a never-ending obligation to monitor unsolicited traffic. It detracts from important messages, which often get mixed with spam, and it requires time to be properly disposed of. For Internet service providers it represents extra cost in server time and the risk of clogging. For corporations it means spending extra financial resources on filtering unsolicited messages using technologies that, although constantly improving, are not fully reliable. For spammers, on the other hand, the issue may be observed as one concerning freedom of commercial speech.

Spam can be defined as any unsolicited communication by means of electronic mail. Such communication is usually commercial, although it does not exclusively have to be in order to qualify as spam. Political speech, for instance, is covered, meaning that the definition of spam is

---

[40] Proposal for a Directive of the European Parliament and of the Council on attacks against information systems and repealing Council Framework Decision 2005/222/JHA, COM(2010) 517, 30.9.2010.

not particularly important for the attempts to fight it. The interesting question, however, is what the legal treatment of similar categories is. Such categories comprise pop-ups and pop-unders and other adverts that appear on the user's browser outside the main browsing context. Also, the status of viruses, Trojans, adware and an increasing arsenal of ever more sophisticated tools for exploiting users' computers is an unknown area.

Attempts to regulate spam worldwide have not been particularly successful. This is probably a result of the Internet's architecture, which allows not only easy transfer of computer hosts actually responsible for sending messages but also hijacking of hundreds of computers for the same purpose. The businesses advertised through spam are equally difficult to trace, either being classified as online services or operating from jurisdictions with lax legal regimes and poor consumer protection.

In the United States, an attempt in 2003 to fight spam saw light in the form of the Controlling the Assault of Non-Solicited Pornography and Marketing Act 2003 (CAN SPAM).[41] Its main purpose is the imposition of penalties on the transmission of unsolicited email. The Act defines spam as 'any electronic mail message the primary purpose of which is the commercial advertisement or promotion of a commercial product or service (including content on an Internet website operated for a commercial purpose)'. 'Transaction' and 'relationship' messages are excluded from the scope. In order for an unsolicited commercial email to be sent legally under the Act, it must have an opt-out mechanism, a legitimate subject line and header, a legitimate physical address of the mailer and a label if the content is adult. Religious and national security measures are exempt as are messages regulated in other laws.

The CAN SPAM text was widely criticized as being inadequate. Its main weakness is the choice of regime, which fails to actively prohibit unsolicited commercial messages. The Act chooses the opt-out approach, which specifically requires the recipient to take action once they get the first email. In fact, the Act specifically allows a first email to be sent, as long as it contains an opt-out clause. Arguably, an opt-in approach, requiring the recipient to sign themselves up for the services, provides a better protection.

A number of EU instruments apply to some extent to unsolicited commercial communications. Before the implementation of the E-Privacy Directive, the first instrument of relevance was the Data Protection Directive.[42] It did not specifically address spam but it could indirectly be

---

[41]   Pub. L. No. 108–187, 117 Stat. 2699 (2003).
[42]   See Chapter 8.

applied to the gathering of email addresses falling under personal data. The E-Privacy Directive explicitly recognizes its link with this instrument in Recital 10 and in Article 1(2). Another instrument of relevance is the Distance Selling Directive,[43] which limits the use of automated calling systems on the opt-in basis, but in Article 10(2) seemingly introduces an opt-out regime for 'other means of distance communication'. The Tele-communications Privacy Directive[44] introduced an opt-in regime for direct marketing by automatic systems in Article 12 but left it to Member States to choose between an opt-in and opt-out regime for all other means of communication. Finally the E-Commerce Directive itself expli-citly recognized the problem of spam in Recital 30 but did not go far in fighting it. It limited itself to introducing an obligation to clearly label commercial communication when this communication is permitted (and this was left to Member States) and on introducing an obligation to consult opt-out registers.

The inadequacy of these solutions is apparent. The early instruments (such as the Data Protection or the ISDN Directives) were drafted long before spam became a problem. Some of their solutions (such as those applying to purchasing and processing email lists) were, although useful in themselves, inadequate.

4.2 E-Privacy Directive

Directive 2002/58/EC on Privacy and Electronic Communications was drafted to tackle some of the deficiencies of earlier instruments and to deal specifically with problems from the perspective of electronic com-munications. Specifically, it regulates 'the right to privacy, with respect to the processing of personal data in the electronic communications sector' and ensures that such data and communications move freely.[45]

The provision that relates to spam is Article 13.[46] Paragraph one provides that the use of electronic mail for the purposes of direct

---

[43] Directive 97/7/EC of the European Parliament and of the Council of 20 May 1997 on the protection of consumers in respect of distance contracts, OJ L 144, 4.6.1997.

[44] Directive 97/66/EC of the European Parliament and of the Council of 15 December 1997 concerning the processing of personal data and the protection of privacy in the telecommunications sector (incl. Annex), OJ L 24/1, 30.1.1998.

[45] For more on this Directive, see Chapter 8 on privacy.

[46] For a more detailed treatment of spam, see Asscher, L. and Hoogcarspel, S.A., *Regulating Spam: A European Perspective after the Adoption of the E-Privacy Directive* (T.M.C. Asser Press, The Hague 2006).

marketing is only allowed in respect of subscribers who have given their prior consent. This is the opt-in regime. However, in paragraph 2, natural and legal persons who have obtained personal details in the course of previous business, may use these details for marketing their own similar products or services as long as the customers are given the opportunity to object without charge. The opportunity to object must be given with each communication, if the customer has not already taken advantage of it. Unsolicited communications other than those previously mentioned are not allowed unless the subscriber gives consent. Especially prohibited[47] are messages that conceal the identity of the sender.

The provisions of Article 13, except that relating to concealing, only apply to natural persons. Member States only have an obligation to ensure that the 'legitimate interests' of other subscribers are also protected. They have to ensure this obligation through their national law. This is somewhat disappointing, as corporations are subject to spam as much as natural persons.

An earlier version of Article 13 referred not only to electronic mail but also to 'other personally addressed electronic communications'. This would have been a welcome addition, as it would have covered SMS and other messages directed at mobile phones of newer generation. It is unclear why this has been left out as national laws sometimes tackle unsolicited SMS messages in the same way as fax messages. Although it is correct that spam SMS has not been as much of a problem as spam emails, this is still a gap in the regulation.

Article 4 of the Directive may also have an impact on the issue. It talks about security, obliging the provider of a publicly available electronic communications service to take appropriate measures to safeguard the security of its services. The duty extends to informing the customers of any breaches.[48] Applied to spam, this introduces an obligation of an ISP to apply all technical measures to combat spam or viruses. This should probably be interpreted as meaning 'state of the art' technological measures.

Spammers are in the practice of 'harvesting' email addresses. This simply means obtaining as many valid email addresses as possible within the shortest period of time. This is done either by trawling the Internet for emails scattered on various web pages, or more effectively, by breaching the security measures of companies which keep the emails in

---

[47]   Article 13(4).
[48]   Article 4(2).

their databases. The latter can be also done by purchasing the addresses from those who illegally sell them.

Certain provisions of the Data Protection Directive along with the E-Privacy Directive may be used to combat this practice. Articles 6 and 7 of the Data Protection Directive prohibit the unlawful processing of personal data, introducing a number of safeguards that determine when data processing is lawful. Emails collected on the Internet would be against these Articles, as they do not constitute fair and purposeful processing within Article 6 or meet the legitimacy test under Article 7. In terms of the E-Privacy Directive, Article 4 imposes the obligation on the ISP to protect the system against harvesting and Article 12 ensures that the customer's consent is obtained before being placed in the email directory.

5. HARMFUL CONTENT

The criminal regulation of harmful content in the EU is limited. The Community regularly drafts 'safer Internet' programs. The latest is the Safer Internet Action Program 2009–2013.[49] It promotes safer use of the Internet and emphasizes the distinction between illegal and harmful content. It has three aims: to increase public awareness; to fight against illegal and harmful content; to promote a safer online environment; and, finally, to establish a knowledge base. The new program includes emerging online technologies and specifically addresses certain categories of harmful conduct (grooming and cyber-bullying).

According to the Program, national authorities, such as the police, must deal with the illegal content but the industry should have the ability to introduce self-regulation schemes, such as codes of conduct and hotlines, in particular in the areas of reducing child pornography, racism and anti-Semitism. Harmful content, on the other hand, should be allowed but should have a restricted circulation, such as rated movies or adult magazines, including content which is offensive to certain categories of people but not to others. The latter category is specifically linked to freedom of speech in the document and includes various forms of hate speech.

The financial resources allocated are limited. The budget of the action plan was €25 million, which is adequate for the aim of promoting a safer

---

[49]   See Decision 1351/2008/EC of 16 December 2008 establishing a multiannual Community programme on protecting children using the Internet and other communication technologies, OJ L 348/118, 24.12.2008.

internet but not for establishing effective protection. Although activities
such as police cooperation are funded under different arrangements, it is
significant that a separate funding project does not exist in the EU for
combating cybercrime.

5.1 Obscenity

Pornography is not always the subject of regulation. Although trading or
even possession is illegal in a number of countries in the world, in others
it is allowed and in some it forms a significant contribution to the gross
domestic product. Regular pornography as content traded on the Internet
is not regulated in the EU. The subject of this section is only child
pornography which gained the special attention of EU and other legislators.

There are a number of EU measures directed at preventing the sexual
exploitation of children. The European Police Office (Europol) was
established in 1995[50] and a joint action (as amended) was drafted as an
extension to it and to combat trafficking in human beings and the sexual
exploitation of children.[51] According to it, the Member States undertook
to review their laws in view of eliminating sexual exploitation by use of
coercion, violence, deceit or abuse of authority, trafficking, the sexual
exploitation and trafficking of children. Member States have the obligation to classify the offences as criminal and to punish them effectively.
Although the joint action does not specifically apply to the Internet its
general scope ensures that providing child pornography on the Internet is
criminally punishable.

The Human Trafficking Directive on preventing and combating trafficking in human beings was adopted in 2011.[52] It replaces Framework
Decision 2002/629/JHA[53] with a wider instrument achieving better

---

[50]   Council Act of 26 July 1995 drawing up the Convention on the establishment of a European Police Office (Europol Convention), OJ C316, 27.11.1995.

[51]   Joint Action 97/154/JHA of 24 February 1997 adopted by the Council on
the basis of Article K.3 of the Treaty on European Union concerning action to
combat trafficking in human beings and sexual exploitation of children, OJ L63,
4.3.1997. Amended by Council Framework Decision 2002/629/JHA of 19 July
2002 concerning trafficking in human beings, OJ L203, 1.8.2002.

[52]   Directive 2011/36/EU of the European Parliament and of the Council of 5
April 2011 on preventing and combating trafficking in human beings and
protecting its victims, and replacing Council Framework Decision 2002/629/
JHA, OJ L 101, 15.4.2011.

[53]   Council Framework Decision 2002/629/JHA of 19 July 2002 on combating trafficking in human beings, OJ L 203, 1.8.2002.

harmonization at EU level. The new directive introduces criminal provisions including a common definition of the crime, aggravating circumstances and different, higher, penalties. Article 1 emphasized the gender perspective, recognizing the nature of the victims. Furthermore, it includes provisions on prosecution of offenders extraterritorially for crimes committed outside the EU. Special sections protect the victims, in particular, the vulnerable, and introduce provisions for victim support. Finally, preventive and monitoring mechanisms are introduced.

5.2 Child Pornography

The early regulation took place through a Council Decision to combat child pornography,[54] which addressed Member States and required them to take steps in several areas. First, they were to encourage Internet users to inform law enforcement authorities in cases where they suspected that child pornography material was being distributed on the Internet.[55] Second, they were to make sure that offences were investigated and punished.[56] To this end, they were to set up specialized units within the law enforcement authorities. Finally, they were to make sure that the law enforcement authorities reacted rapidly upon receiving information on alleged cases of the production, processing, distribution and possession of child pornography.[57] The Decision then envisaged wide and fast cooperation between Member States, who should set up points of contact, cooperate both between themselves and with Europol and 'engage in constructive dialogue' with the industry. Of special interest is the important Article 4 which obliges Member States to:

> verify whether technological developments require, in order to maintain the efficiency of the fight against child pornography on the Internet, changes to criminal procedural law, while respecting the fundamental principles thereof and, where necessary, shall initiate appropriate new legislation to that end.

Effectively, this obliges Member States to review their criminal procedure to make sure that it is keeping up with developments in technology. This refers to new methods of investigation, special police task forces and gathering and presentation of evidence. In fact, a number of Member

---

[54] Council Decision of 29 May 2000 to combat child pornography on the Internet, OJ L 138, 9.6.2000.

[55] Article 1(1).

[56] Article 1(2).

[57] Article 1(3).

States are reporting that they are overwhelmed by the effort required and stated that police investigation of this area is still in its infancy. Member States then have to cooperate with the industry to produce filters and to prevent the distribution and ease the detection of child pornography.

A general Framework Decision has been adopted to harmonize the laws of the Member States (i.e., set the minimum standards) in matters concerning the sexual exploitation of children and child pornography.[58] It has been replaced with the 2011 Child Pornography Directive.[59] The new Directive criminalizes serious forms of child sexual abuse and exploitation and increases penalties. Furthermore, it introduces aggravating circumstances and deals with jurisdiction and extradition. Conduct that is punishable as 'an offence concerning sexual exploitation of children' (whether undertaken by means of a computer system or not) includes the production of child pornography, the distribution, dissemination or transmission of child pornography, offering or otherwise making child pornography available or the acquisition and possession of child pornography. Importantly, the Directive recognizes criminal and civil liability for legal persons, which supplements that of the liability of natural persons. A legal person is made liable if the infringement is committed on its behalf by another person, acting either individually or as part of an organ of the legal person, or who has authority to take decisions on behalf of the legal person.[60]

Article 5, which regulates child pornography, criminalizes acquisition or possession (Article 5(1)), obtaining access (Article 5(2)), distribution, dissemination or transmission (Article 5(3)) and the offering, supplying and making available of child pornography (Article 5(4)). The Directive is specifically targeting offences committed online or with the aid of telecommunications technology (ICT). Article 2(e) specifically mentions online pornographic performances. Article 5(3) provides that obtaining access to child pornography with the aid of information and communication technology shall be punishable. Article 6 criminalizes ICT solicitation of children for sexual purposes, with the attempt also being

---

[58] Council Framework Decision 2004/68/JHA of 22 December 2003 on combating the sexual exploitation of children and child pornography, OJ L13, 20.1.2004.

[59] Directive of the European Parliament and of the Council on combating the sexual abuse, sexual exploitation of children and child pornography, repealing Framework Decision 2004/68/JHA, OJ L 335/1, 17.12.2011. The Directive incorporates the Decision but includes significant new elements

[60] See Articles 12–13.

punishable. Grooming, which is defined in line with the Cybercrime Treaty provisions to include recruiting a child, is covered in Article 4.

Article 25(1) obliges Member States to promptly remove web pages containing child pornography 'hosted in their territory' and 'to endeavour to obtain the removal of such pages hosted outside'. Article 25(2) authorizes selective blocking of child pornography websites operational only towards the end-users in the Member State in question. This specific form of filtering must be proportionate and transparent.

In terms of jurisdiction, Article 17 of the Directive provides that a Member State will have jurisdiction either where the offence is committed within its territory (the principle of territoriality) or where the offender is one of its nationals (the active personality principle). Further to that, it is possible to extend the Directive's field of application to situations where the offence was committed against persons habitually resident on the Member State's territory or where the offence is committed for the benefit of a legal person established in the territory of the Member State or where the offender is habitually resident on its territory.

11. Concluding remarks

A comprehensive analysis of the EU Internet regulation leaves the reader with four dominant impressions.

First, a commonly repeated assertion concerning the Internet is that it is changing rapidly. This rapidity is all too apparent in the European Union where lawmaking is a combination of traditional law, soft law and self-regulation in a continuous state of flux. Competing proposals, multiple revisions, changing agendas and policy statements, to use computer jargon, leave the law in a state of permanent beta. Rather than be seen as a sign of weakness, this fluidity must be understood as an inherent feature of Internet regulation. Many framework EU instruments call for periodic reviews while major policy documents (agendas) are replaced at regular intervals. These reviews will almost certainly remain a permanent feature of EU Internet regulation.

Second, the EU readily experiments with new regulatory models. The introduction of the country of origin principle in the E-Commerce Directive, the increased role of alternative dispute resolution or comprehensive data and consumer protection frameworks are some of the examples. These new regulatory models result from the need to coordinate a large number of national jurisdictions in a dynamic field. The EU desire to act as an incubator for new governance models may make it adapt more flexibly to the reality of the modern Internet as a platform rather than a product.

Third, the EU has not demonstrated a desire to deviate from the boundaries set for Internet regulation in the United States. The 2005 Tunisia Internet governance negotiations, the copyright laws and ACTA negotiations, among others, serve to demonstrate that this is a rule rather than an exception. While European privacy and consumer protection can generally be said to be stronger than American, the electronic commerce, intellectual property, ISP liability and jurisdiction regulation in both countries follow the same patterns. Historically, this can be seen as a missed opportunity to hold a more distinct position.

Fourth, the relationship of the Commission's complex system of regulation to innovation and growth is as yet poorly understood. The legal language, which contains frequent references to 'more protection' or 'stronger protection', may make consumers/citizens feel safer but may ultimately not be the crucial factor for growth and development of the digital society in Europe and may, in the worst case scenario, hinder it.

In summary, the EU Internet regulation will continue to be fluid and occasionally experimental but it also needs to be more independent and assertive and foster innovation as well as (and not at the expense of) consumer and user protection. Ultimately, the EU's ability to tackle the challenge of Internet regulation will probably depend on its ability to strike the right balance between prescriptive and reflexive law-making. Rather than taking over legal responsibility, the EU would do well to show restraint and continue the effort of fostering self-regulation. That way, it will be in a position to respond adequately to the challenges of a modern collaborative decentralized Internet.

Index